PENGUIN BOOKS

ISLAND OF HOPE, ISLAND OF TEARS

David M. Brownstone and Irene M. Franck are prolific authors and editors who share a very special feeling for the story of Ellis Island, the gateway to America for his parents and two of her grandparents. Their many collaborations include the recent historical books *To the Ends of the Earth* and *The Silk Road*. They are married and live in Chappaqua, New York.

Douglass L. Brownstone, a busy author and journalist, lives in High Falls, New York, with his wife and two children. His most recent historical work is *A Field Guide to America's History*.

DAVID M. BROWNSTONE
IRENE M. FRANCK
DOUGLASS L. BROWNSTONE

ISLAND OF HOPE, ISLAND OF TEARS

PENGUIN BOOKS

PENGUIN BOOKS
Viking Penguin Inc., 40 West 23rd Street,
New York, New York 10010, U.S.A.
Penguin Books Ltd, Harmondsworth, Middlesex, England
Penguin Books Australia Ltd, Ringwood, Victoria, Australia
Penguin Books Canada Limited, 2801 John Street,
Markham, Ontario, Canada L3R 1B4
Penguin Books (N.Z.) Ltd, 182–190 Wairau Road,
Auckland 10, New Zealand

First published in the United States of America by
Rawson, Wade Publishers, Inc., 1979
Published in Penguin Books 1986

LIBRARY OF CONGRESS CATALOGING IN PUBLICATION DATA
Brownstone, David M.
Island of hope, island of tears.
Includes index.
1. United States—Emigration and immigration—Biography.
2. United States—Foreign population—Biography.
3. Ellis Island Immigration Station (New York, N.Y.)
I. Franck, Irene M.
II. Brownstone, Douglass L.
III. Title.
JV6450.B76   1986   325.73   85-32054   ISBN 0 14 00.8820 2

Page x constitutes an extension of this copyright page.

All the people quoted in this book are real, though some are quoted pseudonymously, as indicated in the Acknowledgments. Grateful acknowledgment is made to J. B. Lippincott Company for permission to quote passages from the book *The Making of an Insurgent: An Autobiography 1882–1919*, by Fiorello H. LaGuardia. Copyright 1948 by J. B. Lippincott Company.

Printed in the United States of America by
R. R. Donnelley & Sons Company, Harrisonburg, Virginia
Set in Electra

Acknowledgments

~~§~~

A great many people helped us in preparing this book. We especially thank:

Mary Cygan, Project Director of the Chicago Polonia Project; Harvey Dixon, Librarian, American Museum of Immigration, Statue of Liberty Island; Archie Motley, Curator of Manuscripts, Chicago Historical Society; Samuel Proctor, University of Florida, formerly President, Oral History Association; James Shenton, Professor of Ethnic History, Columbia University; and Irene Silverman. Without their help in locating people who had stories to tell, this book might not exist.

We owe thanks to the people who helped us locate the photographs used in this book, who are named elsewhere in this work.

Central to the book, of course, are the people who shared their stories with us. Whether or not we used their actual words, their recollections have informed the whole. We thank:

Esther Almgren, Charles Bartunek (interviewed by Robert Jakoubek), Libby and Sol Glick, Sarah Hershkowitz, Sarah Hirschhorn, Fannie Kligerman, Louis Miller (interviewed by Gail Kaplan Guttman), Hedvig Nelson, Stephen Pakan, Solomon Siegel, Frieda Seligson Siegel, Adele Sinko, Bessie Spylios, Sylvia Tannenbaum, Hilde V. H. (in this book, called Irma Busch), Irene Meladaki Zambelli (private manuscript) and Mary Zuk; and the others who appear under pseudonyms: Vera Gauditsa, Theodore Lubik, Leon Solomon (interviewed by Alan Silverstein), Arnold Weiss and Judith Cohen (Weiss); as well as those who wrote to us of their experiences: Fay Batmasian, Joseph Hornick, Grace Adourian Kalyn, Karol M. Pacanovsky, Mrs. Mark Simek, Shohig Sherry Terzian and John Vallo.

We also thank the people whose recollections are in the oral history archives of the American Museum of Immigration at the Statue of Liberty National Monument, listed here by the pseudonyms used in this book: Sarah Asher, Helen Barth, Hans Bergner, Marta Forman, Rachel Goldman, Paula Katz, Ida Mouradjian, Michael Pappas, Frank Santoni, Rosa Martino (Santoni), Anna Vacek and Greta Wagner. All were interviewed by Margo Nash, formerly of the American Museum of Immigration.

We thank, too, the people whose stories are in the Oral History Archives of the Chicago Polonia collection, on deposit at the Chicago Historical Society, listed here by the pseudonyms used in this book: Sophia Belkowski, Catherine Bolinski, Casimir Cybulski, Sister Wanda Mary Dombrowski,

vii

Stella Jedryka, Martha Konwicki, Stanley Roszak, Celia Rypinski, Stephania Szymanski and Roman Umecka. All were interviewed under the Ethnic Heritage Studies Program grant No. G007602227 of the U. S. Department of Health, Education and Welfare.

Many other people gave us helpful suggestions—and passed us on to others —as the book developed. While we cannot possibly mention them all, we would like to thank: John Badovinac, National President, Croatian Fraternal Union of America; Teymuraz K. Bagration, Executive Secretary, Tolstoy Foundation, Inc.; Deborah Bartnoff, Hillel Director, Florida International University; Ellen Bishop, Acting Chief, Visitor Services, U. S. Department of Interior, National Park Service, Statue of Liberty National Monument; John Bodner, Director, Division of Archives and Manuscripts, Ethnic Heritage Studies Center, Pennsylvania Historical and Museum Commission; Saul Bronder; Diane Doyle, Fraternal Services, The Danish Brotherhood of America; Lee Engel; Otto and Pauline Franck; Marcia Frumerman, National Council of Jewish Women, Pittsburgh Section; Diane Glass; Ara Gostourian, Professor of History, West Georgia State College; Miriam Halberstadt, President, Daughters of Jacob Geriatric Center; Rosetta Hurwitz; Tom Hurwitz; Robin Hutchins; Arnold Johnson, Editor of Monitor, Scandinavian Fraternity of America; Susan Kelekian, Editor, Hoosharar, Armenian General Benevolent Union; Randy Kandel, Florida International University; Richard Knight; John Kowalski, Acting Secretary, Association of the Sons of Poland; Corinne Krause, Western Pennsylvania Historical Society; Ruth Krauss; Irma Krents, Director, Weiner Library, American Jewish Committee; Leopold S. Malinowski, Secretary General, Polish National Alliance of Brooklyn; Elizabeth Branch Mason, Butler Library, Oral History Collection, Columbia University; Jerry Masters; Carol Micheluz; Elizabeth Delza Munson; Carl Oblinger, Pennsylvania Historical and Museum Commission; Irene Odorizzi; Thomas M. Pitkin, formerly Supervising Historian, National Park Service; Carlton C. Qualey, Minnesota Historical Society; Peter Sammartino, Chairman, Committee to Save Ellis Island; Jacques Sartisky; Jonathan Schneer; Robert Shapiro, Head of Recreation, Daughters of Jacob Geriatric Center; Ruth Siegel; Steven W. Siegel, Secretary, Jewish Historical Society of New York; John Stack, Florida International University; Joyce Stedman; Lynn Sussman; Bernard Wax, Director, American Jewish Historical Society; Paul Weinbaum, American Museum of Immigration, Statue of Liberty Island; Rev. Silvano Tomassi, Director, Center of Immigration Studies; Lillian Vandemark; Martin Wadler, Albany Bureau of Cultural Affairs; Marek Web, Archivist, YIVO Institute for Jewish Research; Martin and Helen Weiss; Lilla Wilson; Olga Winkler, National Council of Jewish Women, National Headquarters; Frank Zabrosky, Pennsylvania Ethnic Heritage Studies Center, Archives Section, University of Pittsburgh; and Miriam Zatinsky, Project Director, South Beach Activities Center, Miami Beach.

And our special thanks to:
Deborah Bostwick Brownstone, who opened the doors to many people in the mid-Hudson area;

ACKNOWLEDGMENTS

Gregory Brownstone, whose photographer's eye was so valuable in selecting the photographs;

Gene Hawes, whose advice and counsel were, as always, so very useful from the beginning;

Shirley Fenn, who patiently and efficiently typed it all, from tape transcriptions to the final manuscript;

Kennett Rawson, whose continued support and encouragement have meant so much; and

Eleanor Rawson, whose editorial comments were so perceptive and valuable at crucial stages in the development of the manuscript.

Picture Credits

Our thanks for helping us locate the photographs used in this book go to: Sam Daniels, Library of Congress, Prints and Photographs division; Joseph Dwyer, formerly Curator, Immigrant History Research Center, University of Minnesota; Harvey Dixon; Gunther Pohl, Chief, Local History and Genealogy Division, New York Public Library; and Lynn Schweitzer, Acting Curator, Immigrant History Research Center, University of Minnesota. The list below indicates sources for the pictures shown throughout the text.

Lewis W. Hine Collection, The New York Public Library, Astor, Lenox and Tilden Collections:
  Pages 9, 36, 76, 85, 90, 138, 155, 156, 158, 162, 169, 178, 186, 189, 191, 202, 217, 238, 241, 243, 262, 269, 289

National Park Service, Augustus F. Sherman Collection:
  Pages 25, 31, 41, 51, 69, 81, 97, 173, 212, 228, 232, 234, 256

National Park Service:
  Pages 127, 143, 146, 153, 193, 209

Immigration History Research Center, University of Minnesota:
  Pages 48, 58, 117

Library of Congress, Prints and Photographs Division:
  Pages 139, 167, 176, 181, 253

Contents

❧ষ্টা❧

CONTENTS

I

THE
GOLDEN LAND

"When I was dreaming about America all the time as a kid I was playing with rag dolls.

"And my father said, 'You're not going to play with dolls any more. I am going to throw them out on you.'

"I said, 'No, Dada, please, I'll put them away myself somewhere. Don't throw them out on me.' I felt so bad; he wanted to take my dolls, throw them away on me.

"I put them in a little cigar box and I went to the brook and I said, 'Goodbye, my dollies. I'll meet you in America.'

"That was my dream."

ANNA VACEK
Czech, from Austro-Hungary
Arrived 1901

THIS IS THE STORY of some wonderful people—bright, alert, enormously alive, and very, very wise—and of a voyage they took.

Told largely in their own words, this story is about them, their world, and their hopes and dreams when they were quite young, as told half a century and more later.

They are of remarkably diverse backgrounds, but share this— they are all survivors of the Great Migration to America in the final years of the last century and the early years of this one.

And they all share an extraordinary sharpness of memory, particularly the memory of that voyage from the old world to the new, of the hopes they had and the realities they faced, of the great statue in the harbor and of Ellis Island, the Island of hope and tears.

In a larger sense, it is the story of all those tens of millions who came to America searching for peace and several kinds of freedom —and in the main found what they were searching for; the story of the wit, humor, irony and compassion of ordinary people made extraordinary in the process of braving an extraordinary time. In short, this is the story of our parents, grandparents, great-grandparents and neighbors; of their voyage to America and their passage through Ellis Island to freedom.

Anna Vacek sent her dolls to America when she was ten years old. The year was 1897. Four years later, when she was fourteen, she undertook the long journey from Czechoslovakia, then part of Austro-Hungary, to the United States. She arrived at Ellis Island in 1901, on the day President McKinley was buried. And in her late eighties, having spent her life in the America of her dreams, she was as bright and alert as that child of fourteen must have been, coming to join her dollies in America.

Nineteen hundred and one was, as are all years, an extraordinary year. It was the year Queen Victoria died, to be succeeded by Edward VII; the year William McKinley was assassinated by Leon F. Czolgosz—the end of an era, the beginning of an era.

In 1901 Marconi transmitted his first transatlantic radio message; the United States annexed the Philippines and Puerto Rico; a gusher was brought in at Beaumont, Texas, to start a Texas oil boom; and Mrs. Anna Edson Taylor went over Niagara Falls in a barrel.

H. G. Wells' visionary *The First Men on the Moon* was published; Picasso started his Blue Period; Toulouse-Lautrec died; André Malraux and Walt Disney were born.

And it was the first full year of operation for the brand new Federal Immigration Station at Ellis Island, which had been rebuilt from the ground up after a disastrous fire had destroyed the entire installation in 1897. The then new station later received over ten million immigrants during its peak years, between the time Anna Vacek arrived in 1901 and the sharp restrictions of the early 1920s.

THE IMMIGRANTS

The story of Ellis Island is the story of the "new immigration." In the nineteenth century, the main immigration to America— the "old immigration"—was from northern and western Europe. Then, in the 1880s and '90s, the balance began to shift. Although the northern and western Europeans continued to come in substantial numbers, a truly massive migration started from the countries of eastern and southern Europe. These "new immigrants" were Italians, Russians, Poles, Hungarians, Serbs, Czechs, Slovaks, Slovenes, Greeks, Jews from all over Eastern Europe, Christian Armenians and many other nationalities seeking freedom and a better life in America.

The "new immigration" dropped off sharply in the mid-1890s due to depression in America, and then soared to about a million people a year between 1900 and 1914. During World War I, travel within Europe and across the Atlantic virtually stopped, and immigration very nearly stopped with it. Between 1919 and 1922, it soared again, even though new American immigration laws made entry into the United States much harder. Then much more restrictive legislation passed in 1921 and 1924, and virtually closed America to southern and eastern Europeans.

The people in this book came to America through Ellis Island between 1892, when it opened as the first Federal Immigration Station, and the early 1930s. Most of them came in the peak years, 1900–1914 and 1919–1922, from all over Europe, but mainly from southern and eastern Europe.

Although they came both before and after World War I, and encountered progressively more restrictive American laws and attitudes, their experience is clearly all of a piece. They are all people from a certain time and set of places; they came on the same trains and boats; encountered the same European and American officials and attitudes. Together they share a single, seamless, epic voyage and experience.

And they exhibit a common pride. Not the pride of the survivor, though now in their seventies and eighties they are certainly that, but much more. For what you quickly understand when you talk with them is that for them the voyage to America worked. The voyage to the land of the free brought what they clearly feel was freedom. The trip to the land of opportunity was just that; it brought a better life than that they would have lived in Europe. These are people who made a choice, won through, and carry with them enormous pride of accomplishment.

The people in this book are not naïve. Many of them know quite well that America is far from perfect. Some of them participated in the great labor struggles of twentieth-century America, were active in both union and political movements. Many mention Watergate as a blot on the America they love.

But make no mistake about it. It is the America they love. Their America is the land of Lincoln, whose name symbolized "freedom" all over Europe; of Wilson, who helped bring independence to many of their homelands after World War I; and of Roosevelt, who let their unions be organized, led the way out of the Great Depression and took them through World War II.

In interviews for this book, many immigrants criticized America, but the answer to "How do you feel now about having come to America?" almost invariably was something like, "I love America. It's my country, and I'm glad I came."

In this book, the immigrant voyagers of those years from the old country to America tell the story of their journey in their own words. We will follow some key people every step of the way to America, and many others will talk about portions of the journey. Among them are the stories of:

- The bright, alert eleven-year-old Greek girl who came all the way to America with her thirteen-year-old brother to join her father, and immediately went to work twelve hours a day in a Massachusetts cotton mill, to earn enough money to bring the rest of her family to America.
- The Jewish family that set tables with liquor and food for the Cossacks who had come to kill them during the pogroms, sold all their property, and slipped out of Russia that night, headed for safe haven in America.
- The Polish girl who walked through the forest at night to leave Russia, crossed a continent and an ocean, passed through Ellis Island, and then almost fell short of her goal when a "white slaver" tried to take her off the immigrant train to Chicago.
- The dedicated teacher who survived the Armenian holocaust, World War I and the loss of her whole family, only to be detained at Ellis Island and nearly sent back to a home that no longer existed—and who survived to marry another "orphan of the storm" and raise great-grandchildren in America.

6

- The Czech boy, youngest of seventeen children, who fled his tyrannical father to make his own fortune in the land of his choice, carrying halfway across the world a bundle containing four feather beds and four bottles of whiskey.
- The Polish patriot who survived German occupation of his land, successfully fought for Polish independence, and then came to America to join his brothers.
- The Sicilian family that carried a handmade trunk in a wooden cart out of the hills, to the boat that would take them across the sea to join their father in America.
- The eleven-year-old Jewish boy who convinced his widowed mother to leave Poland—and then had to play "Charlie McCarthy" to get her through the literacy test on Ellis Island.
- The German woman who came to America and went back to Germany years later to marry, only to find that her Germany was gone and that Hitler was in power—and who then unhesitatingly returned to America alone, to live her life in freedom.
- The Ukrainian boy who came to America to avoid service in the Austrian army and possible death in World War I, and instead lived to work at Ellis Island and meet his childhood sweetheart there on her way to America from the old country.
- The sheltered Jewish girl, chosen as the one member of her family to be sent to America for safety, who traveled under heavy guard from Russia through occupied Europe and across the ocean, in the middle of World War I.
- The Greek boy, forced into the Turkish army at fifteen, who escaped and was helped by the Russian Orthodox Church to come to America.
- The Czech woman who fooled the doctors into letting her travel eight months pregnant to join her husband, so she would have her baby in America.
- The university-educated Jewish brother and sister who survived German invasion, the Russian Revolution, civil war, and two years in transit from the Ukraine to make a new life in America.
- And many, many more.

For them and for millions more, America was open then. It was the promised land across the sea, a land of freedom, gold and safety.

And they came. Alone, in families, in congregations, in whole towns and by the millions, they came. As wide a range of people as the world could provide sailed across the seas to America.

They sailed to a word—America! To the vast majority of them, it was only the vaguest of destinations. To some it was a place where their children could walk the streets without fear of beatings. To others, a place of gold, where anybody could move from poverty to riches, where a person's place in life wasn't irrevocably fixed at the moment of birth. A place of food, of land—America was all things to all people. It was the place where it was better than it was at home.

Their America was the mythical promised land translated into a concrete destination, that could be felt, grasped, possessed. And they made that promised land their own. The men, women and children who came to the New World and touched ground at Ellis Island were ending one voyage but beginning a larger one that would help shape the United States into the America they sought.

GOLD AND FREEDOM

Gold drew the most. No respecter of national boundaries or social classes, gold called to an impoverished Europe from across the ocean.

The tens of millions of European poor from Greece to Poland, from Ireland to Hungary, from the small towns and countryside, heard the call of Golden America. To the farmer endlessly struggling for mere subsistence, to the skilled artisan barely able to feed his family even after years of apprenticeship, to the young with no prospects of becoming other than what they could see all around them, America offered a chance of change. Gold was the key word, but the lure far transcended a crass desire for money.

All the promises of America are reflected in the face
of this Jewish grandmother,
come to find peace and bread and freedom in a new land.

All across Europe lifestyles and opportunities were frozen by the accident of birth. European poverty was a life sentence. America was the only reprieve.

Even from the relatively comfortable countries, the call of the golden land brought over the young and unestablished. Life in England or Sweden might be cozy and known, but it was also closed. The doors to movement in life were few and hard to open. Everything, from the kinds of work available to the foods in the market, was a known quantity. Reassuring, perhaps, but terribly constricting in the face of Golden America's call to the young and restless. In America there were still frontiers to explore, room to expand, new directions to try.

And then there were the fugitives, seeking the America of safety, of freedom and sanctuary. For these people, for the Jews fleeing the Russian pogroms, for the Armenians fleeing their holocaust at the hands of the Turks, for the Poles fleeing the triple oppression brought about by the more than hundred-year-old partition of their country, for the young men and their families flying from the imperial armies, the choice was simple. America was the land of life. For them, gold and opportunities were wonderful, but it was the hope of life itself that drew them to America.

To all of these men, women and children, the Statue of Liberty sang her paean of welcome. And lying low in the water next to her, Ellis Island carried the harmony. "Give me your tired, your poor, your oppressed," sang the Statue. And those who were not too tired or too poor, and who were in good health, heard Ellis Island echo that song.

But to those from the poorest places, to those who were ill, to those without sponsors, Ellis Island growled a discordant counterpoint: "Keep out. Begone from whence you came. Sully not these pure shores with your ignorance, poverty and need. This gate is closed to you."

Still, they came. The people of southern and eastern Europe and many more from northern and western Europe packed up and prepared to leave their ancestral homes.

THE JOURNEY

Usually fathers came first, joined by eldest sons or daughters, who could also be breadwinners. These first travelers said goodbye to their families and went to work in the new land. Family ties stretched across a sea where they formerly had strained to stretch across a province.

A father became a series of letters: "Dearest family, I miss you all and live for the day you can join me here. The work is good and there is so much food and people of all types you wouldn't believe. Write me that this money reaches you in safety. May God bless you . . ."

And the money flowed back to the old country for the families to join them. What better proof that the land was indeed golden than those dollars sent back for the family's journey? Little by little the money reached the magic sum needed for departure. One year, and another child followed to help earn money. Two years, and two more joined them. Three years, and a wife and young children journeyed to join them all, wondering what their new life would be like in that strange and magical land. Ellis Island waited for their reunion.

Their leavetaking was not unaided or unnoticed. The great steamship companies shilled for immigrants at every turn. The streets were lined with posters telling of the golden land and the ease of travel on their ships. Everywhere agents vied for lucrative immigrant business.

As the day of departure drew near, the travelers made the hard decisions about what to take with them to the new world to remind them of the old. The harsh necessities of the trip precluded any large or heavy mementos of a life about to become memory. A few hand-embroidered clothes and a down quilt to bring warm recollections, a bottle of rye whiskey and home-cured sausage to preserve the flavor of a former life, and very few other odds and ends became a large bundle to be dragged and carried to America.

Everything else was either sold or given away to those remaining. The precious money thus saved was carefully placed in a small pouch and hung around the neck. It must not be lost, because the agents have said that Ellis Island demands $25 from each immigrant as a proof of self-sufficiency and worthiness to enter America.

The journey began at the outskirts of home, be it town, village or farm. With the first few steps down the road, or onto a wagon or train, the immigrants became people in transit. The familiar borders of their lives had been broken and there was no turning back.

Often the hardest and most uncertain part of the whole journey was the overland trip. Some travelers had visas, permission to emigrate, and simply had to deal with the ordinary perils of travel with a large family in a foreign country, where illness might strike or accident separate them. They also had to beware of the legion of professional thieves and swindlers on the lookout for immigrants traveling to the port cities. For most, however, leaving was neither easy nor leisurely. Many of the young, healthy and impatient people looking towards the shores of America were the cannon fodder and bread producers of their countries. In an age of widespread imperialism and large armies, midnight flights and furtive border crossings became the only way for large numbers of immigrants to leave home.

The overland journey from interior Europe to the seaports might take weeks. In the late 1800s and early 1900s, millions of Russian and Polish Jews made hurried flights to America from a series of genocidal pogroms. Whole families and villages fled, sometimes within sight of the pursuing killers. Many Jews left their homes with deep regret, not wishing to break the pattern of their lives, but compelled to do so for survival.

Using any means at their disposal, people contrived to get to the ports. Those with money spent it freely in bribes and train fares; those without relied on luck and a wary avoidance of officialdom, as they made their way to one of the ports. Bremerhaven, Riga, Piraeus, Hamburg, the name didn't matter, only the docks and the waiting ships.

The shipping companies were overjoyed by the American fever. A law unto themselves in the early years of the century, they were only too willing to carry as many bodies across the ocean as could possibly be crammed into a hull. Happily laboring under the sole regulation of the profit motive, they shipped over many immigrants who were clearly excludable under U.S. public health and immigration laws. Infectious diseases such as the dreaded trachoma of the eyes or favus of the scalp were automatic bars to entry at Ellis Island; a host of other easily detectable health defects might also cause an immigrant to be excluded. The ships had to pay the return fare for anyone rejected, but profits were so high that they would take a chance on immigrants being admitted. Immigrants rejected and returned, however, were deposited back on European soil far poorer than when they had started.

Gradually, as U.S. government pressure increased, the steamship lines instituted the first of many medical scrutinies the immigrants had to face. After braving the overland journey to the ship, the exhausted travelers were examined by company doctors. Rejection meant a wait until the medical problem cleared up—and possibly journey's end unless a properly placed bribe or alternate route could be used. Acceptance only guaranteed being bunked in cruelly uncomfortable tiers of cots and segregated by sex in the bowels of the ship, packed cheek to jowl with hundreds of other steerage passengers. The Ellis Island examination, however, was widely known to be a much more dangerous obstacle than that of the shipping company doctors.

The ocean voyage was an experience permanently stamped on all those old enough to remember their surroundings. Children marveled at the shipboard life and scenery. The older passengers were far more prone to worry about the future as the shores of Europe quickly receded. But for most steerage occupants, all thoughts were washed out of existence by the ship's first wallow in the North Atlantic swells. Seasickness became the universe.

Those spared the torments of seasickness had a magnificent time, since the ship was their exclusive domain. Dining rooms were the province of the hardy few, who had their choice of food in inexhaustible supply.

Ultimately, they reached America, to be greeted by the Statue of Liberty in the harbor. Journey's end—but not quite. There was still Ellis Island.

ELLIS ISLAND

Not until the ship was fairly past the Statue did the turreted brick of Ellis Island's receiving station become visible. As they sailed past Miss Liberty, the knowing among them wondered why the ship did not turn toward Ellis Island, which could be seen swarming with activity on the left. The question was resolved hours later when the ship docked at a pier and the steerage passengers were forced to stay on board, often within sight of their long-separated families, while most first- and second-class passengers disembarked onto the soil of America. America welcomed the richer immigrants with minimal inconvenience but required closer scrutiny of those traveling less luxuriously—they were ferried to the Island for the dreaded inspection.

Ellis Island lay before them, the final gateway in the journey that had begun when they left home so many miles ago. It was the magic portal of transformation from Europe to America, yet some looked at it and wondered if it might not have a trace of the infernal about it, too.

After waiting sometimes for hours on barges, the immigrants' first step onto American soil was onto the pier opposite the main entrance at Ellis Island. From here, they struggled with their bundles across the fifty feet to the building, up a long stairway to the main receiving point, the Great Hall. Before them was a maze of bars, high wire pens, walkways and locked gates, along with uniformed guards and inspectors. America waited on the other side. The final sifting of the harvest of humanity began in earnest.

The immigrant's bona fides as a potential American were checked at Ellis Island. First and most evident was the physical exam, to screen out those destined for welfare or afflicted with infectious diseases. Immigrants feared rejection of anyone in the family, but especially of a child, for American law required an adult to return with the child. Who would make the journey back to Europe with the rejected child? Would the whole family return, or be broken forever at the Island of Tears?

Beyond that was questioning by the immigration inspectors, checking the immigrants' past, current resources and prospects.

Even with interpreters on hand, immigrants were often frightened and confused by the questions. Relatively few were actually deported—sent back at the expense of the shipping company that brought them over—but detention happened often enough to tie another knot in the stomachs of those waiting in line behind them. The majority passed the inspections and went on into America, to build a new life for themselves and generations to come.

The immigrants made a voyage not only across the sea, but across time to land at Ellis Island. It was a journey from a Europe and a way of life that had not changed for hundreds of years to an America that was changing too rapidly to know its own nature. Ellis Island was the crossroads where the immigrant's journey and America's became one. From its construction in 1892 to the passing of restrictive immigration laws by Congress in 1921 and 1924, Ellis Island was the gateway where the lives of millions and their concept of America found both confirmation and betrayal.

THE CLOSING DOOR

As the nineteenth century flowed into the twentieth, America had begun to feel that it was an old and established nation. The frontier spirit and the wide open land that had called out for more and more people to tame the wilderness had begun to pass into memory.

America was beginning to acquire the snobbery and disdain of the newly respectable for too visible reminders of a less wealthy past. Long-time Americans whose families had come to America in the 1880s and 1890s cried out for a halt to the influx of unwashed foreigners. The old immigration had been from northern Europe, while the newcomers were "greenhorns" from southern and eastern Europe. "Since they are different," sang the new chorus, "they are inferior. Restrict their numbers and protect the American way of life."

But the Statue of Liberty's song was not to be reduced to a whisper for a long while yet. As the United States whirled into prosperity with the century, the flow of immigration surged, taking

America by surprise. Close to a million immigrants a year passed through the Port of New York, overtaxing the facilities at Ellis Island—which became a wonderful source of sensational and occasionally true exposés.

Just when the flood of immigration began to totally overwhelm Ellis Island's resources, the outbreak of World War I reduced it to a bare trickle. The seas were closed to commercial traffic and American boys went to fight and die in a European war. Armistice Day brought joy and relief, but it also dawned on an America that had grown bitter and disgusted with all things European, including immigrants and refugees. Immigration restrictions tightened, spurred by the Red Scare that followed World War I and the Russian Revolution. In spite of this, the tide of immigration began to rise again. Europe was poorer than ever and devastated in the wake of the war. Golden America seemed more of a salvation than at any time before and people adjusted to meet the restrictions.

But the call for an absolute restriction on immigration and a return to good old American ways became a roar. It spilled across the newspapers, the radios, and even onto the pages of Western novels, crying hysterically against "race suicide and the incoming horde of foreigners . . .*" Ultimately the door closed to all but a few—and the Great Migration was over.

This book is the story of the extraordinary people who came to America during that Great Migration. It is a history of memory and a history of emotion. Their story is ours, and listening to it, we learn about ourselves, as people and as facets of an idea—America.

* Zane Grey, *The Call of the Canyon*, 1922.

II

MEET YOU IN AMERICA!

"There was absolutely no chance for the common man over there to get ahead. You just lived, and you finally died, and probably the county had to bury you.

"We'd have meat about once a year. We had goats and we had a cow, but most of the time we were brought up on goat's milk, me and my three younger sisters. And once in a while, Mother would buy one of those short bolognas, cut it up, put it in the soup, and everybody would get a little piece. I used to think, 'If I could get enough of that to fill my stomach!'

"Well, when we came to America, for a few cents we ate like kings compared with what we had over there. Oh, it was really heaven!"

&✌&

CHARLES BARTUNEK
Czech, from Austro-Hungary
Arrived 1914

WHO WERE these new immigrants? What dangers and desires were powerful enough to move them from their family homes, their roots, their ties, all of the personal history that is bound up in a life lived in the same place, generation after generation? For each individual, the decision to come to America was unique, wrought out of the special circumstances of a particular life. And yet, each person's reasons and feelings reflect those of millions of others who decided to leave their homes and try for a new and better life in America—when the old country promised only more of the same poverty, oppression and starvation.

The stories of the people in this book form a mosaic, representing those millions of people who left the old country for America. Three-quarters of a century later, they recall, step by step, their journey to the land of their dreams.

The power of the dream of America is reflected by Anna Vacek, who sent her dollies to America when she was ten years old and promised to meet them there. And meet them she did! Life hasn't always been kind to Anna Vacek—she married young and lost her first husband early. Not until 1929, twenty-eight years after she arrived in this country, did she meet her second husband, John, a Czechoslovakian engineer. At the age of eighty-seven years and after forty-five years of marriage, with John at her side, she retells the story of her dream of America—a dream that still has the power to move her, as well as her listeners:

"Look at these, my dreams of America, from a child. My sister, before she came to this country, she was a young lady already. I talked with her about all kinds of things, like teenage girls do. And she said, 'I heard somewhere that if you see a star fall from the heavens, you should make a wish and never say anything to nobody—and you'll surely get your wish.'

"Well, that was something for me! Every night I went to close the door on the geese that I took care of. One evening there was such a beautiful sky with a lot of stars. I said, 'My dear stars, I wish I could go to that America!'

"While I said this, I saw a star falling down to the east. Oh, this is fine! Oh, I wish! I'm going to keep my wish, that's true, and never say anything. I was ten years old. I said nothing to nobody when I saw the star coming down.

"So, sure enough. My sister had a sweetheart, he shot himself. She wanted to go to America, so my brother gave her money and said, 'Go ahead, girlie, you go.'

"And then when she got here, she started to write that she's lonesome and cries all the time, and she wanted me. My brother was a soldier already, so he said, 'I'll help you. I will take you with me to Germany anyhow. You're too nice for the village, you're too delicate.'

"And so that was the way it happened. When I got to this country, I said, 'Thank God, I got to America from the star.' It showed me the way to go to America. This is the God's truth about how I got to this country. I prayed to get to this country. And I love it."

For Anna Vacek, as for many immigrants, the dream of America is still sharp and fresh. They are not sheltered innocents—they have had life's usual joys and disappointments. What is striking, though, is that so many of them have spent their lives trying to make their dream of America a reality. And in truth, there were many different dreams of America, many different reasons for leaving the old country for the new.

LIFE, LIBERTY AND THE PURSUIT OF HAPPINESS

Many people came to America seeking the traditional American freedoms of life, liberty and the pursuit of happiness. Such freedoms were rare in the Europe of the early years of this century—a

Europe very different from the one we know today. The old country—the land the immigrants left and the lives they lived there—no longer exists, except in their memories. Even the names on the landscape are different—empires no longer exist; new countries have since been created, some only to disappear in a generation; towns are called by different names, and some are gone forever.

It was a time of czars, kings, emperors and sultans. Western Europe's constitutional monarchies, such as England, Belgium, the Netherlands and the Norway-Sweden Union, offered their people a large measure of democratic freedoms, as did Italy and the recently re-established republic in France. East and central Europe, however, was dominated by four massive autocratic empires: the German under the militant Kaiser Wilhelm II, the Russian under the doomed Czar Nicholas II, the Austro-Hungarian under the aging Emperor Franz Josef and the Ottoman under the soon-to-be-deposed Sultan Abdul Hamid. In that whole region, only a few Balkan countries—Greece, Serbia, Montenegro and more recently Rumania and Bulgaria—had won their independence from the Ottoman Empire. The Balkans were a trouble spot largely because the Ottoman Empire had weakened its hold—major powers, such as Britain, Russia and Austro-Hungary, wanted to expand where the Turks had retreated, while the various Balkan nationalities were making a strong drive for self-determination.

Such nationalist aspirations, which had led to the recent unification of Germany and of Italy, had grown increasingly powerful during the nineteenth century among the captive nationalities of all the empires. In the west, Ireland was still protesting British rule and Norway broke away from the Swedish monarchy only in 1905. In the heart of the continent, central and eastern Europe were the main source of the "new immigration" to America precisely because freedom and self-determination were not available to the ethnic minorities held in the grip of the four major autocracies.

Four years before the American War of Independence, Poland had been partitioned and, despite several nationalist uprisings, it was still held by Russia, Germany and Austria. Other nationalities that gained their independence only after World War I were also yoked under these large empires. Lithuania, Latvia, Estonia and Finland were all then under the rule of Czarist Russia, while Jews were a persecuted minority throughout eastern Europe. Ukrainians, Czechs, Slovaks, Slovenes, Serbs, Croats, Rumanians and many other central European peoples were under the dominion of Germany and Austro-Hungary, while the Turks increasingly persecuted Greek and Arab minorities and massacred over a million Armenians in the first two decades of the twentieth century.

Much of turn-of-the-century Europe, then, was a tangle of ethnic groups under the pressure of alien and oppressive governments. The result was persecution of one group by another, across the map, with the oppressed often being themselves oppressors. The Poles, for example, felt oppressed by the Russians, but in turn were seen as oppressing the Jews and Ukrainians. In such a world, liberty was hard to come by, life was often threatened, and pursuit of happiness was a will o' the wisp. And in such a world, tales of America—the land where that great man, Mr. Lincoln, had fought a war to free the slaves, the land where you were free to say whatever you liked—tales of such a land were eagerly circulated, offering hope to the hopeless.

Russian Jews had long since been forced to move into "the Pale," which was a restricted area (primarily the Russian portion of Poland) between the Baltic and the Black seas. Even within the Pale, few Jews were allowed to live in cities, and those who did usually had to pay dearly for their special privileges. From the 1880s organized massacre and looting of Jews was so widespread that they gave it a special name: "pogrom." A surge of pogroms in 1903, centered on Kishinev in the southwestern area of Russia, killed an estimated fifty thousand Jews in four years, and sent hundreds of thousands to America in search of safety and freedom. One person who lived east of Kishinev and felt the impact of those pogroms was Fannie Kligerman.

Fannie was a very tiny thirteen-year-old when she carried her youngest sister in her arms as her family fled through the night from a murderous pogrom in Russia. Today she is constantly accused of lying about her age—in reverse! She's so small and lively that she looks much closer to sixty-six than to her actual eighty-six.

She remembers that flight of seventy-three years ago vividly—the sounds and sights, the fear and excitement:

"In Europe, I can remember the house where I was born, in a small town close to Kiev. We lived there quite comfortably—we weren't poor but we weren't rich. Food we always had on the table. And clothes. I didn't have six dresses, like now. In school, we had to wear uniforms, we couldn't wear anything else. So I had two—one to wear and one to wash. It was a small town, and everybody was comfortable, see?

"But every night the pogroms were all around. I hate to tell you. They were chasing us out. They were chasing after us, to kill everyone. I remember the pogroms, the Kishinev pogroms, how they frightened us to death. One night we were hidden in a basement with a two-or-three-month-old baby. And we had to 'shush, shh, shh' the baby. We said, 'Keep still! Maybe somebody is going to hear us!' This I remember very well. We had working for us a girl, a Gentile girl—she had brought up my father yet. While we were hidden in the basement, she gave us food through a little crack. I'll never forget it.

"The best friend my father had in his life came to see us one day. My father didn't recognize him and said, 'Who are you?'

"The man answered, 'Don't you recognize me?'

"My father said, 'No.'

"The man said, 'I'm so-and-so.'

"My father almost fell on the floor. His friend's hair had turned white—and he was only thirty-two years old. They had taken one of his children and tore her apart. They tied the child to a truck and another truck and they tore her apart.

"One day there was a rumor that they are coming to us, the pogrommers. What are we going to do? My father took all the knives and the scissors and everything, and he buried them someplace, so they can't kill us. He had a friend, a lawyer, who said, 'Look, we have nothing to lose. Let's do something.' So we set tables outside—it was summer—we put tables out with plenty of whiskey. We would get them drunk and they would not touch us. And so it was. They came to the house with sacks to load, but they never made it. They all got drunk and they didn't bother us and they disappeared. He was clever, that lawyer.

"But my father said, 'That's going to be the end of it. We're going to get out. Let's get out while we're still alive.' He sold the house as soon as I am talking to you—it didn't take two hours. The house was only a couple of months built. We had just got into it, but my father said, 'I don't want to own anything. I want my family alive.'

"We left the same night. We went to somebody's home for supper, and we had to walk to the station about four miles to get a train. We

23

were afraid, but nobody followed us. They were still drunk. You see, they got drunk when it was light yet, but we went through the night. We had to walk miles to run away from Europe, carrying our belongings—and diapers. My mother had such small children and I carried my youngest sister. She couldn't hold three children, so we had to help. We had a lot of little children among the seven families that traveled together, so we changed off. I was thirteen years old, and I had to carry a baby, and that is how we got out—all seven families.

"We hated to leave. I had a grandfather and grandmother living in Europe and my father was an only child. It was terrible to part with the two of them, but they wouldn't go along. They wanted to die in Europe. My father said, 'Why don't you want to live in another country?' No. So they died there. But we wanted them along.

"We got on a train that we had ordered—one train for the seven families. There were a lot of people in there, more children than adults. Each family had at least three or four children, you can imagine. My family had eight. The youngest wasn't walking yet, I think she was about ten months old. Some of the other children were two months old, four months old.

"After we got away from there, we had to stop and buy some food—we were without it. Everybody had a little money, because each one had sold his property. So we would stop off at a station and one person would go and get some food for everybody. We wrote down what we wanted. You would buy the food today. Tomorrow it would be my turn to buy the food, see, we alternated very, very nicely. But one woman missed the train! She went to open up a bottle for the baby or something and the train went away—she was left behind. They had to detour the train to pick up that woman and they missed two or three days of riding. But still we made it in time for the boat. You can imagine, we traveled from Purim night to the seder*—we came on April 5th to America. What a long trip we had!"

Russia's loss was America's gain. Among the hundreds of thousands of Jews who left Russia during the decades of pogroms was the family of Israel Baline. Arriving at Ellis Island at the age of five in 1893, Israel became the quintessential popular composer and celebrator of America—we know him as Irving Berlin. Born in Siberia, with the burning of his home in a pogrom one of his earliest memories, he had good reason to write "God Bless America."

The imperial governments of Europe sought in many ways, offi-

* Two springtime Jewish holidays, approximately a month apart, the seder being the first night of Passover.

These eight children, orphaned in one of the many massacres—the pogroms—against Jews in Czarist Russia, were brought to America to start a new life.

cially and unofficially, to stamp out ethnic beliefs, practices and language. But in this century of nationalism, captive minorities sought to maintain their identity through practicing their own religion and language—underground, if necessary. The secretly circulated writings (what the Russians today call "samizdat"), the hidden libraries, and the underground schools that still exist in central and eastern Europe have a long history.

Poles, Armenians, Jews, Catholics and other groups often could not freely speak their languages or practice their religions until they left their homelands for another—America. Stanley Roszak's family, for example, founded a Polish community in Wisconsin, which they called Poznan—while back in German-held Poznan, people were being arrested for teaching Polish!

Stanley was one of those people who was unable to develop his many talents and interests in Europe because of discrimination by the Germans who controlled his area. Rejected by a German engineering school because his name identified him as Polish, Stanley blossomed in America. While he earned his living as a pharmacist, on the side he also has been a philatelist, a linguist, a gardener, and an amateur historian and archeologist, traveling all over the world to visit archeological sites—from Homer's Troy to ancient Polish settlements to Mayan ruins in the Yucatan. Here he describes his family's reasons for leaving Europe for America:

"When I came here, I was seventeen years old. I came with my parents and my sister and brother—just before the First World War started. My brother was two years older, my sister one year older.

"We came from Poznan. That was under the Prussian regime at the time. We had schools, of course—we had to go there; but it was all in German. Some noble ladies tried to teach Polish at home. Police found out; they captured the ladies, took the books away, put the ladies in jail so nobody could learn Polish. Everything was supposed to be in German. You had to speak German in the school, in the bank or the post office or anywhere. The only way to learn Polish was at home— there we spoke Polish."

◆§ "Why did your parents decide to come here?"

"First, there were already rumors of war. My father had connections with the so-called politicians—they were warning him. Number two, the business was very hard—my father had a bakery. The taxes were very high, so he decided to close up and come over to America."

◆§ "Business was difficult in the bakery? After all, the people have to eat bread all the time."

"Yes, but the conditions were so different because of the German bureaucrats, you know. They used to take the goods, we had to pay by the month, but many times they didn't pay us by the month. We would take it to the court and you know what happens—you have to settle for a penny on a dollar. So the business was no good at that time and he was disgusted.

"Also we came here because it was getting harder and harder; take, for instance, school. I was interested already in engineering, technical stuff like that. I applied to what they call a technical school. Well, they wouldn't take me because my name was Polish. They said they were overfilled, which was not true, because other boys who went with me to the regular school, they were German, so they were accepted. So we had all kinds of trouble.

"But my father decided to come over here because most of the family was here already; he had sent them all out while he was in business—two daughters, two sisters, grandmother and grandfather, he sent them way ahead."

◆§ "Four, five years ahead?"

"More. We were the last ones to come. My grandfather was here long before. Same thing on my mother's side, grandparents and uncles, *they all came here way ahead—fifteen, sixteen years maybe, ahead of us. They moved to Wisconsin and started a farm there. As a matter of fact, they started the Polish community and called it Poznan; it's near Chippewa Falls.*

"You see, my father had a bakery and the others didn't have anything. They came from a small village, so he helped them, everyone. And there he was, it took about seventeen years or so, before we decided to come here."

⋙ "Did you want to come to America?"

"Oh, sure. I was anxious. I thought I might scalp a couple of Indians and all that stuff. I thought they were running all around here. I got the sight of an Indian in front of the tobacco store, a wooden Indian."

⋙ "That's the only Indian you ever saw?"

"I saw Indians later on—I went where they were, but not in Chicago."

In the Polish areas controlled by Russia, conditions were worse. Often there were no schools at all, in any language. The old saying, "It takes money to make money" applies as well to education. Often those who had a little education passed it on to the children of the village—or imported teachers to do so. Stella Jedryka benefited from this kind of education—once in America, she even patented her own model for creating needlework designs, and traveled around the country demonstrating and selling it successfully to stores like Macy's, May's and Marshall Fields'. Resourcefulness runs in the family, with her mother running an underground school, as Stella describes:

"Oh, we had problems. We couldn't do anything that we wanted. We didn't have even a school there. The Russians didn't care about teaching their children or us, so many parents used to bring a teacher to the house, or to the whole village. But that was only during the winter, for a couple of months or so.

"Later they built a school, but I was already a big girl. They could take only two from the house—they took my brother and sister. So we went in a night school."

⋙ "What kind of things did you study in night school?"

"Well, there were no planned subjects. We were learning to read and write and history, but my mother used to read to us Polish history. She would close the windows and teach us, read to us the whole Polish history, but what she did with the book later, we never knew. She had to hide it, because we weren't permitted to learn anything about Poland.

My mother had come to the little town from a city and she could read and write and speak Russian. But she was teaching us only Polish—the history particularly.

"We couldn't stand the Russian people—soldiers. We were running away from them. The soldiers were right on the edge of our place. My parents never let us go alone, because they were savages."

In such a world, independence movements, too, moved underground. In a country where teaching your own language could lead to imprisonment, political activity was extremely hazardous to health. Martha Konwicki's father had to leave the country because of his political activity. Martha shows her bewilderment at her father's disappearance—and her family's difficult decision to join him in America, knowing they could never return. How especially difficult it must have been for Martha's mother, pregnant when her husband went into exile, to prepare to travel with a two-month-old baby. And for Martha at thirteen, it was terribly hard to leave behind all of her family and friends for good:

"In school we couldn't talk politics. We couldn't even sing, because we were under Russia. The teachers, they were trained by the Russians. In their minds maybe they were, like my father, for freedom. But they had to be quiet. With grownups, maybe they discussed things, but we children, we never heard anything.

"Our apartment had a little kitchen and then one big room—a living room—and the beds were there. We had a rug on the wall—I don't know if it was oriental, it was these patterns, designs, some flowers, some with horses and buggies—and the beds were against that."

◆§ "Did you all sleep in the same big room?"

"Yes. We were traveling quite a bit, because like here the company opened a new factory, so my father was sent there to teach as an instructor.

"I was too far away from the school, so—at the end, before my father disappeared—my mother had tutors for me. They were two sisters, they were princesses, but they were poor. Their land and everything had been taken away from them. One taught me music—one of our cousins had a piano, so I went and practiced there a bit. Then I wasn't too anxious to take music. The other sister taught me reading and spelling. Later on, my father's nephew used to help me. He was in gymnasium—he was already sixteen years old."

◆§ "Did some of your friends also have tutors?"

"They all had them. That was common.

"Then in 1911, that's when the problems started. I didn't know about it at that time, I don't remember much, only when I was eleven-and-a-half, my father disappeared. And we didn't—I didn't—know what happened to him. And at that time, I just remembered that ten prisoners from Warsaw escaped. They were going to be sent to Siberia by the Russians. However, the underground helped those ten men to escape . . . And that's when my father disappeared, too."

◆§ "Did your father help them to escape?"

"No, he couldn't, because he was an outsider. And that would have to be somebody who was in charge of the prison. But his disappearance was tied to that.

"At that time I didn't know what happened at all. But mother— she had a little delicatessen store—she sold the store to her brother. And we moved by my grandma and her sister. We didn't know anything about my father.

"And one night, I was sleeping on the davenport by the window and the window was open, and I was dreaming that my father came towards the window and he bent down and he kissed me. So the next morning, I was telling my mother and they all started to cry, my mother, and my aunt, and they didn't say anything to me. Later they had a letter from my father when he got as far as Austria. Then my mother said it hadn't been a dream. He had been there.

"It took him about five months to get to Austria—he could have walked maybe in a week's time. There it was free. We Poles were under Austria's occupation, too, but the Poles were free there. Not like in Russia or Germany. Later I found out my father's nephew was working in the office at the same factory as my father. He called my aunt, and left the message: 'Uncle John has a terrible toothache. He should go to the dentist.' My father didn't go to work after that night. That was a signal. That's why he disappeared."

◆§ "So your Dad was a true patriot for the Poles."

"Yes. He came to America, to Chicago, and located my mother's nephew. My father didn't take the nephew's address, so he had a notice in the Polish papers, and somebody saw it and they located my cousin. My cousin was married with three children, but in six months, he and his wife and my father scraped together enough money to send us tickets to come to America. We left Christmas Day, 1913, my mother, my brother, Stanley, who was four, and my sister Clementina, who was only two months old when we came—she was born November 13, 1913. We couldn't take much because my mother had three of us that she had to take care of and everything was left behind in Warsaw, valuable things we had. When we were moving from Warsaw, we left everything behind—we took just clothes."

❦ "After the prison break and your father's disappearance?"

"Yes. Oh, the family was crying because they knew whoever came—especially like my father—he wouldn't be free to come back. My cousin, he couldn't come back to Europe because he ran away—he didn't want to serve in the Russian army."

OUT OF THE OLD WORLD

The trip to America was part of a much larger movement from centuries-old rural life to modern urban life, a movement that was taking place throughout the Western world. Rapid population growth, partly from medical advances cutting the death rate while the birth rate was still rising, and industrialization both prompted migration from farms and small towns to the cities, where more wealth and opportunity were concentrated. In countries that were industrializing rapidly, such as Germany, Great Britain and the Scandinavian countries, the cities were able to absorb many of the workers off the land—though many people chose to move instead to America, which was also industrializing rapidly and seemed to offer unlimited opportunities.

In less developed countries, however, the cities could not provide enough jobs for all the people who left the land, and the countries as a whole were at an economic disadvantage in relation to developed countries. The result was to make the poor people on the land even poorer, in Greece and the Balkans, and especially in Poland, Italy, Ireland and other Catholic areas, where no attempt was made to control the birth rate. Rural people had to move to other countries to find work and opportunity, as immigrant workers continue to do today. They moved to more industrialized parts of Europe, to South America, but most of all to America. Once in the Americas, many of them chose to re-establish a rural life, made possible by the vast stretches of country to be filled and farmed. Either way, America—with its double promise of wealth and freedom—was almost irresistible.

Before it was outlawed in 1885, many American companies imported cheap "contract labor," but in fact then, as now, the best

A Scottish family on its way to a new home in Alabama in 1905.
Long after the industrialized Northeast had cried "Halt!" to importation
of contract labor, the South still cried for more workers,
a need large families like this one helped to fill.

advertisement is word-of-mouth. Most people came to America because they heard success stories from families and friends who said, "Come! You'll find a job here easy." Frank Santoni's experience is typical of this passage from old world to new.

Frank Santoni is a quiet man. His story has less drama than poignancy, with its echoes of a world long gone. That pastoral, old-country world could not provide the life he and his family sought, but it still evokes feelings of nostalgia in him—and in us. Like many other immigrants, Frank kept alive the spirit of the old country and his childhood by later marrying someone from his native area. Coming to America at the age of seven in 1900, he followed in his father's footsteps to become a butcher, and married at thirty-seven to Rosa Martino, a later immigrant from Sicily. Frank's story conveys much of the flavor of the old world at the turn of the century:

"I was born on November 19, 1892, in Campofiorito, Sicily, Italy. My father was born in 1846 and at the age of twenty-one he entered the

31

service of the Italian government. He was a lancer—as you have perhaps seen in the movies, because you don't see them now any more—a soldier on horseback with a long spear, with the armor that they hold in front to protect themselves from others' spears. He was in the honor guard of a baptismal of one of the kings in the House of Savoy, King Emmanuel III. My father was in the campaign of the Capture of Rome and I have the medal which he received from the Italian government.

"Now, after his five years' stint, he went back to his home and found that he could not make a go of his life. Our family had had a business, from way back, as butchers. But he went back and found that he could not make a living as a butcher there—all he knew was horse riding. So he got himself a job as a bodyguard for a very rich man, near the town where I was born.

"His job took him through the town of Campofiorito with his master. You can imagine two horses and wonderful-looking men! All the girls in the little town, which is on just one avenue, watching and singing. And, of course, my father being then around twenty-eight years old, naturally he had his eyes open also. And he saw this little girl— he made up his mind that she would be a good wife. Being that his boss had influence in the town, my father was able to find out who she was and proposed. Her father said to him, 'No, you cannot have my daughter. You don't come from this town.'

"My father said, 'That's all right, I don't expect to go back where I came from.' He knew her father owned quite a bit of property in the town. He said his vocation was the meat business, and if her father would give him a place to live in and open a store, he would marry the daughter and stay there. And that's what happened. My grandfather gave him a house.

"As time went on, one child came after another. I was the seventh child and, naturally, to feed seven children was a lot to do. My father struggled here and there, doing his chores, going out to buy animals, slaughtering them, selling them, but still couldn't make both ends meet.

"We heard of America. My uncle and aunt, my mother's sister, had gone to America before, so that is how my father came to know that America was the place for him and his children to come. Finally, in 1898, he decided to come to America with two of my sisters. He borrowed money for the passage, and he came to this country and began work. Even though he had never done any laboring, he thought fit to start in as a laborer, what we call 'hod carrier,' carrying bricks on his back, mortar and so forth. But that didn't last long. He wanted to work at what he knew. So he opened a meat market on 18th Street and prospered enough to send for another daughter in 1899. Finally he got enough money together to send for the rest of the family in 1900.

"*The night before we left, we received the clothing of my oldest brother, the firstborn. He had left for the service three days before and the government returned his clothing. He served his country three years and came to America in 1903. We left town the next day.*"

Traveling out of rural areas—whether the hills of Sicily or the steppes of Russia—was not so easy in those days. There were no cars, the trains mostly connected major cities, and for poor people, suitcases and hotels were an unthinkable luxury. So many, like Frank Santoni, carried homemade trunks or huge bundles made of sheets or blankets to hold all their belongings. They rode in a cart when they could, walked when they had to, and slept wherever they found themselves, until they reached a railroad center or port city, as Frank describes:

"*I remember that we left in a cart, a two-wheeled cart with a big homemade trunk, I would say perhaps five feet wide, three feet deep, and three feet high. It was well made, because it took the whole trip to America, and we had that trunk for many, many years. I think I can remember it being in my family even when I got married, and for twenty-five to thirty years after we got to America.*

"*So this trunk was our baggage. It was in the cart, plus my mother, my brother James, myself, my brother Stephen, my sister Lena, and we also had a cousin who came with us. And we started off for Palermo, which is forty miles away, with one horse and a driver.*

"*We stayed overnight in a small town, where we slept in a stable, where the horse slept, on top of the hay. Even my dear mother slept there with us. And we started the same way the next morning and we got to Palermo. I do remember that we took a small launch. We hopped onto it—there was no such thing as a dock. And the Mediterranean was very rough. We had to travel some distance to get to the boat. It was an overnight trip. And I remember so well that there was really a lot of crying going on because of the frightfulness of the Mediterranean. Now this boat was not a boat to come across the ocean. You had to go to Naples—there you take the ship.*

"*We were leaving Naples about five or six o'clock, approximately dusk time, and as we left I could see on my left the Vesuvius—and that stood out so vividly with big smoke coming out of the mountain! On this trip that I took in 1970, I made it my business to see the same view as I saw at that time. And sure enough, it was the same, except that there was no smoke coming out of it. I understand that Vesuvius has not been active for many years now. But on that trip we stayed in the hotel which overlooked Etna, which is very eruptive now, and at night you could see the flames of the mountain."*

If we feel jet lag today, what a tremendous shock these immigrants felt, wrenched from an isolated country life and set on a trek to the seaport, followed by an ocean voyage, a passage through the Tower of Babel at Ellis Island, and their final arrival at a country of bustling cities, with skyscrapers and elevated trains!

Many people who came to America were indeed poor people, with little or no resources but an enormous capacity for hard work. Poverty was not the province of any one nationality. And for many Europeans, being an ethnic minority under an alien government was perhaps less important than being poor. Poor people from all over Europe came to America looking for food, work, maybe even gold in the streets, most of all a chance for a better life. Charles Bartunek was one of those people.

Charles grew up poor on a farm in Austro-Hungary but then came to America—and ah, the difference! In Europe, he and his family struggled on a little piece of land and had meat "about once a year." In America, he and his brothers became skilled workers and independent businessmen—one becoming a pharmacist, Charles setting up his own appliance business. He gives a very personal view of what it was like to be poor in Europe at that time, in an almost feudal society with emperors and little scattered plots of land:

"I was born in what is now Czechoslovakia—it was Bohemia in those days. It was under Austrian-Hungarian rule, Franz Josef was the Emperor. We were a family of four girls and three boys with our mother —we lost our dad when I was six years old, and times was pretty tough for us. We were one of the poorest families in the village—probably a little over a thousand people lived there. We had a couple or three pieces of land that wouldn't amount to more than two acres altogether —it was separated and in different places.

"There were farmers who had quite a bit of land and they lived pretty good, a lot better than the common ordinary man. And, of course, my older sisters and brothers, they worked in the factory up there, making rugs and stuff for a few dollars. It was hard for us to get along, but then Mother was a good manager, and we just managed to struggle through it.

34

"*In 1913, my brother, Joe, was scheduled to go into the army. He had his examination and everything. He was supposed to report, but instead he and my brother-in-law left the country and went to the United States. They arranged things for us to come over to America. We sold what we had over there. That brought us about under $300 in American money. That plus the difference that my brother borrowed from the banks in America, and we made it here. We came to this country in 1914. On my fourteenth birthday we left for Prague.*"

Coming out of the old world meant leaving behind old customs, including old patterns of marriage, such as dowries and match-makers. Some young people emigrated to America for the freedom to choose their own partners. Even where the parents no longer made the match, the old-world pattern of giving a dowry of money, property or goods as a marriage settlement remained.

The dowry was Stephania Szymanski's concern—she didn't want to make her father a beggar. But more than that, she was a woman forging an independent life by working in a factory, which put her father to shame. So at age nineteen she came to America on her own and made her way to Chicago. With the husband she met there, she raised a family—and while he worked in a factory, she ran the two apartment buildings and the store they bought. For Stephania, hard work has been a tonic. As she says:

"*I put some pants on, put my hair up, nobody knows who is that.*" ·§ "They didn't recognize you?"
"*No. But you know, all the people they laughed at me, they said I am working so hard. I am still living, but you know, they died.*"

Here's how Stephania describes her decision to come to America:

"*There were three parts to Poland. There was Prussia, and Russia, and I was in Austria, about three miles from Krakow. But we had it good over there—we had freedom, we sing and everything. We had a nice school, all kinds of subjects. And religion, once a week, the priest came in. I went to school right up until the time I started to work in a factory, when I was sixteen. In the evening I went to sewing school.*

"*I was working in a factory making men's hats. My father didn't want me to work. He said, 'Your mother didn't go to work. I am ashamed of you.'*

"*I said, 'Father, I make money. That's why I work. That's no shame at all.' Sometimes I made sixteen or seventeen corona a week. That was* big money. I did piecework. I worked there for two years.

"I had a boyfriend in Europe. My father was still a young man, you know, and he was thinking we were going to get married and he had to give me something. Because that was the Polish custom, they give the girl something. Today, they love each other, they marry, and that's all—the parents make them a wedding. But in Europe then, they give some money or a piece of land or something. But my father, he didn't have too much money. I heard him say to my mother, 'Pretty soon probably they are going to get married, and we are going to be beggars, because we've got to give them something.'

"I heard that and I was thinking, 'My goodness, I don't want to make my father a beggar.' So I saved the money from my wages, special, and I sent the deposit for the boat.

"And I came in 1914. On the 30th of March I left Europe and I came over here on April 16, Easter Sunday."

ONCE UPON A TIME

For many people, life in the old country was the stuff that fairy tales are made of—not the kind with fairy godmothers, but the kind with wicked stepmothers. In a time of hard labor and large families—a time before wonder drugs, modern sanitation and easily available health care—one or both parents might well die before the youngest children grew to maturity. Many children were left to relatives who often had their own interests in mind.

This young Slovak woman,
arriving in 1905, wears the "babushka,"
or scarf, worn by most women from
eastern and southern Europe.

Such was the case with Celia Rypinski. Celia is a delightful, motherly woman, full of enormous warmth and vitality. In her case, the villain of the piece was a wicked sister-in-law. Even the terms of their parting argument could have come from Grimm's fairy tales: Deprived of the money she had earned to buy a scarf (a babushka), Celia said, "Listen, I'm going to dress beautiful when I get to America. I'll wear hats!"

Even in her mid-eighties, she tells her story with great verve and ebullience, occasionally calling her young man interviewer "Honey":

"Well, I was born—the thirteenth child—in Poland. My parents didn't want the child, where my mother was fifty-three and my father fifty-six. And it happened to be a girl. My mother cried and cried for being old, because she knew she wouldn't raise me—she was so old and worn out from other children, twelve children before me. Some few oldest died, but nine of us lived. And it happened—my mother died when I was a little girl.

"Then I lived with my father. All the older children begin to pick on parents when they have so many children. And that's the way life went on. Some of my older sisters got married, and four of my brothers went to America, gradually . . . not all at once. My other brother got married and brought his wife home. She was a very mean sister-in-law, my brother's wife. After she came to the house, she took everything. She locked up a lot of things, and my father took the crow bar and pulled the locks off. He said, 'I did not raise thieves. You're not going to hang locks on my attic or on my place. My children are not thieves.' I still had three brothers at home, at that time."

᪥ "The mean sister-in-law, did she take your mother's place?"

"Oh, God no! Not like my mother. Wanda was very cruel to me. She was even cruel to her own children. Many times I got a licking for being good to those children. She asked me for forgiveness when I was real old already and I told her to pray to God for forgiveness, but not ask me."

᪥ "What was it like, living on the farm?"

"My father had a ninety-acre farm. They were making everything by hand then—linens, cottons, wool. We worked hard, but we never were broke or hungry. The food we had was cabbage, beets, peas, grits—everything that grows—and dark bread. We had plenty of food. Of course, for holidays, they used to bake white bread and different things and for St. Pancras in the fall, they baked buckwheat bread. That was very good. But in general it was dark bread, a very healthy bread, from homemade ground flour. You know, my brothers used to grind it on the stones. We had plenty of milk, plenty of things, but everything we grew on our land. My father never bought anything. They used to kill pigs, kill a calf in summer, lamb and chicken here and there. Food we had plenty and good. Because we worked hard, we had the food.

"And one summer the rye was so big! My brother used the scythe to cut that rye near the ground. I was picking up the rye. He had promised to give me, like in America, fifty cents and a handkerchief on the head. And my whole chest was sore from picking that rye with the heavy stem and pulling. And there was a hired man and my father to stand it up and cover it up with another bunch for the rain not to get to it until it dried out. That was a whole July.

"And you know my brother never gave me that fifty cents? I asked and asked for it and he said to his wife, 'Give her fifty cents.'

"Wanda said, 'She doesn't need it. She doesn't need a handkerchief. Let her sisters buy it for her.' My sister-in-law! I cried.

"And then we got through with the rye that July, we cut the oats. And there is where my father died. He fell in the field. He got a cerebral hemorrhage. And when he died, I was lost. I fixed up a rope in the barn. When we came from the funeral, I thought to myself, 'I'll never live here. I'm going to hang myself.' But a neighbor of mine went to the church where the mail was, and she brought me a letter. My brothers from America asked my father to send me to America. That was really the cure for my life! If it wasn't for that letter . . .'"

Even so, twelve-year-old Celia had to live with that mean sister-in-law for almost a year before she could leave for America. And she had a decidedly ungracious send-off to boot, with no preparation for the long journey she was to make:

"That fall we had a festival in a nearby church. And I wanted that fifty cents so I could buy myself some fruit. They had a lot of fruit in the market. And they had girls coming from Krakow dressed with all the European costumes. And I walked and I looked at them, how beautiful they looked, how different they are dressed. They had those Polish Krakovsky costumes, with a lot of beads and ribbons and beaded jackets. It was gorgeous. The jackets were red and the skirts were white. Blouses were white, but trimmed with red ribbons. On their heads they had little wreaths, with ribbons hanging down. It was beautiful. And I came home . . . I cried. I knew already I was going to go to America, so I said to my sister-in-law, 'Listen, I'm going to dress beautiful when I get to America. I'll wear hats! You can have your handkerchief on the head—babushka. And maybe you'll ask me to send you a hat.' That's God's truth as I'm talking to God, that's how I'm telling you.

"She was so cruel. She made me sit down after I came home from the church and peel a bag of potatoes. The hired girl that used to take care of her children, she went out to play and I had to peel potatoes."

◄§ "You had a hired girl?"

"Yes, for the children. About my age, maybe a year older or so. She was supposed to work. I was supposed to have some freedom. And I cried while I was peeling the potatoes to think that the other girl went out to play and I had to work. That's how cruel she was to me.

"And then my sister-in-law's mother came, and said, 'Why is Celia crying?'

"And Wanda said, 'Because she has to peel potatoes!'

" 'Where is the other girl?'

" 'It's her day off. She had to go out to play.'

"And her mother said, 'Don't be so cruel. Don't you see that Celia has no mother and father?' She was a wonderful lady, her mother.

"Anyway I stayed until about the middle of the next May. Still they wanted me to stay to help them dig the turf from the ground. I said, 'Oh, no.' I did help them seed the potatoes. I had calluses on my hands and on my back from that big thing that you carry the potatoes in. You seeded after the plow, and then you came to the end, they turned around, they covered the potatoes, and you curved around again. So when I came to America, my brother took a razor and cut the corns off my hand I got from shaking the manure on the ground for the potatoes. I worked like a man, not like a girl of twelve or thirteen years old, which I was when I went to America. That was in May 1909.

"When Wanda shipped me to America, I did not even have underwear, but lived in two shirts; I had no snuggies. She gave me old torn shoes and her skirt—that's what I had for my better clothes. What my sister made for me and linens left by my mother, Wanda kept for her own daughter."

◄§ "Now who paid for your trip to America?"

"My brother John in America. He waited to be married three weeks for me. I was to be a bridesmaid or flower girl. But I sat in Rotterdam. I sat in New York. And when I came he was already married. But his wife took me like a daughter."

◄§ "What about your trip after you left the village?"

"I went with my brother to the border of Prussia, to Germany. All that part is now under Poland. But up to that time I never saw a train. I saw such a big train—tracks and trains—and I said, 'What is that?'

"And my brother said to me, 'You're going to ride on one like that, maybe a couple of hours. You'll find out what they are. They make a lot of noise and ring the bells and whistles.' And I did.

"I had with me a basket of linens that my brother from America had paid for—I was to come and bring it, beddings and everything. But my brother, he turned his horses and the wagon and went back home—and took my trunk! The basket I had everything in. My brother in Poland wrote after a while that he could not mail it because I had the ticket with me. That's true. I had a ticket that was to be torn off and pasted on the basket. But I never got the basket back."

◄§ "So did he forget? Were you just so excited you forgot to take your luggage with you?"

"No, no . . . what did I know? He was responsible for that. He had been in service four years in the Russian army. He knew. He bought me a little kettle for hot water and a little box of lump sugar and a little box with tea, so I could have some hot tea on the ship. And a little bottle of some kind of stuff, whiskey or some kind of juice, that I could put in the tea. That's all I got from my Godfather—my brother. And he took all the other stuff home.

"My brother John collected the money for the basket later. It was $19 he got back from that, because they never shipped it. And I'm glad they didn't, because I didn't have a place to keep all that. Of course, I wouldn't waste it. My sister sent me a lot of linens from Poland, later. I still have scarves and tablecloths from Poland. My sister made them and mailed them to me, or sent them with other people that were coming to America.

"Well, then the train went to Berlin. And it was some kind of a German holiday. We stayed two days in Berlin."

◄§ "How did you get from Berlin to Rotterdam?"

"Well, on the same train. We were sitting on the train for two days! And I got hungry."

◄§ "Did you get off the train and go to Berlin at all? You stayed on the train?"

"Honey, I was thirteen years old! I had a sign on my side. I didn't know how to read or write or anything or talk German. I couldn't. There were no schools then. I came all the way to Chicago with a sign pinned up on my chest. And it says on the sign, in different languages, that I was Polish, and my name. That's all."

◄§ "Did it say where you were going or anything?"

"Yeah, I suppose. So we sat there in Berlin for two days. That's how we got late in Rotterdam for the boat that I was to be on."

Celia had had no schooling, so she could neither read nor write in any language. If she had arrived in America just a few years

Although most immigrants in the peak years came from Europe, people came
from other continents as well, including these three, their names typed
on the photograph years ago, who arrived on the S.S. *Adriatic* in 1911.

later, she would have been unable to pass the literacy test and would have been returned to Europe—and we would have lost a delightful friend and neighbor.

Celia Rypinski was an orphan without a protector after her father died, but many others were troubled by being the youngest child in a large family, even when both parents were alive. It's one of the oldest stories in the world: younger children being abused by their parents and going out into the world to make their own fortune.

One such youngest child was Steve Pakan, born in Czechoslovakia in 1890, the last of seventeen children, six by his father's first wife and eleven by the second wife. His father was so harsh and exploitative that all the children left as soon as they could, some to come to America. As the only child left at home, Steve bore the full brunt of his father's rages. And yet it's sad to see misery repeating itself: in an aside, Steve notes that his father, an orphan, was treated badly in his own youth.

As for Steve, America gave a happy ending to his story. You can see it as he plays cards—his winning hands slap the table. His voice is constantly active with stories and anecdotes, entertaining his playing partners as he lulls them into foolish blunders. His self-confidence and good humor seem unshakable, which isn't surprising since they've stood the test of eighty-eight years. Since he fled from his father in 1908, Steve has packed in careers as a musician, master machinist and successful farmer without ever losing a stride or missing a beat. He laughs and gestures and enjoys the memories as they flow:

"My town was called Miala, not far from Bratislava. There was a big mountain there and you could see the lights of Vienna at night. In school, I went to the sixth grade and wanted to go on. But when I was thirteen, my father said, 'I need my son not to be just some kind of white collar, easygoing guy. I want a worker.' So he broke me into the weaving trade, into the looms from the beginning.

"When I was a little older, he took me on this trip to a faraway part of Czechoslovakia. He went with a team of horses to the first railroad station, three or four kilometers away. From there we rode a train for maybe a half an hour, and then we started to see different mills, on the big rivers and small creeks. We went way up in Czechoslovakia, almost near the Polish border. Then we walked from the railroad station and my father said we had to go a certain distance to this mill where we were going to sleep overnight. I remember it was in June, a hot day. We got there maybe six o'clock. I was all sweaty and had a carrying pack on my back, just like my father did.

"Then, of course, the miller welcomed us, and the mistress of the house made a nice meal for us. We were going to sleep, but the miller was sitting on a bench outside the house. He and my father had a bottle with them on the table; they were drinking and talking about their experiences. My father, he really got a head. But I was tired and I wouldn't take any kind of an alcoholic drink. I lay down on the green grass on my stomach, and I fell asleep in ten minutes, I was so tired. I don't know how long I slept, maybe a half an hour. My father by that time had had quite a bit to drink. The miller had a meter ruler, a long stick. And, as I was laying on my stomach, my father came over and Bing! he hit my back with the stick. He said, 'What's the matter with you? Can't you stay awake?' He hit me terrible and I couldn't get up—I thought he broke my spine, that meter stick was solid oak or some kind of hard wood.

"The miller's wife saw that and she cried, 'Oh, did you hit the boy just because he is sleeping? He is a child, young and tired.' Well, of course, then they picked me up.

"The next day, when I told the story, my father said, 'Don't repeat that. I didn't mean to hit you like that.'

"I said, 'Well, of course, that alcohol does it. I know.'

"So he mistreated me like that. At home once, my belt buckle made a hole in the cloth while I was working the loom. I had to have my stomach against the cloth, and there was a strong stick in front of me to brace myself while I worked with my hands and feet on the loom. And somehow the belt buckle snagged the cloth and made a hole in it. And of course, as the cloth advanced, it was rolling under. My father was making bobbins and he said, 'What's that hole?'

"I didn't see the hole myself. I didn't know. He took a big bamboo stick to me and he cut the skin on my hands. My hands swelled up and I told Mother, 'I don't want to have anything to do with him. Please, send me someplace else for another trade. I don't want this.' But he was the boss, so after a few days it healed up and I had to work again.

"Even though I was working, he didn't pay me. I didn't even have ten crowns, you know. Nothing. When I was eighteen years old, I said to my mother, 'Please, if you haven't got the money, borrow it. I'll pay you back. I want to go to the United States.' I had three sisters in America already. I wanted to make my living some other way, any old way. I said that was all right, maybe, when he was a boy—he was an orphan, and nobody took care of him, and he didn't know his father even. But that—that was no way for people to have to live nowadays. So she borrowed the money.

"She told my father, 'The boy doesn't want to stay, he is afraid. You've got to let him go.' She hired a team and took me to a railroad station about twenty kilometers away. When she was giving me my last goodbye, she told me she prayed that I would have health and luck. But father, he was awful sore at me. Even when he bid me goodbye, he didn't like me."

Traditionally, young people traveled with their money in a pouch around their necks, and like Celia, often a name tag pinned on their jackets. The pouch or tag could call forth help from kind strangers, but it also marked them as easy prey for predators along the way. Steve, having traveled some with his father, was wary, but others were not so lucky:

"I took the train from what they call Moravia, a part of Czechoslovakia. I went on a train to Silesia—that belonged to Germany. They had taken it in the war from Queen Maria Theresa.* On the train, a couple of guys were sitting in the coach all alone. The trains had benches along the wall, not like here with one bench after another. These two guys came to my coach and said, 'Hey, where are you going?' They asked me and looked to see if I had anything hanging around my neck, you know.

"I said, 'I'm going to Berlin to get on a train.' I didn't really tell them where I was going. The other guy was watching the door. In the meantime, after he talked to me for five minutes, the conductor came through to inspect the tickets. He saw them and they moved to another coach.

"In about ten minutes or so, the train slowed down and these two guys jumped off. All of a sudden a boy started to cry, a boy about fourteen years old. He was going to his parents in the United States with the money in a little bag around his neck. These two guys had ripped it off of him and taken everything, all the money he had, and they ran away. That's the way they were doing things on trains in those days.

"At twelve o'clock, the train came in to Troppau*—it was a big city. I got off the train because it wasn't going any further until eight o'clock in the morning. A couple of German police officers asked me in German—I could speak German—if I wanted a place to sleep. So they escorted me to a building four stories high. I went up to the third floor and there were about forty beds—and no heat on December 15th. No

---

* The Wars of the Austrian Succession in the 1740s.
** Now Opava, on the border between Czechoslovakia and Germany.

heat and no lights. They lit up a match and showed me that I could pick any bed.

"I didn't want the one next to the door, so I took about the tenth one. I lit up a match and I saw blankets—it looked all right. It was so cold that I didn't want to undress, so I just took my boots off. I decided I was going to rest that way until morning, and we'll see. But it was about fifteen or twenty minutes and I felt something crawling on my back and then I felt something crawling on my face. 'Oh,' I said to myself, 'that's something alive!' And I got up and lit a match and I killed them—they were bedbugs! Down under the sheets I saw lice. Holy gee! I can't wear my underwear now. I took my underwear off, what I had, and I threw it away. Then I put clean underwear on and I put my boots on and I walked the floor until morning. I was afraid to take another nap.

"Well in the morning—they had locked me in, you know—they opened up the door and said, 'It's time to go to the train.' Was I glad! It was about 7:30. I left there and had a ways to walk to the train. Then we came to Bremerhaven."

For people like Celia and Steve, the bridges were burned. The old country no longer held a home for them. Whatever lay ahead, good or bad, America was where they had to make their life.

MAKING THE MOVE

Making the move from the old country to America was no easy matter in the best of circumstances. The Kligermans were lucky and very unusual—they had enough property so that, even in a forced sale, they had the cash to move their whole family together, help charter a train, pay for the ship's fare, and still show a bag of money to the inspectors at Ellis Island. Few families could do that.

The usual pattern was for just one person to make the first move —a father, a mother, an older brother or sister, anyone who could be a breadwinner. A young person would get a stake from another member of the family, such as Anna Vacek's brother or Steve Pakan's mother provided, or would sell his "portion"—his piece of land or share of an inheritance.

Most often, the move to America was a planned family move, as it was with Frank Santoni's family. The family would scrape together enough money to send one person across to America; that person would get a job and begin to save money enough to bring another person across, then another, finally the whole family.

Helen Barth, the child of immigrants fleeing earlier waves of pogroms in Russia, worked for the Hebrew Immigrant Aid Society (HIAS) at Ellis Island, from 1914 to 1917. As a HIAS representative she saw many families come through this way, one by one, as she describes it:

"Now, Jewish immigration was heavy in the early 1900s on account of the pogroms that took place in Russia. In order to bring a family over the father had to make arrangements with the various banks and so forth and buy a ship's card, a passage, at a great sacrifice. Once these fathers got here they lived on practically nothing but a herring and a piece of bread. Herrings were sold from big boxes on cellar steps, for 2 cents a herring.

"The fathers would save and plug, they worked very hard, especially in the needle industry, in the sweat shops, rolling tobacco, and that was the way. And the sweat shops were—oh, very, very bad places. The immigrants never had decent machines, they worked on fruit boxes and so on, and that is the way they accumulated their few cents to bring their families over. Some of them had five to seven children, and they had to pay for every child."

Such a pattern posed tremendous hardships for everyone. The first person, often the father, suffered loneliness and deprivation, along with the shock of adjustment to the new country, as he tried to save up enough money to bring over the rest of the family. The mother, left behind with the children, had to run the family farm or business and deal with the normal problems of growing children without the aid of her partner. And she had to rely on uncertain mail service to keep in touch with her husband, service that broke down completely during World War I.

Nor was it easy for the children of these families on the move. Because many families were large and the ship's fare took a long time to earn, the middle children often formed the second wave of arrivals, traveling alone to the new world. Then, because America did not yield her riches so readily as picking gold out of a mountain, those children often went to work, too, to help earn the fares for their mothers and the youngest children.

Bessie Spylios' family followed this pattern in emigrating from Greece to America. Life hasn't always been sweet for Bessie, even though her candy and ice cream shop was an Ellenville, New York, fixture for forty years, until her recent retirement. Running Bessie's was a lot of hard work, but she loved doing it. It was certainly more rewarding than the cotton mills where she worked twelve-hour days as an eleven-year-old immigrant from Greece. Yet, though the work has been hard, you can believe Bessie when she says that she's had one heck of a time. Her spirit is contagious, and she's still as forthright and observant today as she was leaving Athens in 1909:

"I lived outside of Athens, in a small town, which is now bigger. I went to school until I came here. There were six kids in the family and we had a very happy life, like all the Greeks, until everybody in the family decided they wanted to come to the United States. Everybody was saying it was a land to make money, to have freedom, to do whatever you please—all those things, I guess.

"My father got the notion to come here with my older sister. They were here about a year—both of them worked—then they sent money for myself and my brother. We came by ourselves. I was eleven, my brother was two years older than I. We were both young kids, but we weren't like the kids nowadays. We were different kids. We went to work. I came here and I went to work.

"We traveled with other people. You see, this man used to come to America, where he used to work sometimes. He made a trip back, and it didn't cost him anything because we paid his fare to bring us here."

* "He was a kind of agent for you?"

"Yes. That's right. So we just came along to the United States and we are thankful."

With long-distance arrangements and family members traveling by ones and twos, the role of agent became more and more important. Agents came in all shapes and sizes, responding to immigrants' needs and to their own greed. Often they were "landsmen" —people originally from the area they served. Like travel agents today, they set themselves up in a major city, often a seaport, in Europe or America, and there they were contacted by villagers moving from Europe or by earlier emigrants ready to bring others over. Some agents, not so established, were little more than shills, painting glorious pictures of the golden land, for their own profit— and the ship company's benefit.

І. рік. **Цьвітень, 1911** 4. і 5. ч.

ЕМІҐРАНТ

часопись „Товариства св. Рафаіла" для охорони руских емі-
ґрантів з Галичини і Буковини

Адреса редакциї і адмінїстрациї:
ЛЬВІВ, ул. Кспериика ч. 36.

›Еміґрант‹ виходить з додатками 5
разів до року і коштує 1 кор. річно.
Поодиноке ч. 20 сот. — Для членів
›Товариства св. Рафаіла‹ висилаесь
даром.

Засади дїяльности Тов. св. Рафаіла.

☞ *Дорогі Земляки! Рідної землї не покидайте легко-
душно і на все! Коли Вас доля змусив еміґрувати, то бодай
не продавайте батьківских ґрунтів, щобисьте мали до чого вер-
нути. Ідьте радше на зарібки, щадїть, не розпивайте ся; з за-
робленими грішми вертайте і потравляйте ними Ваші госпо-
дарства. Не лиш зарібків пильнуйте, а вважайте також на
Вашу душу — не дайте ся пірвати в море зіпсутя, бо втопите
ся на віки! Не забудьте порадити ся перед виїздом в „Товариствї
св. Рафаіла".* ☜

Що в тім числї є:

Дороговказ для переселенцїв : 1. Перед рішенєм до ви-
їду. — 2. Домашнї мужі довіря. — 3. Головні напімненя му-
жам довіря і переселенцям. — 4. На желїзницї. — 5. В чужім
містї. — 6. Переселенцї в Нїмеччинї. — 7. На кораблн. —
8. При приїздї. — 9. Висїдане з корабля. — 10. Реґісрация,
або записи. — 11. Білети їзди зелїзницею в Америцї. —
12. Мінянє гроша в Америцї. — 13. Пакунки на зелїзницї
в Америцї. — 14. Приїзд до Ню-Йорку. — 15. На зелїзницї
в Америцї. — 16. По всдорожі. — 17. Адреси руских парохів
в Америцї. — 18. Для тих, що їдуть на зарібки особливо
до Прус. — 19. Охорона женщин. — 20. Не так ті вороги, як
ті добрі люди. — 21. Вибір дороги і єї кошта. — 22. Закони
для переселенцїв. — 23. Добрі ради і пригадки для переселенцїв. — 24. Просьба Тов. св. Рафаіла.

Лист про пекло.

The front page of this newspaper, published by the "St. Raphael Society for
the protection of Ruthenian emigrants from Galicia and Bukovyna," urges:
*"Dear Countrymen! Do not forsake your homeland for always! When
fate forces you to emigrate, at least, don't sell your lands, so that you
will leave something to come back to. Go for the sake of making money.
Be thrifty and don't lose your savings on drinking. Return with the
money earned and use it to improve your farms/households."*

First comers would make arrangements through banks, which advertised and vied actively for this business, and agents, to send back the "ship's card" (the ticket or boarding pass), as well as sufficient money to show at Ellis Island on their arrival, to those who waited in Europe. Emigrants who lived far from the seaport, or were traveling inland in America, often would be "ticketed through," as Celia Rypinski was, with all their train tickets paid for and in hand when they started from home.

Working the towns and villages were professional immigrants. Early weatherers of the passage and entry at Ellis Island, these men became commuters, returning again and again to their old neighborhoods as agents for the new emigrants. For a fee, commonly paid in the United States by those already landed, these agents returned and shepherded the greenhorns, like Bessie Spylios' group, through the perils of the trip.

Money and travel arrangements were not the only problems; many countries were unhappy about losing some of their youngest, strongest, most productive members. Permits were required by many countries, government propaganda against emigration was common, and as strains of war were heard in the distance, young men found it harder and harder to leave their homelands.

Charles Bartunek was one of those young men. His brother and brother-in-law had fled to America just before they were due to report to the army. They then arranged for the rest of the family to follow them—which turned out to be more difficult than they had anticipated. But Charles and his family had some good advice from their agent—and a lot of luck in meeting an official who sympathized with their desire to leave:

"When my brother wrote from America, he praised the country. But people in my village said, 'Don't go. He has to write like that. He is really under regulation. He is a slave over there. They'll get you over there and you'll all be slaves.'

"They also said, 'The Indians will kill you. There are snakes. You will go to bed and you will find snakes in your bed.' Oh, people told us all kinds of discouraging things, because the government over there had kind of a propaganda against America—they didn't want men, especially, to leave the country.

"I was fourteen and my older brother was not quite sixteen. We were small boys—over there, you know, you are undernourished, you are nowhere near as big as a boy fourteen years old in America, who is a pretty good-sized boy. I think I weighed eighty-five pounds. Well, when we got to Prague, this agent who was arranging our transportation found out that we had to have a permit. I suppose the government already felt that the war was imminent. Mother had to have a permit for us two boys. None for the girls, but us two boys, we had to have permits to leave.

"So she left Prague and went back to our county seat, to get permits for us boys. Well, the guy up there, he just put her off. He said, 'You raise a boy and when he is about ready to serve the country, you scare up some money and say, "Here, go to the United States." You get your oldest son to report for duty like he is supposed to and we will get you a permit for these two boys.'

"Of course, my oldest brother was already in America. Well, mother came back crying. She didn't know what to do. The agent said, 'You can see my position. If I give you any kind of advice one way or the other, maybe I will be in trouble.' But he said, 'Oh, I tell you, if it was me and my family, I would take a chance and I would go without the permit.'

"While she was on her way back to us, they put us up overnight in a haymow. We had to crawl up there on ladders—me and my brothers and the four girls—and we slept in the hay. And in the morning we saw Mother coming back, she was crying. The police had a drill out there in the square, and the captain of the police department saw Mother was crying, so he walked up to her and said, 'What's the matter, Mother? Why are you crying?'

"Well, Mother was honest, she couldn't lie, so she told him the whole thing. Well, he said he didn't agree with the government. In the morning, when we were boarding the train and they were going through the permits and everything, this captain made it a point to be there. When we came up, he just shoved us on the train and told Mother, 'Happy journey and God be with you.'

"After this police chief or captain got us on the train, we had no more trouble. When we got to the border, it was midnight—everybody was half asleep and they didn't bother us up there at all. Once we got into Germany, we were all right. My brother here in America had arranged for us to contact the agent. It was the Holland-American Line from Rotterdam. Our ship was the New Amsterdam. By the way, that same ship was sunk during the war, the First World War. We were on the ship when the message came over the wireless that the Prince of Austra was assassinated in Serbia. And that started the war. Well, we were really lucky that we got out when we did!"

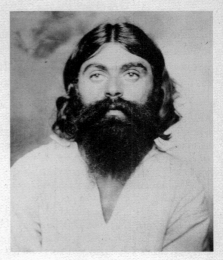

In America, this young man could practice both his Judaism and his vegetarianism freely, which he could not have done in the Russia he left behind, especially in the Czar's army.

CROSSING THE BORDER

Further east, the travel restrictions applied to everyone, not just young men who could be used as cannon fodder. Russia, then as now, had closely watched borders. Fannie Kligerman doesn't describe how she and the seven families were able to cross the border from Russia. We don't know what arrangements her father made, but arrangements there must have been. In order to leave Russia legally, an emigrant had to get a government permit for a heavy fee. People who left in haste had no time to spare for wading through such red tape. Luckily for the emigrants, there was an alternative: bribery. Many Russian border guards were quite willing to take wholesale bribes for turning their backs while emigrants fled across the border, usually into Germany, gateway to many of the major port cities, but also into Austro-Hungary or the Balkans.

One striking description of the whole process of a family move from inside Russia to the sea is given by Leon Solomon. In his child's-eye view, there is no sense of danger, only excitement at the trip, admiration of the soldiers' uniforms, and wonder at the pageants of his Christian neighbors. That Leon has strong memories of religious rituals is not surprising, because in America he became an eminent conservative rabbi, a true teacher who was loved and respected by generations of students graduated from the seminary in which he spent his life. In this interview, just before his recent death at the age of 86, he recalls his journey:

"I was born in Lithuania, when it was a province of the Czarist Empire, in a small town which is probably not on the map. There was a church in the center of the town. When the church bells tolled, we listened with childish wonder and astonishment and awe—especially when the bells tolled at night. We listened until the vibrations finally died away and it came to perfect stillness.

"When Christians in Lithuania would pass a street corner where a crucifix was nailed on the pole, they would kneel and cross themselves and move on. I also recall that on certain Christian festivals, they would have a pageant that would issue from the church, led by the priest in colorful, ecclesiastical robes, with crucifixes, followed by the worshippers carrying other Christian symbols and chanting aloud. We Jewish children would look on from afar in awe and astonishment.

"I was too young to know whether the Jews in town had any relations with non-Jews. Probably the peasants would come to Jewish stores to do shopping, buy groceries, or farmers would bring whatever products their farms would raise to sell to Jewish merchants . . .

"All Jews had one overwhelming motive: to get out of the tyrannical regime of Czarist Russia, where there was no hope for advancement, to come to the free world, the land of promise.

"Young men ran away from military service. If they had remained, they would have been drafted into the Czar's army, and served there three or four years of hard labor, with no prospect for promotion. So young people of military age ran away from military service. Married people hoped to find in America an easier way of life, opportunities for advancement, for getting rich. All of them hoped to live in freedom and equality, which were denied them under the Czar's tyranny.

"When I was still a child, my father left for America and waited for a few years, until he had saved up enough money to buy tickets on an ocean-going steamship to bring us across. It must have absorbed all his savings to pay for the passage of Mother, my brother and myself, because he worked very hard in America. His savings were earned with great effort over a long period of time—he had to live very frugally to save up enough to pay for our passage.

"We left behind my paternal grandmother, my father's mother. I remember a moving scene when my grandmother came to bid us farewell, prior to our departure for America. She and my mother embraced each other and they wept long and copiously.

"This is my recollection of my first journey from my home in Lithuania to the United States. In order to leave Russia legally, it was necessary to purchase a certain document called in English translation, 'a governor's permit.' We couldn't afford to pay for that, so poor Jews who emigrated from Russia had to steal across the Russian-German boundary, which was guarded by Russian soldiers, and this is the manner in which we emigrated from Russia. It was done through intermediaries, who were people specialized in leading emigrants across the boundary illegally. They bribed the guards to look away, so, at the proper moment, when it was safe, they signalled to us.

"Let me recall the manner of transportation. My mother and her sister, who came with us, engaged the services of a hack driver. Our belongings were wrapped, encased in suitcases and boxes, and we sat on our luggage in his two wagons, which took us out of the town and brought us to the border.

"Before stealing across the border we, and many other emigrants, concealed ourselves in a barn. We were told to stay there and make no noise. At the appropriate moment, when those who were experts in helping emigrants across the border, when they thought it was safe, they called to us and said, 'Now, run!' So we picked up our luggage and we ran. And I remember how breathlessly we ran and crossed the border until we were told, 'Stop running!'

"Of course, the rest of our luggage came several days later. We arrived in a boarding house, which specialized in accommodating and giving hospitality to Russian-Jewish wanderers, emigrants who stole across the border and waited to take a train.

"This was in Prussia, across the border from Lithuania. I have childhood recollections of Prussian-German policemen, and I marveled and looked at them admiringly, as children do when they look at soldiers in uniform. How they were so tall, and handsome and strong. I must have been about six or so, and my brother about four years older.

"I have no recollections of our stay in Prussia except that we waited for a train that would take us from Prussia to Brussels, Belgium. That was the first time in my life that I saw a train. I saw a locomotive that belched fire and smoke from the chimney. And when our luggage followed us across the border from Lithuania to Prussia, we were taken to the train, a special train for emigrants. None of the comforts and the cushioned seats for wealthy passengers, but third-class passage on trains with crude benches. The passengers who were old, poor emigrants from Russia, like ourselves—who stole across the border, like ourselves—were packed into these emigrant trains like sardines.

"We stopped in Brussels, Belgium. And there, too, we were put up in a boarding house, which was maintained to accommodate emigrants *like ourselves. We had to wait about a week until the ship, which our father had arranged to take us across the ocean, had entered port."*

Tales of the exit from the Russian Empire almost always include a dramatic escape, like Fannie Kligerman's or Leon Solomon's. The routes of emigration were well established—Jews had been fleeing pogroms in Russia since the 1880s. Along these routes to the seaports were way stations such as those Leon described. These way stations were run mainly by "landsmen" of the main group they served, but were open to anyone who crossed and waited at crucial junctions. So the route that Sophia Belkowski, a Polish Catholic, took out of Russia had been established and was maintained by Jews, but served others who also wanted to escape across the border to freedom.

Sophia was one of those naïve, vulnerable young girls who made the trip to America alone. From the way people reacted to her at every step of the trip, her whole demeanor must have cried out, "I have never been away from home before!" But she had a great deal of help from kind strangers and by the last leg of her trip to Chicago, her instincts had become good enough to warn her away from a "white slaver," who would have sold her into prostitution. Sophia needed all her strength later, when her husband died of cancer, leaving her alone to raise their two children, ages ten and twelve. Over forty years later, she concluded her interview by saying, "I never cry, never—much." Here Sophia describes her background and midnight escape:

"My mother died in 1912 and two months later my father got married. When my mother died, my brother Pete wrote to my father from the United States. He said he would come back home to Poland, to help him out. You think my father listened? He don't listen that. He married himself and that's all. In eight weeks he brought another woman home.

"So I wrote to my brother Joe—I had three brothers in America, Joe, Bill and Pete. I said, 'Joe, my father he got married. I don't want to stay there. Could you send me money, and bring me here to the United States?' He did. He sent money right away.

"So I came to the United States from Europe on October 16, 1912. I was sixteen years old—a young girl—and I came all alone to my brother. We started September 12 from Poland. To cross the Russian zone we walked from the village through the forest preserve all night,

to Germany someplace. There were twenty-one people and two were girls, I and one other girl. A man came with a horse and buggy—part of the way we two girls rode in the buggy, but the boys walked all the way to Germany.

"When we got near the border between Russia and Germany, this older man, that was taking us across, he saw I was a young girl and he said, 'You stay with me, because if I go and leave you all alone, you'll get lost.' The man had to go see the Russians, the people who watch—what they call the border guards. I sat there on the ground and fell asleep. When he came back, he woke me up so we could walk farther.

"We walked farther. Then the man said, 'You sit here till I come back.' He went someplace else and reached the borderline—the Russian soldier was there. There was a deep trench and they put a board over the trench—then the man put his coat over it and we walked across the Russian border into Germany. It was five in the morning already. All night we walked.

"When we came into Germany, we went to this house. The man called out and this woman opened the second-floor window. She said, 'How many people you have?'

"He said, 'Twenty-one people. Open the door.' So when he brought us over there, the people bought beer, you know, and some drank. I didn't drink—I was a young girl, I didn't know how to drink. Well, this man—he was a Jew—had watched me, so I bought him a glass of beer. I said, 'Here, you watched me all night, while I walked.'

"He said, 'Don't buy any beer, because you need money.' I think I had three dollars with me only. Well, he took the beer. He drank.

"The next day they left me all alone there in Germany. I stayed, I think, four days over there. I was young, I didn't have papers. The people said I had to wait for some papers. I said, 'Where do I go and get the papers? Who will send me papers. From Europe?' Then, in four days I got permission—I don't know from who—to take the train to the ocean, where the ship was.

"I rode in the train four days or something. But when I was a young girl, I had never gone anyplace. I didn't know a thing. I was sitting alone there, with a little package. I saw that people would, like now, go and buy some food or something. I had from home a piece of dry bread. Usually when you went, they dried the bread, and they gave you cheese or something. So I saw that people was eating in the train, but I was ashamed to eat. An older man, who rode there in the train, he said, 'Miss, you have to eat because you're going to get sick if you don't eat.' "

Oddly enough, Sophia had very little idea of where she was going and what it would be like—only that America was the place to go.

It was surely better than a place where people were watched all the time, even in church:

&§ "What did you think America would be like?"

"Well, I knew it would be better because when I was in Europe, I don't like, I don't like. I like something good to eat. But in Poland they cook soup. They have milk, macaroni, barley, sauerkraut. They cook it for two different meals with baked potatoes in the morning, so I don't like. I liked something different."

&§ "But you had no idea what it might be like in America?"

"Nobody explained. Nobody said anything. They never talked about America."

&§ "Why did so many people go, though?"

"Boys—girls, some, too—when they reached a certain age, then they go to United States.

"We Polish people, we don't know much over there. We worked on the farm and that's all. We didn't have no school—it burned down when I was a baby and they never rebuilt it. But my father every year brought a teacher, a man who gave up studying to be a priest, to our village. He would go house to house to teach, one day for each child in the house. We learned to read and write."

&§ "In what language?"

"Polish. My father wanted us to learn Polish. The same teacher used two languages—Polish and Russian."

&§ "Oh, so he would use that as a disguise."

"That's it. They thought we were being taught Russian, but we were really being taught Polish.

"And we went to mass every Sunday, there was a Russian policeman sitting there in the choir. If the priest said something wrong, he's gone. You never see him again."

&§ "You mean at that time they were watching the people?"

"Yes, sir."

I'LL BE BACK!

The traffic was not all one way. Looking back years later at the distance, the difficulty, the cost of the journey, often the sale of property back home, we might think that the move to America was final and virtually irrevocable. Not so. People traveled back to their homelands more often than we might suppose. Sometimes they went back to visit family, like Frank Santoni's aunt and uncle;

occasionally they brought out with them other family members who wished to emigrate. Sometimes they went back as agents to bring others across to America, as Bessie Spylios' agent did.

People who came to America to earn money and then went back home to buy land or build a new house sometimes were called "birds of passage." One such "bird of passage" was Jerzy Cybulski. Jerzy's son, Casimir, came, married and stayed. Casimir founded a family that by the time of this interview had grown to five children, eighteen grandchildren and eleven great-grandchildren, a number of them professional people in the law, nursing or corporate management. But Casimir's father made a different choice— Jerzy came to America not once but twice, and would have come again if his eyes had allowed it, but finally he settled for good back home in Poland. Casimir tells us about himself and his father:

"The reason I came here was that in Poland there wasn't enough work. I didn't come from the big city; I just come from the farm. In the summertime there's enough work on the farm, but wintertime there was no work.

"My grandfather had been a carpenter making wagons and wheels and everything for the farmers. That was his job the whole year round."

⋖ "How about your father?"

"Well, my father didn't have much of an education. When he was single he was in the Russian army for three years; then he got married and worked on a farm. He was in America a couple times. I was a small child yet when he came here the first time."

⋖ "What did your father say when he came back to Poland?"

"He said America is a nice country. You can make a good living there. You can make money. He did make money, and when he went back to Poland he bought a ten-acre farm. About a year or so after that he went to America a second time. He made good money to pay for the farm. So, he wanted to come a third time, but he couldn't come because his eyes were bad.

"When I was seventeen years old, my father gave me money, and told me to go to America. He said, 'You get there. You find yourself a job, regular money. If you like it over there, you can stay there. If you don't like it over there, you can always come back to Poland.' So I came —I left Poland in November 1913."

Jerzy Cybulski was not alone—there were many such "birds of passage." Between 1908 and 1923, fifty or more people returned

These two farmhouses near Pilzno, in the Russian-held part of Poland, show the result of the return migration. The farmer originally lived in the thatched hut on the right; the fine house on the left was built with money earned in America.

for every one hundred immigrants that arrived for many nationalities, such as southern Italians, Russians, Slovaks and many Balkan peoples. While some returned only to visit, not to stay, this proportion of back-and-forth migration is still astonishing. Other groups had much smaller proportions of return migration, among them Armenians, Czechs, Finns and the northern and western Europeans who made up so much of the "old immigration." The lowest proportion of return migration, only five out of one hundred, was that of Jews—not surprising, considering the pogroms of eastern Europe.*

In the early decades, those who later wanted to return to the United States had to go through the complete immigration check again—with the risk of being turned back, as Jerzy Cybulski feared —unless they had become American citizens. Clearly these were

* These figures are from the table "Immigration and Emigration, and Net Gain or Loss, 1908 to 1923, by Race" from Eleventh Annual Report of Secretary of Labor for the fiscal year ended June 30, 1923, as quoted on p. 210 of *Immigration Restriction*, by Roy L. Garis (New York: The Macmillan Company, 1927), reprinted by Jerome S. Ozer, 1971.

people who had *not* burned their bridges, but had been able to raise the fare without selling everything they owned. Often they had family back home to keep watch over their interests there, although families are not always completely reliable, as some found to their sorrow.

Sophia Belkowski's family reveals some of the tangled interconnections that these repeated migrations produced. Sophia's father had come to America when she was very young, had earned a few hundred dollars and returned to Poland. Three of her brothers came to America in the first decade of the twentieth century and, when Sophia's mother died, one of the brothers, Joe, brought Sophia over. Joe had married his childhood sweetheart in Poland and they had come to America together, where they had three children. But Joe's wife was homesick, so he sent money back to buy a farm— and found he had to handle the deal himself. So the whole family returned to Poland sooner than expected. Joe's granddaughter, child of one of those three American-born children, later came to the United States, and she is the interviewer here as her great-aunt Sophia tells about why Joe returned to Poland:

"My brother Joe made $600. At that time, they didn't pay much, a dollar a day, two dollars a day. That's all. But he saved $600 and he said to his wife, 'Let's send the money back to my father. He'll buy a farm; then, we will go back to Europe, we will have more land.' Well, they sent the $600 to his father over there to buy a farm.

"Later on, somebody told them, 'If you want to buy a farm, you better come back yourself, because your father didn't buy a farm. He kept the money. If something happens, you have nothing. You will lose those $600.' So they went back to Poland and bought that $600 farm."

&§ "Would he have preferred to stay here?"

"Well, he preferred to stay here, but when he had sent the money over there, he was scared he's going to lose it."

&§ "But why did he send the money?"

"He wanted to buy a larger farm."

&§ "So he was planning on going back there. He wasn't happy here?"

"Joe's wife, she didn't feel good. She was sick, sick. She couldn't eat. So they went back."

More often, however, immigrants arrived in America never to return to their homelands—or at least not until most of a lifetime had passed. Like so many of us, these people sometimes made one of life's major decisions without realizing the finality of it—often they intended something much less permanent.

One immigrant who came for only two or three years, and didn't return for forty-seven years, was Mary Zuk. A short, compact Ukrainian woman, Mary Zuk wears rather thick glasses. Many older people do, but Mary has worn them since her youth to correct for the effects of typhus-related cataracts. (As one immigrant put it, "Typhus over there was as common as colds over here.") Eye problems kept Mary from school in the old country. Seeing her drive and power, even today, you would not suspect that she could neither read nor write when she arrived in America. In fact, just five years later, she would have been turned back at Ellis Island, being unable to pass the literacy test required after 1917. Yet in this country, Mary and her husband built up two successful family businesses, one in New York City and the other in rolling country much like that of her homeland. Sunning herself beside her lakeside summer cottage sixty-five years later, she recalls that she never intended to stay in America:

"I was born in what was at that time Austria—Franz Josef was the President. The big town nearby was Lubachov—it had the big stores, church and everything. I was on a farm in a little town—just a few people. Everybody had a little farm and they made a living. In our town was just one little store, but you could buy whiskey, flour, whatever you needed for the house when you ran short—when you didn't have it from your own farm. When you had it from your own, you didn't go. Most of the people, farmers, when they were tired, they went to get whiskey . . .

"When I was a child, I had typhus. It went to my head and to my eyes, you know. My hair was falling out, my eyes were just as red as a beet and hurting, bloodshot completely."

⋖§ "Were you in a hospital?"

"No. The doctor came to the house, because it was going on in the whole village. So he came to whoever was sick, one after the other, he tried to save them. Some of the others died, but I came through. Later on my eyes were getting bloodshot and I was getting cataracts. Then I went to the hospital and they put something like a vaseline on—this burned the cataract out. I came home and in a couple of weeks or so, the same thing started again. I was in the hospital nine times before I came here."

⋐§ "It finally cleared up?"

"After a while, yes. Oh, my God, I was going for a long time. I didn't go to school over there because I was sick. After I got bigger, when my eyes hurt me no more, they put me in the first class. But you know, I was already big—I was twelve or thirteen. I went half a day and came home—I didn't want to go any more and they didn't force me to go. If they had forced me, maybe I would have gone."

⋐§ "So when you came over from the old country, you couldn't read or write, even in Ukrainian?"

"No. I had to learn. I took a book, you know, and from the book I learned. When you are young, language is easy to learn. American is not easy, but I learned it—not very good, but I learned it! Enough for me. To get around and, like, find the name or address of somebody. I cannot read much. But I never really learned to write, except my name and a few things like that."

⋐§ "Why did you come to America?"

"Because my sister came before me and two years later I went. My cousin came first, then she wrote for my sister, and after that my sister wrote for me."

⋐§ "And did they do well over here?"

"Very good, oh God, very good, all the while."

⋐§ "What did they write about America?"

"Nothing. Just, 'Come over,' and they sent the ship's card. What did they know? My sister was here a year already, maybe two years, working for $10 a month."

⋐§ "But she thought it would be better for you to be here?"

"Oh, sure. It is better. I expected to find that I was going to be happy—and I was happy. I was happy because I could make a dollar and send it to my mother. Pop died the year before I came here. What else could I do over there? We wanted to take my brother over, we sent a ship's card, but he turned it back. He didn't want to leave Mama all by herself, running the whole farm with the younger children.

"I came over here when I was almost seventeen, in 1912. Before that I would go to church in Lubachov and then walk home. What else? Where else do you go? You go no place yet, at that time. Today, yes. But not then."

⋐§ "What did you take with you?"

"Oranges! I had oranges. But oh, God, I couldn't eat. I got very sick as soon as I got on the train. I brought them to America—this is true. I took nothing else. A few clothes. That's all."

⋅◦§ "When you came over, were you planning to stay?"

"No, just two or three years. Everybody had the same idea—make a little money and go back home. But the war started and that finished everybody. You get so used to it here—and after a war, where are you going to go back to? So everybody decided to stay. You didn't make a lot of money, but things were cheap, so you made out all right. And I could send money home."

Whatever their original intentions, people like Mary Zuk found that they could *not* go home again—their homes had been destroyed and families dispersed. And life goes on. Before the war was over, Mary was married to a young Ukrainian man who had come to America also intending to stay just a few years, until the threat of a European war had passed. Like many others they settled in America to stay.

III

THE
SHADOW
OF WAR

"They were taking boys all the time for the army, but I didn't wait until they gonna call me. I skiddoo. I didn't want that they should bother me. If they would take me, it would be a very hard job to get out.

"My brother was in the police over there, on the other side. He left everything and came to America. He was the first one, showing the lead. I was after him second, then my cousin and his older brother. Oh, after that, lines were forming!"

❦

THEODORE LUBIK
Ukrainian, from Austro-Hungary
Arrived 1913

THE WAR changed everything. The Europe of empires was transformed into a Europe of nations. In their lust for power, territory, advantage, the political leaders created a juggernaut that destroyed them—and left millions of people dead or starving in the ruins.

Europe in 1914 was a powderkeg. Germany, Austro-Hungary and Turkey confronted Russia, France and Great Britain, with almost all the other nations of Europe ultimately to take sides.

People in the captive nations and cultures were going to be cannon fodder, and knew it. Poles held by Germany and Austria were being drafted to fight Poles held by Russians. Italians in the South Tyrol and Trieste were being drafted to fight their Italian brothers across the border. Jews were being drafted into the Czar's armies to fight for the greater glory of the Mother Russia which had systematically persecuted them all their lives; Armenians faced service in the Turkish armies, while their families were being massacred by the Turks; Greeks in Turkey and Serbs, Croats, Slovaks, Rumanians, Czechs and dozens of other peoples held by Austro-Hungary faced conscription.

The kings, czars and emperors might have denied that war was coming, but many people heard the rumblings in the distance. There had been local wars, border skirmishes, punitive raids, revolts, uprisings—and there was every prospect of more such "troubles." In the beginning, that's what people were fleeing—a continuation of those regional conflicts that had all the governments call-ing up the armies. Few expected that these local wars would coalesce into one massive war that would have most of the world choosing sides in a monstrous waste of life, as the old world died.

Many of the people who left Europe in those years left precisely because they did *not* have a side. Poles, Greeks, Jews, Ukrainians, Armenians and other minorities had no wish to fight in the armies of their oppressors. In fact, many young men who emigrated to avoid imperial armies, went back later to fight for national inde-pendence, in such countries as Greece and Poland. And some served in the American army, as volunteers or draftees. As one immigrant put it, "I was a Polish patriot—fighting in the American army for Polish independence." However, immigrants who were legally still citizens of the Central Powers—Germany, Austro-Hungary, later Turkey and Bulgaria—were considered enemy aliens and were barred from service. While the war did not make the world, in Wilson's phrase, "safe for democracy," it did—for better or for worse—make the world safe for nationalism, at least for a while.

THE LINES WERE FORMING

In those prewar years, imperial armies were being mobilized and draft-age men were fleeing in droves from the shadow of war. One young Ukrainian who left Europe to avoid service in the imperial army of Austro-Hungary was Theodore Lubik.

Dressed in a dark suit and white shirt and carrying a summer straw hat, Theodore Lubik has less formality than easy dignity. He looks not like the working farmer he was most of his life, but like a gentleman farmer of the old country. His face, at first im-passive, soon loosens into warm wrinkles as he recalls meeting, sixty years later, a friend from his hometown:

"He has a different idea, I have a different idea. We don't agree much."

ᴥᣘ *"Then or now, or both?"*

"Now. Before, we had one idea—nothing! Empty heads! We were

66

sixteen and seventeen when we came over to this country. Today, a seventeen-year-old boy is—'oh, a baby yet! Oh, oh!' Then, I made a couple of thousand-mile trips and I worked for my living and everything."

He laughs now at the "empty-headed" mischievous boy who came to America to avoid the army—and also to make his fortune. In fact, the man who gave him dreams of getting rich in America turned out to be bilking immigrants at Ellis Island—as Theodore later learned when this man got him a job at the Island. Theodore's story illustrates the complexity of motives that drew people from the old country to America, from the classic orphaned youngest son going out on his own to the draft-age boy fleeing conscription to the ethnic minority seeking freedom from oppression:

"When I left home, I just got on a train, with no suitcase, nothing —only the shirt on my back. I didn't even have money or a ticket—they were waiting for me in Hamburg. And nobody from my house to see me off, crying. They did their crying at home, so the officials wouldn't try to stop me for the army.

"I was born in what was Austria at that time—on July 24th, I'll be eighty-two years old, so that would be 1896. My town was Lubachov, a small city. It was near the city the Jews call Lemberg—that's the German name. But Ukrainian or Polish people called it Lvov. Finally, I figured, this fellow go, that fellow go, maybe I should go. Not because there was poverty or nothing like that, like some of them. I was pretty well off—my family were middle-income farmers. But I decided to come to America because I got a little bug in the head and that's all!

"I came in before the war—everything was nice and peaceful. That was in 1913. The war broke out next July, but I was lucky, I got out of it. One year ahead of time, that's all. But I was thinking about what's coming. There was too much talking and mobilization and all that kind of stuff. So I said to my brother, 'You give me the money because I don't have any.' He knew that if he gave me a certain amount—enough for the fare, the ship's card, and so on—I'm going to leave him what I used to own.

"I had my own piece of farm. My father died when I was ten years old, my mother died after him, and I was left. The farm was divided between five of us. So my brother was pretty lucky, he had the money to give me—$200—and I was off. In effect, he took what I owned there and what my brother already in America had. We made a paper and signed it over officially to his son.

"They were farmers, but I was the youngest. They always said something like, 'Go on, you shrimp. Go take care of the horses.' They wanted older ones to work. I was tending the cows, working in the pasture, nothing important. But I had eyes, I saw them, that's all.

"We had a well there. And a friend of mine, the first from our area who worked at Ellis Island, he came to Europe once on a visit. He always stopped by our well to water the horses. I saw him coming, oh, far away. I was already waiting for him. He looked just like a governor, horses, wagon, dressed fine, giving his pocket change to us. He gave me ten cents or a quarter—that was big money. And we had fun sometimes.

"He had gone to America. He was just lucky. Somebody gave him that job or something. But he was cheating the immigrants! He was so experienced and he had learned the language and he knew what it was about. Because when an immigrant came in, he didn't know how much a piece of money was—a dollar or quarter or whatever. The immigrant showed his money, this man took it. How did the immigrant know how much he took? So he helped himself. But he was a nice man, anyhow. Over in Europe I didn't see what he was doing."

✎ "So he was one of the people who made you think, 'Maybe I should go over there'?"

"Yes, that's the one. You see, I was looking for a still better life. That was a bad place to live for the Ukrainians. I shouldn't maybe talk like that, but the Polish people would persecute them, wouldn't let them talk their language. Everything was in Polish—the language in homes, in schools, and so on. In Ukrainian, we studied one hour a week. Of German, I think we had two hours a week. I still have my school report card! I've pasted it with tape and everything, but still you can read it clear. It says how good I was in Polish, Ukrainian and German. There was one school and that's all—six classes, that was the top. After that, they had college, or what they call gymnasium. I had a couple of years and was supposed to go on, but I didn't want to keep taking tests in Polish.

"We knew one man from my hometown who found himself a job as an agent in Hamburg. He spoke good German, he knew how to behave there, and finally—like here, with an agent working for some different trade—he was the one everybody wrote to. People were glad to get acquaintance with him. He fixed them up with the ship ticket and everything.

"So I had a deposit with this agent. He was waiting with the ship card and the money. Getting on the train, I had no ticket and no money —even if they searched me, I was clean."

✎ "So they couldn't stop you and bring you back into the army?"

"They couldn't prove I was going to America. I told them I was

Enrico Cardi, a fifteen-year-old war hero nicknamed "The Little Corporal," was wounded thrice and awarded the Croix de Guerre, and was brought over by an American soldier. Adopted briefly by singing star Elsie Janis, he was later deported when it was found that the "orphan's" parents were alive and well in Italy.

going to Germany. They examined me on the border, at Krakow, but they didn't bother me. You have nothing with you, so they take you for a traveler or something. I had with me only my identification book.

"Once I crossed into Germany, already, I was all right. I bought myself a valise, I bought myself another shirt. I bought whatever I needed, a piece of kielbasa and salami—that was German—because you need food on the ship."

For some, the danger was not a shadow, but a reality. Ethnic minorities were, indeed, often the first to be drafted into imperial armies and were often pushed into the front lines. So it was with Michael Pappas—or would have been had he not managed to escape the army, and the certain death that all of his friends met.

Michael, a Greek living within the Turkish Empire, was a classic immigrant. Aided by the Russian Orthodox church, which paid his fare to America, he had no training and no resources, only a name and address on a piece of paper. Although times were hard for him in the early years in America, he was able to build a successful restaurant, buy a 105-acre farm, and have a winter place in Florida—a far cry from the poverty and danger he left in those years before the war:

"I was born in a little village twenty miles outside of Constantinople. My father was dead. In 1913 there was the Balkan War. I was only sixteen years old and they tried to draft me in the army. The mayor of our town knew they were going to try to get us, so he told us to have our birth certificate with us. That way I could prove I was only sixteen, not twenty-one—which was the age when you had to go into the Turkish army. But one day I was standing in a street in my little town, and a cop came over and grabbed me by the neck and took me over to the coffeehouse. I saw there another fifty boys, all my age, all sixteen and under. At the same time, my mother found out that they got me. She came to the coffeehouse crying, so the Turk captain asked the mayor who she was. They told him that I was her son. He said, 'Why is she crying?'

"'She is crying because her boy is only sixteen.'

"The Turk told the mayor to call me up by name. So the mayor said, 'Michael Pappas, get up.'

"I got up and the Turk captain said, 'Sit down—you're in the army.' Then he told one of the guards to get this woman out of the coffeehouse. They got her out and I was told to sit on one side. It was September, drizzly outside and getting dark. So the captain told the mayor to notify the parents of the boys to bring clothing, underwear and a piece of bread or something, because we would have to walk all night, walking to Constantinople.

"Right back of this coffeehouse was the house of my grandmother. So they notified my grandmother and she brought me a little valise—not a valise, a little towel, a piece of bread, a little cheese and everything. She hugged me and she kissed me and she looked around and said, 'There is no Turk around here. Why don't you quit?'

"This coffeehouse was narrow and long and had two doors, one in the front and one in the back. The one door on the front was guarded by policemen. On the back, there was nobody. So I saw there was nobody, and she told me where to go.

"I went to a house where only girls were living, because the Turks

were going and breaking down the doors of the houses that had boys—
men. This house had only three girls. They were surprised, so I told
them all about it. They let me stay there.

"At five o'clock, the captain gave orders to call out all the boys.
Everybody came out of the coffeehouse and they called the names—no
one answered to my name. So they knew I was missing. The captain
said, 'Go out and search. Find him.' They started to blow the whistle all
over town looking for me while I was hiding in this house. But they
couldn't wait for me, so they went on to Constantinople. The next day
the local cops were looking for me all over but they couldn't find me.

"Now my grandfather had a nephew who was captain of a sailboat
—he had ten boats that sailed from our little village to Constantinople
every day, bringing grapes, vegetables and everything from Constantinople. That was the only place for me to go. The cops were watching
the sailboats. And all the roads were blocked. But they hid me in a
basket and got me on the sailboat. It took us nine hours to get to Constantinople.

"At Constantinople, a Russian, our patriarch—you know, a patriarch
is our religious leader—had fixed it up with the Russian Embassy to
help protect us boys who weren't army age. The Russian Embassy and
the patriarch had come to some kind of understanding with the Turkish
government, so they could let us leave Turkey. One of these Russian
representatives was there at the pier where all the sailboats parked. This
embassy man asked the captain, 'Daniel, you got any boys with you?'

"Daniel said, 'Yes, I got one boy.'

"So I got out. I was scared, you know. The embassy man told me,
'Don't be scared. The Russians will protect you. Get in line.' There
were about one hundred boys all my age. All Greeks. They had three or
four buses, and they put us all on the buses into Constantinople.

"You know, in 1884, there was a war between Turkey and Russia,
and the Russians reached outside Constantinople. When they signed
an agreement, the Russians built a big monastery. They called it San
Stefan, and it is still there now, I think. Well, they took us over to that
monastery. They had beds and they had the kitchen ready for us. The
man said, 'We will keep you here, you will stay here, eat here, sleep
here, until we have a boat from Russia or Rumania. Then we will put
you in the boat and then you go to Greece.'

"And sure thing, after a week there was the Queen Olga from Russia with the Russian flag. They took us to the boat. As I said before, two
guards were watching all the people who used to go on the boats. But
we were all fixed up so they let us go in there. It took us a day or two
maybe to cross from Constantinople to Piraeus—that's the big port of
Greece. On the boat I met four other boys from my village—but they

were grownup, about thirty-five or so—that were going to America. One of them was my godfather. We stayed in Piraeus two days and then we had to go to another port, called Patras, to get the boat for America. We stayed in Patras for a week and then the boat came from America to Patras and was going back. The name of the boat was Martha Washington, Austro-American Line."

◆§ "When did you decide you wanted to go to America?"

"Well, the Russian Embassy had my tickets all ready. The arrangements were made by them."

◆§ "In other words, the Russians were sending you to America?"

"The Russian patriarch. They bought the ticket—everything was ready. A few of the boys came to America. The rest of them stayed in Greece. But myself and a few other boys, we got tickets for New York."

◆§ "Why did you decide to go to New York?"

"They advised me to go. Greece was poor—I had no future there. It was better to go to New York which was in those days, like we know, the richest country in the world, with more chances, more future. I was only sixteen. That's why I decided to come to America."

◆§ "Did your mother know that you were going to America?"

"Oh, yes. They notified her. And you know, when I had been hiding in the town for three or four days, it was all fixed up that I had a few dollars. My mother, she had nothing, but my grandmother had a few dollars—so they gathered the whole thing. They told me, 'You'd better go to America because you have a future there. You are a young boy. It is better to go to America than to go to Greece.' "

◆§ "What happened to the boys that went into the Turkish army?"

"None of them came back. All got killed, died. I came to America in 1913."

IN THE MIDST OF WAR

If governments are, as Quebec's René Lévesque has said, judged by how they treat their minorities, then the governments of southern and eastern Europe and of the Near East did not show up well in those years. While the Western Front saw carnage in the trenches and ghastly new weapons—the poison gases, aerial fighting and bombing, huge guns like the Big Berthas, submarines—further east and south the plight of the people, especially innocent civilians, had its own special terror.

Like the Jews, Armenians had long been a persecuted minority, dispersed from their original homeland and subjected to periodic massacres throughout their history. The story of the Armenian holocaust, as told by Ida Mouradjian, reflects the fate of many thousands of Armenians at the hands of the Turks—and strikingly foreshadows the later holocaust under Hitler.

Ida herself is a strong, articulate woman, who speaks fifty years later with the pride of a survivor. Her salvation was education. Education, along with the experience of living in an international city, gave her the resources to survive the holocaust. And in her later life in America, education allowed her to make her living as a teacher in the schools of Chicago. But first she had to survive those terrible war years:

"I was born in the small town of Hadjan way up in the Toros mountains, that's Cilicia. It was a town of ninety percent Armenian population, a settlement that came from Armenia proper in maybe the ninth or tenth century. At the age of ten I was sent to boarding school for girls in Constantinople, where I really spent my growing up years. I was there until the summer of 1914.

"In 1914 I went back to my hometown for the first time. It took two weeks of traveling on horseback, wood-burning train and slow boat to get from Hadjan to Constantinople—that is why I went home on vacation for the first time after four years, with full intentions of going back to school. At fourteen, I had done one year of high school already and it was time I had a rest, my teacher decided. Unfortunately war started in 1914, or news of Turkey's implication with the world war, and I was not able to travel back. All the roads were closed to civilians."

◆§ "Tell us something about your family."

"My family was a typical family of Armenians. My father was a farmer, who had land in the valley, but he died of an accident when I was seven years old. My mother decided that I should have an education and that is how I was sent to school. I came from a background of education-minded people. An uncle of mine, my maternal uncle, had been educated in America. He had a Ph.D. from Yale, believe it or not, halfway around the world. And they believed that even girls should have an education. And with my father gone I suppose my mother thought that her daughters should be educated."

◆§ "Was that unusual?"

"Not at all unusual after the Revolution of 1908 in Turkey. Before that traveling was not very easy. You didn't even travel freely in your own country, let alone travel to foreign countries. It wasn't unusual, but it wasn't everyday practice. Every family did not believe in education for girls at that time and every family did not have the means or the ambition. But that wasn't the case with my family. You see, my family was influenced by American missionaries, and this is where, also, probably the ambition to get a higher education came in.

"Anyway, let's go back to 1914. I wasn't able to go back to school to Constantinople and in 1915 Armenian deportations started. Turkey was allied with Germany. The Allies thought that they were fighting a noble war, they were going to make the world safe for democracy, and then give back minorities their lands, and their countries, and their freedoms. Big talk. Big ideals which irritated the Turks and probably with the help and suggestions of Germany they thought, 'Well, if there are no Armenians, if Armenia is without Armenians, to whom are we going to give a country?'

"They proceeded into a diabolical plan of creating an Armenia without Armenians. Of course, they did not have sophisticated gas chambers, then. How would they accomplish this—Armenia without Armenians? They would displace every Armenian, get them out of their own homes, out of their own towns and drive them into the Syrian Desert. The idea was to get every Armenian there, and by the time they got there they would either die of hunger or exposure or pestilence. You might think it is unusual to find a desert in green Asia Minor, but there is.

"So they deported practically every Armenian family, young, old, blind, lame. Everybody had to go, including my family. Without regard to the fact that there were not even any male members in my family— my father had died, my brothers had been taken into the army, and there were only my mother and my old grandmother and we three sisters. The youngest was seven years old, and the oldest was sixteen. Well, we walked in the summer heat through impassable roads, mountains—that land is mountainous—and valleys, and across rivers. We became parched, hungry, and had sore feet, and we were resentful."

❧ "Did you go en masse? Whole villages?"

"En masse. For instance, there would be 500 to 1,000 in a group. They couldn't drive out a 48,000 population in one group. This would be impossible. So they divided them in groups. First they took the young males separately. Then the older males—I think that the idea was to take the male population first and kill them along the way, someplace, but later on they changed their minds. And then the rest of the population—men, women, old and young. Probably they wanted to leave us helpless. Who knows? Because if the young males were with us, they might start some rebellion, but what can a bunch of old women and helpless children do?

"After three months we reached a place that was an area of concentration. There they concentrated the exiles and from there they sent again separate groups to the desert. Well, this place was hell on earth, you cannot imagine, I cannot describe. If I tell you only that it was impossible to breathe the air from the stench of the dead and the rotting, maybe this will give you an idea. We wanted to close our noses and choke up to that, so we wouldn't have to breathe that air.

"Well, it would take too long to describe the circumstances, but a group of very young people, like sixteen, seventeen, they found a way. They hired Arabs with horses to put a few belongings on these horses and we would walk at the speed of the horses to reach Aleppo, which is a large Syrian city. There we might be able to find a way to get into the city and hide in the crowd. Well, I was young, I was daring and had had some exposure to the larger, freer world. You didn't live for four years in Constantinople and remain a backwoods little girl. We walked at the speed of horses. After three months of walking already, my feet were bleeding, my head was like a great big sore, but for the sake of saving my little sister and my mother I walked, I walked. We reached Aleppo in nine hours."

◆ઙ "Was the idea to get help?"

"You always hoped for help. Somewhere beyond that other mountain there might be help. We got to Aleppo and were put into another concentration camp, detained again, guarded again day and night. But I must have been quite intrepid. I can't believe it myself, I can't believe the daring, but when your life is threatened you get some kind of energy, courage from nowhere. I did escape. I entered Aleppo."

◆ઙ "How did you escape?"

"I was clad in rags. I always saw that my face was a mess because I was also afraid that I might be abducted—although to tell the truth this did not happen very often. But I took some rags and I said to the guard—there was a little stream, I noticed, running around the concentration camp—I said, 'These are my child's rags. May I go to that stream and wash them?'

"He said, 'Don't you dare to try to escape because I won't let you.' Well, I escaped. I saw a road, and I followed it, and he with a couple of others, they tried to catch me. I went back to that road afterwards and tried to measure the distance. It must have been at least two miles before I reached the outskirts of a city, where a Mohammedan, they call them mullahs,* got out of his carriage. He talked Arabic, which I don't understand, to these guards, and I think he scolded them for persecuting a poor, young little girl, 'Aren't you ashamed of yourselves?' And so I want to say that people mustn't think that just because the government planned this atrocity there weren't kind Mohammedans or even kind

---

* A learned teacher and interpreter of Islamic law.

75

Arabs, too, came to America. including this Syrian woman. The photographer notes that tattoo marks on her face and hands—a sign of marriage—did not show in the photograph.

Turks. That would be very wrong to say, because I did see extreme kindness, later on, too. So he asked me in Turkish where I wanted to go. I said I am looking for the pastor, the Protestant minister of the Armenian Church. He got out of his carriage and told his driver to take me to this minister.

"The minister wasn't home when I got to his home. I waited for him—I don't know how long, it seemed centuries. He came in. How should I describe him? He was not a man, he was a saint. He had devoted his life, his energies, to saving as many exiles as possible from the concentration camp. He said that I would not go back to the concentration camp, that I would stay there, and that he would do his best to save my family too, which he did, eventually. I won't go into the details, but at great difficulty, at probably great expense, he did save my family, and I and my family were in Aleppo. This was the optimum of good luck.

"Okay, we did not go to the desert, we were in a civilized city. For two years we hid in sub-basements and in God-forgotten attics. Several times they caught us and sent us to the concentration camp, and we escaped again. Oh, that would take a thousand pages, those experiences.

"Then there came a time when the Turkish army was defeated in

76

Jerusalem by the Allies, and the entire city of Aleppo became a hospital center. And who was going to take care of these wounded, sick, torn, burnt soldiers? The Mohammedan woman does not show her face to any other male but her immediate family. Therefore, the military government sent news through various ways to Armenian exiles who were hiding in Aleppo to come out, because if even one member of the family was accepted to serve in the military hospitals, her family would be saved from deportation. They could come out from their hiding places and live like free persons.

"This was, of course, too much to resist. I went and applied and again through some miracle was accepted. I was waiting to be interviewed. A military doctor, tall, good-looking, walked into the waiting room. He looked around and said, 'Child, what are you doing here?' I didn't recognize him. I had been away from school for two years. He was our school doctor. He took me in and introduced me, and I was accepted without question.

"I served in the military hospital for two and a half years. I did a very good job. The chief surgeon once called me in and said, 'My child, if I defer you, separate you in my heart and my mind from my own beloved daughter, may I be deprived of heaven.' This is kindness again. He was a Turk, an educated Turk, a Turk with a heart. He was a Sorbonne graduate. He loved speaking French with me, and I even tutored his daughter in French, during a war when we were fighting the Allies, including France. This takes nobility.

"Then the Turks lost the war completely. Aleppo was occupied, and the Turks vacated it. We went back home to a ruined city."

Ida hoped that she and her family, having survived those terrible war years, would yet be able to rebuild a life in that devastated land. Not until later was she to learn that her hope was in vain.

Other peoples, too, were forced to leave their homes during the war. One of them was Solomon Siegel, who here became a dentist, his son a doctor, and his grandchildren active in music and dance. Had the war not come, he might have spent his life in Lithuania; had his engineering school not closed seven years later, he might now be living in Russia. But, like millions of others, his life was wrenched from its foundations during those years, and his family was set wandering:

"I was born, actually, in Kovno,* capital of Lithuania. When I was ten years old, in 1914, the First World War started. Kovno was

* Now Kaunas.

one of the cities occupied—but the Jewish people were banished before
the Germans occupied it. Kovno was a fortified city and they thought
the Germans couldn't pass through it—they could stay there for months
and years. But what happened when the Germans came—they just went
right through it, they went so fast. It didn't make any difference whether
it was fortified or not.

"In 1914 they sent us out from Kovno. We had to leave all our
things. Of course, as a child, it was big excitement. I didn't realize—I
had no comprehension about the holocaust that was coming. And we
had to leave the town in forty-eight hours after the decree was passed.
Just imagine, Kovno, a city where roughly fifty percent of the population was Jewish—and they all had to emigrate within forty-eight hours.

"They had supply trains for us to go, but we do not know where.
On the day that we left, it was very hard to get a wagon to take us to
the station. There weren't that many wagons and that many horses at
that time. They were paying all kinds of prices for them—but my
brother had a derby hat. Well, the son of the janitor for our courtyard—
we lived in little houses around a courtyard—had a wagon. And he loved
that hat of my brother's. He wasn't interested in money so much—we
were going to leave things anyway. But he wanted that hat. He put on
that hat—he was so happy! And because of that derby hat, we got the
wagon and got out of Kovno."

Sol and his family went to stay with his aunt in Russia, to the
east, but not for long:

"We lived there for a little over a year. And then the Germans
started coming out fast, in about 1915, and everybody was running away.
It was not a case where they picked on the Jews alone. Whoever could,
ran. At that time, really, there wasn't any real reason for running, but
it was contagious."

Moving from relative to relative, trying to find a safe place to
settle and some way to earn a living, Sol's family moved on to
Smolensk, and finally ended up near Kiev. There Sol survived the
war and the later civil war that followed the Russian Revolution.
Once things began to quiet down, he wanted to get an education—
and almost ended up staying in Russia, as he describes:

"I was accepted to an engineering school near Dnepopetrovsk. At
that time there was a decision to be made. That was, I think, in 1921.
The Russians and the Germans had had the Brest-Litovsk Treaty. After
that, when the Allies won the war, in order to let the Germans come
out and to restore to the Russians the territories occupied previously,

the Allies had wrested from them an agreement. Lithuania became a state by itself, and Poland became a state by itself, and Latvia, Estonia and all those. All the people who had lived in those territories outside, if we wanted to, we could go back to our country. We were actually not of Russian citizenship but of foreign citizenship. If we decided to go back, they would give us the accommodations to leave Russia. I didn't want to go, because I was accepted to school to be an engineer. It was a privilege we had only for a short time—how short, you can't realize, when people can't leave Russia today. The people who stayed there, they just remain —a lot of them remain, dead."

As it happened, the engineering school closed down and Sol's mother had died of typhus. With nothing to hold him in Europe, he came to America to complete his education and build a new life with his wife, Frieda, who also fled from war in Lithuania. Many others had to make those choices of whether to stay or go, little knowing how permanent those choices might be.

For people caught up in the eddies of war, extraordinary choices had to be made. Rachel Goldman's family had to decide: which child should be saved? (They lived in Poland, in an area held by Russians before the war but occupied by Germans a year before she left.) In this case, the answer was more final than they knew, for although the family lived through World War I, the survivors later perished during the holocaust of World War II, after Rachel and her husband failed in all their efforts to bring her sister to America. Rachel tells of that choice:

"We were under German occupation for about a year and three months when I left my home in Bialystock. There was little food and a great many illnesses. My oldest sister was very ill with tuberculosis and not expected to live.

"I had another sister who had learned about people going to America, and since we had relatives here she wanted to go. When I heard about it, I wanted to go, too. But it was expensive and there wasn't much money—all the banks were closed and there wasn't any business at all. Whatever money my parents hid and saved, we had to use to buy food on the black market, which was very expensive.

"But we felt that somebody should be saved. I was the strongest of the children, and after a great deal of debate, they decided that they would permit me to go, and I left home shortly after my sixteenth birthday."

Various agencies were working in Europe to aid refugees. Most civilians, however, had no help, but had to struggle as best they could to survive those war years.

In many parts of Europe, people could and did use the period of occupation as a time of planning for the independence they hoped would come at the end of the war. Roman Umecka was one such person. Born in 1896, in Russian-held Poland near the border of East Prussia, his territory was occupied very early by the Germans, so he was not drafted. Roman describes how he and his friends prepared for independence:

"Well, we Polish people rose three times against the Czar, if you know the history of it. Of course we lost, but we wanted to get freedom of the Russians. They took so many taxes from Poland. Sometimes when they were taking the taxes to Russia, the Polish would stop the train some place in the woods and take it away because that belongs to Poland. We were fighting with Russia all the time—from the first partition of Poland in 1772 up to 1918. We wanted our own freedom.

"You know, when I was a boy, we were living only about a kilometer from the East Prussian border. People over in Prussia, they knew us. I remember, when we were watching the cows, the Prussians would be doing the same thing. Now we were one with them, you see—they knew that we got no school in Poland, so they were teaching us—these boys were going to school, and they knew everything.

"We had too much food, and we would sell mostly to Germans in the autumn. Us boys would get together and talk. Different people got freedoms—we see they got better. We were looking to the war for freedom. Polish people aren't dumb and never were.

"From 1914 when Germany took our part of Poland, nobody was taking us boys into the army, from 1914 to 1918. So lots of boys filled the villages and towns and there was lots of Polish ready to fight. Then when Poland started in 1918, all those boys went to town to get into the Polish army. Everyone wanted to be a Polish soldier.

"All the Polish army, they forced us to go to evening school, because they knew that Poland had no school before, so we had to start catching up. Evening schools were open all over in Poland to get the soldier's insignia. All those teachers from the part of Poland that belonged to Austria, where they had Polish schools, those teachers right away got into everyone's village in Poland.

"When I was still over there in Europe, my older brother was in the American army. He was a strong boy, and he went himself—they didn't call him—to join the American army in 1917. He was a soldier in that

Albanese soldiers.

Looking at these Russian (above) and Albanian (below) soldiers, we can easily see the fear they might inspire in southern and eastern Europe—but they, too, opted to leave the Old World behind.

first division in France—he got that German gas. All his life, he was kind of a cripple, but he lived to eighty-three. So we Polacks fight for this country. And not only have many brave in the first war, but also in the second war. Nobody, see, feeds us here for nothing."

◄§ "What made you join the Polish army?"

"I heard so much of Polish history from the old people, the way they were talking. In church, sometimes, they would close the big door and start singing Polish songs. So you start planning to get even. When the Germans were over there during the first war, we already were organized—all youngsters belonged to the underground Polish army. Maybe the Germans even knew it, but they left us—what can they do? We went into the army and began to take arms from German soldiers, wherever we caught them. Whenever there was two or three of them, they were afraid to shoot because there were so many of us and they knew we had some arms, so they gave us their arms. We got more and more arms like that and we were even fighting with them in some places."

◄§ "Like guerrilla warfare?"

"It began like that, because Poland had no regular army at that time."

The Germans remembered that disarming, as the fate of Roman's brother later showed. Roman himself, after fighting in the underground, fought in the Russo-Polish War that followed in 1920. But then he found he could not make a living in Poland:

"Poland was poor after the war. You see, everything was smashed. When I came out of the army in 1921, I couldn't find work. Of course, I didn't think that I was going to ever be in America. But such a misery there was at that time . . ."

So, like many others, Roman left his shattered homeland to join his brother in America.

WHERE IS MY FATHER?

Large parts of Europe were cut off from the rest of the world during the war. Europeans who had relatives in America could not know if they were alive or dead—Roman Umecka, for example, had no way of knowing that his brother was fighting in the American army. Such separation was especially difficult for the families who had sent a husband, a father, a breadwinner, to America. Not only could the families not get news of their relatives in America, but also no money could get through to help support people left behind in Europe.

One person who was cut off from her father for eleven years was Catherine Bolinski. Catherine's village, in that part of Poland that had been held by Russia, was occupied by Germans very early in the war. Her father had left in 1912, planning to make some money and then return to Europe—but he was also careful to avoid being drafted into the Russian army, as Catherine describes:

"He didn't go through the government because, as a young man, they might want him for the service. He went through different channels—usually the Jewish people handled it, they smuggled him across the border."

The Russians were out of the war by 1917, but afterward, war resumed between Russia, now the Soviet Union, and the newly formed Poland. The result for Catherine's family was that from the beginning of the war in 1914, they did not hear from her father until 1920 or 1921. Catherine describes what it was like during those years in occupied Poland:

"My earliest memories are when I was about five or six years old— it was the First World War—and we had to run from the village and hide in the forest. My father came to America in 1912; so he left my sister and I and my mother. We lived with my mother's parents, the five of us.

"In Poland, my father had worked for other people. We didn't have land, just a little cottage. We bought a lot, put the house in there, and a little garden. And when we wanted food, we just had to go to other people that had more land, and they gave us certain spaces to put potatoes, and cabbage, and things like that, so we could have them for the winter. Wheat or rye, you buy. And in the meantime, to repay the people that gave you the land, you agree with that person whether you want to work two days or three days a week—it depends on how much land he allowed you to have.

"My mother did the same thing, too, like everybody else. In a village there are no factories, there is no nothing, so you work out. The village had just a row of houses and the land was outside the village. In America, each farmer has a home on his own land, but there, no.

"We had schooling two winters. First, my grandmother's brother was teaching us how to read. In the second winter, they got another teacher from some place else that taught you how to write. So that's the education we had. In the meantime you do a lot of reading.

◆§ "You did a lot of reading. Most people don't.

"Well, you see, when you're home in wintertime, ladies are working on the loom, making things and sewing. Well, they sit the children down, give them a book. While they work and listen, you read to your mother, to your grandmother, whatever . . .

"My father came to America to earn a couple of dollars for a few years and then come back home. But in the meantime, the worst of it was we were cut off."

◆§ "How did your mother feel about your father going?"

"They agreed to it that he should come to America and come back to Poland in a few years. But when the war started, he could not come home. After the war, my father didn't want to. He said, 'Life is better over here.' So he did the papers to bring us here.

"When a distant relative of ours came back from America, I cried all day. I said, 'Where is my father? Why doesn't he come home?'

"My mother said, 'Well, we just have to wait to see if he is still living. If he writes to us—he knows where we are—we will find out what's going on.'

"That's when I was always thinking, 'This one's got a father, that one's got a father. Where's my father?' "

◆§ "When did you hear from your father?"

"About 1920 or '21. During the war you could not communicate at all. So we got the first letter. Then we wrote back, and we were corresponding for a couple of years. He wanted to come back and he didn't want to come back.

"So come to the end of it, my grandparents advised my mother. They said, 'You have young children. They will have a better life in America than we have here. So just go. We are not leaving here. This is our home, so we will get by somehow.'

"My father sent us the papers. We had to wait for our Polish consul in Warsaw and the American consul and had the passports made up. They didn't want anybody that's crippled, anybody that would be blind, that the government in America would be responsible. So they must test the eyes.

"The whole village came to say goodbye. Of course, my grandparents cried, they felt bad about it. We got somebody to drive us to the station. By the time we went down the road with the wagon, bags and all, my grandfather was already at the station—he wanted to say one more goodbye. Then we went to Warsaw, and it was kind of scary. Going on a street car, and the large buildings and different clothes—we stayed close to Mama."

84

People like this Albanian woman from Italy came from homelands where their native costumes had been unchanged for centuries, to a world that changed from full-length dresses to flapper outfits in less than a decade.

Even with an eleven-year separation from her father, Catherine Bolinski was relatively lucky—her grandparents provided a strong, loving, supportive home during difficult times. How much greater the wrench for those grandparents who chose to stay behind, knowing they would never again see their children and grandchildren.

Many people had no such family resources. With the skilled breadwinners in America, and mail service halted so no money could get through, many families literally starved. That was what happened to Judith Cohen.

Today Judith keeps a clean, comfortable house and is proud of it. Having lived in America for sixty years and having passed on to her children and grandchildren her high standards of propriety and cleanliness, she still shudders at how she and her family were forced to live during the war, with her father in America. Her voice drops with embarrassment as she describes their struggle against starvation and lice:

"I remember my stomach swelling from hunger. I remember going to my mother and crying for food. Can you imagine how a mother feels? My mother had five children. All she did was work for people that are better off in town, she was like a maid. She went in like the cleaning girls do here. But she had to be away from home—she left five children at home.

"My sister and I, we had long curly hair. Mother used to come home once a week and she would go through our heads. Why we had sores from scratching. You should excuse me a million times—the lice in Europe are like cockroaches in this country. When my mother came home on the weekend she had to walk the three miles from Warsaw, she couldn't get a ride—she cut our hair and would take our heads and wash them with kerosene and fine comb them.

"God Almighty, I start to think back in time. How we suffered hunger! How could we feel! So we took to stealing. My mother lived by a Polish man, a landlord, and all the Polish people, they all had farms. Isn't it funny, how they managed—couples, families, and they had big families those years. They had a little piece of land, a farm, they planted, they raised pigs, they raised chickens. They were always managing. Now we had a landlord. He had a big apartment, but we had one room—that was our place with five kids.

"We saw how they were digging potatoes out of the ground and getting them ready for storing them for the winter. I think I was maybe five or six years old at the time, but this I remember. They were loading up the basement with potatoes and with all their vegetables and everything—and here we're suffering hunger. My oldest brother at that time was about sixteen. So we fell on a plan—we were going to make a hole in the wall, connected to this basement with all those potatoes. Through that hole, we took one potato, two potatoes at a time—we started to eat. Then he had a fishing pole—a little birch off a tree. He tied a string on it, got worms and he went fishing—he used to catch these little fish. Now we had the potatoes and we had the fish—and my mother made a meal. So we ate!

"But this Polish man was smart. He noticed that his potatoes—they were piled up to the ceiling and, you know, as you take them from underneath they drop—he realized that they were not using that much potatoes that the pile should disappear so fast. So he came in to my mother and said, 'What is going on? I find that I am being robbed.'

"She said, 'I don't know anything about it. Do not accuse me, because I am going to sue you.' But she was afraid already that he might go down and investigate. So this hole was closed up and we had no more potatoes. We had nothing to live on. So we used to go in the garden and steal. But they were smart. They made the fences with those nail heads sticking up. They were high and, as a child, you could climb up, but when you got to the top, you had to go across—and either you caught your clothing in the nails or your flesh. I still have a mark on my foot where I was caught on a fence and I had a rip about two inches long. And that is how we survived—by stealing, actually stealing food.

"But you see, my father was in America before the First World War. He was a very good tailor and he made good money, and there was no reason for our starving. But during the war he could not send any money. *That is why we suffered like that. But after the war was over, our father in one shot sent us $700! Can you imagine in 1919 what $700 meant? So with the $700 we packed up and left. And then we really began to live. We came to this country on a first-class boat, not steerage. The tickets, everything, first class. We came like millionaires.*

"Once my father was able to send us money we were on Easy Street. The only thing that we suffered was because he couldn't send us the money to keep us going."

Despite these hardships Judith's family was at least reunited after the war. But Arnold Weiss, the man she met and married years later in this country, was not so lucky. His father, like her's a tailor in America, died in the worldwide pandemic of "Spanish flu" in 1919.

After his father left, Arnold never had a real home again, until he married Judith. Even when Arnold's mother reluctantly came to America, she had no skills to support her child. She married to provide a home for Arnold, only to have her new husband refuse to support her child—leaving thirteen-year-old Arnold on his own.

AFTERMATH OF WAR

Europe had been devastated by the war. Its young men had been conscripted, and millions of them had died in battle, of cold, of disease, and in prison camps. Its civilian populations had starved, their land had been plundered, their economies smashed. Even after 1918 fighting continued in the east, in the form of the Russo-Polish War and the civil war that followed the Russian Revolution.

The map of Europe had changed dramatically. Austro-Hungary was no more, replaced by a very small Austria, and the independent nations of Yugoslavia (including prewar Serbia), Hungary and Czechoslovakia. Large portions of formerly Austro-Hungarian territory had been taken by Rumania and Italy. And there was an independent Poland, for the first time in almost a century and a half.

The Czar was dead, and Russia had become the Soviet Union, under a Bolshevik government, along the way ceding large chunks of territory to Poland and Rumania and to the newly independent nations of Latvia, Lithuania and Estonia. Not for long—the inter-war period lasted only twenty-one years.

Germany was a republic, weak, disarmed, in chronic financial crisis, having lost western Poland; Alsace-Lorraine, which returned to France; and Schleswig-Holstein, which went to Denmark.

The Ottoman Empire, replaced by the Turkish Republic before the war, lost much of the Near East, but the persecution of its minorities continued.

In Europe, it was a time of continuing personal crisis, starvation, pain—and America, relatively untouched and in many ways strengthened by the war, was more attractive than ever.

In those years during and after the war, education, riches and status were no shield. Old dreams and plans had no place in that shattered world. People who normally would have lived in ease and comfort found themselves totally dependent on their own personal resources and occasional help from friends or kindly strangers.

Ida Mouradjian had thought, after surviving those terrible war years in the desert, in hiding, and in the hospitals, working to save her family, that she might be able to rebuild a life in the land where she was born. But she was tragically mistaken. There is a ghostly laugh in her voice as she tells about the town—and its people—that no longer exist:

"Hadjan, my hometown where I was born, will exist only in this conversation, because the Turks now say that there never was such a town, that we must be mistaken! We wanted to establish my husband's birthdate some years ago. We wrote to the American Embassy, the American Embassy wrote to the Turkish Embassy and word came from the Turkish Embassy that such a town never existed. Because it really doesn't exist now—they tell me that there is a way station, an inn, but there is no town there. You can't even tell that there has ever been a town. It didn't get ruined all by itself. No town gets ruined to that extent by itself. They had poured kerosene over it and burned it down to the ground.

"Well, we went back to these ruins with courage to rebuild it. From 48,000, only 10,000 survivors had remained, which in itself is a miracle. Later on, the Turks, the new takeover Turks, killed those 10,000, too—and there will be many to testify to the truth of my statement.

"But before this happened I wrote a letter in French to the head of the French Occupation,* who was a military man. He was surprised to find someone who could write French in this desert country. And he said, 'I will help you go back to school if you will promise to come back and teach in the schools that I intend to establish here.'

"I said, 'Hallelujah, that's what I want.' Well, I did go back to my school, which accepted me this time without tuition. They were so happy that I had survived. I stayed; then it took me three years to finish school.

"I lost my family during this last, while I was at school—I lost every member of my family in that second murder. All my efforts and my hard work—nothing. I don't know what they did to my mother or my older sister. I don't know to this day what their fate was, and if you think that's not enough to send somebody to the door of insanity, I've got news for you. I sometimes wonder myself how I did survive it and how I retained my sanity . . .

"After that I was lucky enough to get a teaching job in an American-established, American-financed school for boys. This family of very famous rug manufacturers had made it their business to help on their own. They had adopted one hundred boys and gathered them in a beautiful building and saw that they were educated, nursed back to health, and so on. I was one of the first teachers in that school. I taught school there a year. I intentionally took that job because it was a boarding school and it would help me save my money. I wouldn't have to pay room and board elsewhere. I taught there one year. I was very happy at my job.

"Everything was fine, but one morning I got up and the English navy had pulled out from the Bosporus. I felt terribly unprotected and terribly angry and terribly afraid. The principal of the school called me. By this time it was June of 1922. And he said, 'Miss Kazanian,' that was my maiden name, 'are you going to stay with us here?'

"I said, 'No.'

"He said, 'What are you going to do?'

"I said, 'I am going to go as far away as I possibly can.' Since I was fluent in French, France would have been the right place to go to. But France was swamped with Armenian exiles and they were already beginning to call the Armenians 'Sal Armenian,' which means 'dirty Armenian.' That hurt, that always hurts.

"And believe it or not, I had read Uncle Tom's Cabin, Lincoln was my hero, and I thought of a card my uncle had sent to Mother from Pasadena, California, which had said, 'Dear Sister: This is Paradise

* After World War I the French occupied Cilicia.

This Armenian Jew left Turkey in the postwar period,
in the wake of the massacres that wiped out Ida Mouradjian's family
and many thousands of other Armenians.

on earth. Some day I would like to live and die here.' And I thought,
'Well, maybe not Pasadena but maybe America. If there is a heaven
in America in one spot, there might be another one for me.' So I decided to come to America.

"I am here through a series of miracles. It so happened that the
principal of the school was a close friend of the American ambassador—
they had their summer homes adjacent. By the way, the principal was not
just a principal—not that the principal is always a great man—he was a
medical doctor who had married one member of this family that
founded the school. This man had given up his private practice to be a
father to these one hundred boys, and he said, 'Well, I don't see that I
blame you. And what's more, I think I can help you. I will give you a
recommendation to the ambassador, who is my personal friend and he
will give you every possible help.' He did.

"They were putting the ambassador's baggage on a carriage because *he was leaving in half an hour for England, for his summer vacation. But he did read my letter. He signed it and said, 'Take it to the consul this very afternoon.' I took it to the consul. The consul was very angry because this was discrimination—there were so many in line and why should I be pushed? But he couldn't very well go against the order of the ambassador. This is how I got on a boat."*

While Ida Mouradjian was able to make contact with the "proper authorities" in leaving Turkey, many refugees found it hard to know who the proper authorities were. After the war, old empires were replaced by new countries with new governments— who were none too happy to see some of their best or brightest or strongest leave for another country.

And yet "proper papers" were necessary—America was now requiring them. Gone were the days when you could enter America with a strong back, some hopes, and a slip of paper with an address on it, as Michael Pappas and millions of others did. In 1921, America instituted a quota system, with the quota set at three percent a year for each nationality as represented in the 1910 census. This "three percent law" limited overall immigration, as well as requiring that people have proper identification papers and clearance from European authorities. Long waits became the norm—though, as in Ida Mouradjian's case, the process sometimes might be speeded up.

The combined impact of postwar governmental turmoil and the American quota system is shown in the story of Sarah Asher. Like Ida Mouradjian, Sarah was a highly educated woman—she had to be, to wade through the bureaucratic tangles that kept her in transit to America for over two years. Sarah's family was especially privileged in being allowed to live in a major city, be educated at a university and work in the government, when most Jews were forced to live in rural areas in the Pale. But, privileges or no, in Russia the horrors of war, revolution and civil war were felt by everyone.

Once Sarah and her brother left their home, their skills allowed them to earn their keep as they followed their long arduous route to freedom. Listening to her story, you are struck by her buoyancy and irrepressibility—essential qualities for the long trip she undertook:

"We all had very good positions in government. We were all educated in our universities, so my brother was an accountant and I was working in the Justice Department. We were dictating the books of law. I was working on interpreting that, because certain laws that were created one hundred, maybe two hundred years ago, were outlived. Circumstances were so different and every time a different government —like if we had the Communist government come in—even if they were there a short time, they wanted their own way with the law."

◦§ "How did it happen that you were allowed to live in Kiev?"

"We lived in Kiev for many years before the war started. My father was a successful man. He was able to pay every year the taxes, about 1,000 rubles, the Jews had to pay. And we were a big family. We had the privilege to go to the high school and pay very little tuition.

"Well, 1914 the war started. The Germans started to raid Russia and we were in Kiev in the Ukraine, so we were not too far from the battle line. And naturally the army was going back and forth, and we had big hospitals in Kiev to accommodate all the wounded. And then, it was a losing proposition for Russia, because she wasn't ready for the war and everybody, all the population, tried their best to help to win the war, but it was very difficult.

"We were working, but the family was ten people, eight children and two parents, so it was very hard for us to just manage to eat. Not only to eat—we were in such a bad situation that even water we couldn't get. Besides, the sickness, cholera, started to spread in our river so we were cut off from the supply of water from the river we always had. Well, they dug some wells and sent us special purified water, but that was cut off from the apartments. We lived in a big house, six floors, and the water couldn't come, so we got a water supply only from about two o'clock in the morning to six. We were compelled to go some distance to get a little water to have a drink—or to rinse our mouths—but not to wash ourselves, that was impossible. We were also starved!

"The circumstances were unusual, because we went through all the revolutions and invasions—twice invasions by the Germans and then later other people like Poland invaded us. The situation was going from bad to worse. So my brother and I decided, well, we had a brother in the United States, we will try to go to him. Might as well—either die in your own country or, if we survived, we'll survive in the United States, where we really wanted to see our brother. My parents wanted we should go, but they hated to see us leaving the country, and leaving them, naturally. So one day we decided.

92

"We were able to take the train from Kiev, going down south, to where Russia was closer to Rumania. My brother and I came to this spot, where we found an old friend of ours, a young woman. She was a dentist and her husband was an engineer. They used to come to our house in Kiev. We stayed there for a while—it was summertime—and tried to cross the border, which was a river. Well, after two months we found the spot."

◄§ "You mean, during these two months you were trying to find the right spot to cross?"

"Yes, we couldn't just cross right over. Certain spots at certain times, only. So we came to Bessarabia, which was right then under Rumanian government. It belonged to Russia but it was overrun by Rumanians and everything was in the Rumanian language and the population remained there."

◄§ "How did the Rumanians treat the Jews?"

"Very nice. They didn't interfere too much. So we obtained papers as refugees. We found an office that gave refugee papers and tried to help people go places where they wanted to go."

◄§ "An office of the Rumanian government?"

"No. It was in Rumania, in Bessarabia, but the office belonged to the United States. It was the Joint Distribution Committee and they had an office there. While we were there, we didn't know what to do. We couldn't find our brother right away because we lost his address. They offered us positions—I worked as a secretary and my brother as an accountant. And so we thought it wouldn't be long before we got to go to the United States. You had to have a visa, you had to have passports, and in the meantime we were working there. It took about two years.

"We were assisted by another committee to find our brother in the United States. That was HIAS (the Hebrew Immigrant Aid Society), through the American Joint Distribution Committee—they were very nice to us. They gave an advertisement in a Jewish newspaper that happened to be read in Chicago. One of our relatives read it—we had never met him, but he knew my brother. And that cousin cut it out because it said Sarah and Joseph Braverman—that's my maiden name—are looking for a brother, Paul Braverman. It happened that somebody else was reading the paper, and told him about the advertisement. He saw that we were looking for our brother, so he right away wrote to the newspaper with my brother's address in Buffalo.

"So we found our brother. When we got the announcement, imagine how happy we were! We started to correspond with our brother and he said, 'Naturally, you are coming to me.' He was poor; he had a few dollars in the savings bank and he was a married man with a child. He had to send us money, because the money we made just covered our expenses. He had to pay for the passport—not for the visa, the visa was five dollars—but the main thing was to have the passports. Passports allowed a certain amount of people to come to the United States. How do you call it?"

◦§ "Quota?"

"Yes. So it took over two years until we got the papers and at the same time we were working, and we were content."

◦§ "Why didn't you stay in Rumania? Did you consider that?"

"We were anxious to go to the United States and see our brother, because we had studied so much and learned so much, we were really anxious to see the country. So we got the papers and later the passports came. We went to Bucharest, the capital of Rumania, to get the visa for America. But when we came, we found our passports had been annulled by the United States from Washington!

"You see, my brother was a veteran in America, so he had the right to bring us. He sent an application to Washington to the right department that he wanted to bring us there and by the time he got the papers, our passports were annulled. They found out that they weren't good passports, that we weren't really Rumanians; we were Russian refugees. It was different rules.* He thought we were coming on those passports, but the passports were annulled and we were just left without any way of coming. What to do?

"We decided to go back to Kishinev where we were working and explain what happened. Then a few days after we returned, I read in the newspaper that in Bucharest they had a representative—the old Russian representative.** We wrote a letter that if we could come and explain our matter, maybe he could assist us in going to the United States. He answered very nice that we should come.

"So we again took the train and came there in the morning. He was very delighted to see us, I have to say. He was so nice and kind and he heard our poor experiences, bad experiences, and he said, 'Well, while you are here, I'll send a telegram to Washington to see what I can do for you. I may get an answer around four or five o'clock this afternoon. Would you like to come to me tomorrow morning to hear the answer?'

"We stopped in some kind of little hotel and the very next morning he showed us the telegram that we were allowed to come to the United States on our Russian papers. Can you imagine? We had with us our diplomas and some more Russian papers. So we were very happy.

"We had very little luggage with us, and we didn't have too much

---

* They fell under a different quota.
** A representative of the Imperial Russian government, not the new Soviet government.

money. We had just $16 to cover our expenses. We had to have an American visa and a transit visa. If you went through Poland, you had to have a Polish visa, and an Austrian, too. We had to go to Hamburg because my brother wrote that he had sent two tickets for us to Hamburg; that's where we had to get the boat.

"But to have the money, it was very difficult for us. I went to HIAS, but they refused to give us money. They said they did not supply individual money, that is your own business. I said, 'We have to have the transit visas.'

"They said, 'It's up to you how you go.'

"So we decided. Poland didn't want to give us visas because my brother was a man and they said that he should go into the army—he was a lawyer in Russia and didn't have to go. Well, they didn't want to give us, so we went to the Austrian ambassador. He said all right. We had to go through Hungary—Hungary okayed us to pass by or to stay for a day or so. From Bucharest we went to Hungary through Budapest by train. Then we went to Austria and then Hamburg. Germany gave us the transit visas so we were free from that trouble.

"Money we didn't have, the little money that we had in Rumania we had to exchange in every country like Hungary, and then Austria, and then Germany. But we weren't worried that we would starve, that we were hungry, we just didn't worry. You get so accustomed to circumstances. So it took us, I would say, about two or three days to cross all of Europe and get to Hamburg."

WAITING FOR A NUMBER

In 1924, the United States passed even more restrictive immigration legislation, setting the annual quota at two percent of the number of foreign-born people living in the United States as of the 1890 census, with a minimum of one hundred for any one area. Since most immigration before 1890 had been from northern and western Europe, this "two percent law" heavily favored the "old immigration," drastically cutting the "new immigration." While under the 1921 quota law, "new immigrants" could make up about forty-five percent of the year's quota, under the 1924 law, southern and eastern Europe could make up less than fourteen percent of the total.

The effects were tremendous. Polish immigrants numbered 122,-

657 in 1913–14; by 1923, that was cut to 19,371; but the quota for 1924 was set at just 5,982. People from other countries of the new immigration felt the same pinch, with resulting very long waits, even for the lucky few who managed to get quota numbers. The process is described by Irma Busch, who, as one of the relatively favored northern Europeans, had an easier time than did her new immigrant counterparts.

America disappointed Irma. Not the country, or the opportunity, or the people, or the freedom—she appreciated these even more after a later encounter with Hitler's Nazis—but the lack of frontier to explore. She laughs ruefully today. "I would have liked to be here during the covered wagon days. I would have gone West with anybody. I mean it!" Still as slim as she was at age seventeen, Irma talks about how she decided to come to America in 1925:

"Well, you know, this really goes back to the First World War and the starvation we went through. I was six years old when the First World War started. By 1915 or '16 there was no food. I lost three little sisters from malnutrition—we had half a pint of milk a day between us. At four o'clock in the morning we had to stand on line to get a few potatoes. We had three meals a day out of ground turnips. That was all we had. We used to try to get into somebody's garden to pick up the green apples that lay on the ground. There was never anything, really, to eat in those days.

"We had to flee because it was said the Russians were coming. We were living in Brandenburg at the time, near Breslau in Upper Silesia. My father had been drafted, he was in the reserves. My mother packed us up, all the little kids—we were five then; she had lost four children. We moved close to Berlin because she had two brothers who had good-sized farms near there. She hoped that maybe there we would be able to get some extra food. I spent my summer vacation there on the farm, working along with everyone in the fields and boiling potatoes for the pigs and all that sort of thing, but I had good food. Then it became slimmer because the government was taking the food away from the farmers to send to the front for the soldiers.

"Of course, books to me meant everything. I would read anything, even labels, you know. So I read so much the Fenimore Cooper stories, and about the wild West, Buffalo Bill, and all that. I wanted to go to America. When I was about eight years old I wanted to go. Well, I had this uncle, a younger brother of my father's. After the war was over, he came to visit us—he worked on a liner of the Hamburg-American

In the Ellis Island years, many people also emigrated from the
West Indies, among them, this group of women from Guadalupe, in 1911.
Marcus Garvey, leader of the Back to Africa movement,
emigrated from Jamaica in 1916.

Line, sailing between Hamburg and New York. So when he came to
visit, I told him this was where I wanted to go.

"Well, okay, it took awhile. First, my parents didn't want to give permission. They wanted me to be a nun. In the interval, I went to commercial college—I had two years of English there, and had been working
already. When I was sixteen, I got a job right away when I got out of
school. But then when I was almost seventeen, my parents agreed that I
could go, if I wanted to, as long as I didn't want to become a nun.

"So I went to Hamburg in 1924, and it was one year before I finally
got my quota number, in 1925. But first of all I had to have my papers
ready. In those days, if you were an émigré, you had to have a statement
from the police that you were a proper moral person, and then you got
your passport and went to the city where you would sail from—there
you waited for your number.

"At the consulate, they said to me, that if I had been born a little bit
further down in Silesia, in the Polish sector, I couldn't have come here,
because that would have been under a different quota. There were always more people applied from that part than there was a quota for. The
part I came from was different. The borders have been moved so many
times!"

While Irma Busch describes bureaucratic difficulties in arranging for a quota number, in some areas getting in under the quota was almost impossible without "knowing someone." In Germany, the quota under the two percent law was 51,227 immigrants a year. Just over the border to the south, Austria had an annual quota of 785. One person who conveys the effect of that restriction is Adele Sinko.

It's hard to picture Adele in the midst of starvation and suffering. The laugh lines are too deeply etched on her face and she talks with such an easy good humor. World War I left her with the memory of starvation—but she now laughs as she comments that's probably why she likes to eat a little too much. A large woman with twinkling eyes, she could be anybody's grandmother, as she tells her story:

"My childhood was very sad, because in 1914 the war started and I was ten years old. We went through a lot. We weren't in the war, but had had starvation for about three years. The end of it was I had TB, but I got saved, you know, with a big scar on my lungs. To go through starvation is terrifying—there is just nothing to eat!

"We were living outside of Vienna. There was a big factory there, one of the Krupp factories. Three thousand people worked in there, and the factory built up all the houses for the people to live in. But where we lived was all private. Father worked in that big factory, but he was a manager of over thirty men. He did pretty good, but not good enough for such a big family. Because we had my mother's parents living with us and there was eleven in the family—and only him alone to work. I had six brothers, and I'm the only girl. In 1914 I learned dressmaking."

◄§ "Were any of your brothers conscripted into the army?"

"Oh, yes. Three of them were. One didn't have such luck. He got shot in the head, but he lived—but you know you're not all there after that, and something was a little wrong. And one was in a boat in the Adriatic—all this towards the end of the war—but he swam to shore. He was told the war is over and he was so surprised! Then it took him twenty-one days to get home because nobody took care of soldiers, there was just such a mixup in the whole country.

"And the third brother was shell-shocked and gas-poisoned in Italy. That's the one that came over here, and he brought me over then. He never was well the rest of his life, because when you are shell-shocked, all your nervous system is upset. But he met a girl who had an aunt over here, and he wanted to get away from Austria. So they got married and *they came over here in 1921—he was just twenty-one years old.*

"So they decided, 'Adele, let's bring her over.' It took me two years to get a visa. It wasn't so easy, you know. I was supposed to come with another brother, but in the meantime he got killed and I was alone when I came over."

⊷§ "Do you remember what you had to do to get your visa?"

"We couldn't get it at all. There was less than nine hundred people who would be allowed to come in, but those places were always taken. Then my father went to a priest and he talked to him about it. So he said, 'I'll see what I can do.' Through that we got the visa. You have to know somebody."

⊷§ "Did you have to bribe officials or anything?"

"No, no, no. We came to the consulate and the fellow, the big man, said, 'How come they are going through?'

"Another man replied, 'Well, on the recommendation of Senator So-and-So.' So we got the visa."

⊷§ "What did you bring over with you?"

"I didn't take much. My brother said, 'Don't bring any junk, you can buy anything here.' So I really just brought clothes. But I tell you something—me, as a dressmaker, I made all my own underwear, real fancy and all this and that. Then I sent it all back. I liked it here better!"

Under the 1924 immigration law, certain nonquota immigrants were allowed into the country. Among them were children and wives of immigrants, as well as immigrants previously admitted who took a temporary visit abroad. In the postwar years, families of alien veterans of the United States Army, like Sarah Asher's brother, were also allowed to enter as nonquota immigrants.

The 1921 and 1924 immigration laws also gradually shifted responsibility for medical, literacy and other checks to the American consulates abroad. A policy long advocated by reformers, this clearance abroad greatly reduced the number of people rejected at Ellis Island. Vera Gauditsa was one of those who was checked and cleared in her native Czechoslovakia, and who came over as a nonquota immigrant, to join her American husband.

Vera is a traveler. You can see it as she strides along the beach on her daily two-hour walk, in loose-fitting blouse, slacks and visored cap. She's as slim as when she fooled the American doctors in Prague into letting her cross the ocean while she was eight months pregnant. As she says herself, "I like to travel. I like to go by plane. If I was young today, I would probably try to get a job as a stewardess." And lucky for her, the child she was carrying on that first trip fifty years ago is today a pilot, so she has been able to fly all over America and to return to visit her homeland. What was an ordeal then, she describes with a great deal of laughter today:

"When I was traveling here, I was pregnant eight months. It was the law in that time that a woman was allowed to travel* no more than five months pregnant. But I was very thin then and I thought to myself, 'This child has to be born in the United States!'

"When I came to Prague, the American doctor there didn't speak Czech—I couldn't talk to him, but the nurse spoke the Czech language. She said he wanted to send me back home—that I am more than five months. They examine you and look at the veins and everything, and everything shows. But I tell him I am just five months pregnant.

"So then he sent me to the highest clinic in Prague and I began to cry about what they were going to say. But three doctors, they put me on the table and examined me. I almost thought it was over. Oh, I must have been a good liar. I was afraid I'd get mixed up, you know, so I just kept saying, 'Five months! Five months!' I came back to the American doctor again and he didn't want me to travel to America. But the three doctors at the clinic okayed the five months, so he was shut up.

"I was foolish to travel when I was eight months pregnant—actually it was seven and a half. I was eight months pregnant when I arrived. But somehow I was happy that I had fooled those doctors. Maybe they were sorry for me. I would never advise anybody to travel that late. Of course, I grew up on a farm in Estonia and in those days, the food that we used to eat had no chemicals, everything was natural. We had cows and grew our own food. If I wasn't so strong, maybe I would not be able to hold the baby under those conditions.

"The country I came from was far away from Prague, near the Tatras Mountains, in the lower country. That was about 182 meters, or 400 to 500 miles from Prague. Growing up during the First World War was very hard—we starved. I was thirteen when the war started and my father was killed in the war. I was alone and there was no such thing as government support, as they have in this country. My brother, who was the oldest, was wounded and came back and supported me."

⮞ "How did you decide to come here?"

"My husband was born and raised in New York, but his parents had been our neighbors. He was about twenty-four or twenty-five the first time he came to Europe to see where his parents came from. So the first time we met and then the second time he came again and we got

* To immigrate.

married—I knew him only three weeks. I wanted to go to the United States. Before the war we belonged to Austro-Hungary, but after 1918 the Czechoslovakian Republic started. We had a terrible, terrible time, with no jobs, lines and lines waiting for jobs. When I lost my father in the war, I was planning to go to the United States. I had two uncles there.

"Then my husband came to Europe and we got married—but I stayed for five years after that—I left in 1928. Between 1923 and 1928, my husband traveled back and forth. Then I went to Prague—where they had the best medical examination, and then twenty-eight hours on the train to France, where we waited eight days for the boat to land."

THE DREAM STILL ALIVE

Of all the images of America—the land of Lincoln and freedom, a safe haven, a land of opportunity, an open frontier of cowboys and Indians, a refuge—perhaps the most persistent was the image of America as the golden land, a land of ease and plenty. The image was fed in the early years by the propaganda of profiteers who benefited from the transport and cheap labor of immigrants— but it was supported by the many immigrants who visited or returned to live in their homelands, almost always more prosperous than when they had left.

The persistence of the dream is well expressed by Esther Almgren. One of the favored northern Europeans, Esther's image of America in the 1920s is little different from the idea of the Golden Land held by immigrants many decades before:

"I was born in a city called Malmo in Sweden. My father was a carpenter and he wanted to move to the country, to build houses. So we went to the country and he built a home there for us. I went to school there until I was twelve years old. But in Sweden then we had to go out and take a month off every year from school to help the farmers to pick potatoes, from the time you were about eight or nine years old. When I was twelve I had gone through the schools and I asked if I could quit. They said I passed everything and I could.

"So then I went to Stockholm and I worked in a laundry for nine years first. Then I went to work in a department store. And at night, I wanted a little extra money, I was waitress in a big restaurant. You know Sweden was very poor at that time. You lived pretty good when you had a good job, but you couldn't eat like we do in this country. You had to save and do things, so we could go over to this country and pay the boat fare. I was married for three years at that point; I was married in 1920."

❧ "What did you bring with you to this country?"

"I didn't pack. I could have packed much more, but I didn't think I could take it through. We had a lot of crystal in Sweden and my dresser was full of crystals and combs for the hair, nets and all that. I left it all, and my silver from my wedding I left. I thought you couldn't bring it over. It was a shame—I could have. They wouldn't have said anything."

❧ "What did you end up bringing?"

"Only my clothes, that's all, and a few tablecloths and a little embroidery stuff I did in Sweden, but nothing else. We had to start all over."

❧ "Why did you want to come to the United States?"

"I figured you're going to be picking gold out of the mountains, everybody thought that America had no work, you have it easy, that you could make more and more and more. They thought that it was easy here. But I was never afraid of work. God has been with me and been good to me in this country and I love this country."

❧ "But you didn't find any mountains to pick gold out of?"

"I didn't find any mountains to pick gold out of."

But at the end of that decade, the bubble burst. After the Great Crash of 1929, it was clear that America had no gold to pick up from the streets, no automatically easy life. The annual immigration that had for some years before World War I been over a million a year and which by 1930 had been cut back by restrictive laws to under a quarter of a million, had by 1931 dropped to below 100,000, with only about one-third of the year's quota filled. Not until 1946 was the annual immigration to rise again to above 100,000, then for different reasons and from a different world. A flow of people that hadn't been stemmed by a world war or quotas was finally quelled by a worldwide depression. The Great Migration was over.

But the voyage of the people we have been following had just begun. Having left their homes and crossed overland to reach the seaports, they had completed only the first stage of their journey. Now they had to cross the wide ocean to reach "that America" on the other side.

IV

VOYAGE TO THE GOLDEN DOOR

"Seeing the Statue of Liberty was the greatest thing I've ever seen. It was really something. What a wonderful sight! To know you're in this country. God, just think of it!

"I remember as a child people used to say to me, 'In America you'd find gold in the streets.' The streets of gold! And as a child I said to myself, 'Gee, we're in America. Now I can go out in the streets and pick up gold.'"

◆§◆

ARNOLD WEISS
Polish Jew, from Russia
Arrived 1921

PIRAEUS, Trieste, Naples, Marseilles, Rotterdam, Southampton, Hamburg—all the great port cities of Europe played host to generation after generation of southern and eastern Europeans leaving the old world for the new. Streaming across Europe into the port cities, people breathed their first lungsful of salt air and were cut loose from the land, from their former lives. For them, the ocean air carried the heady aroma of freedom and gold mingled with the bracing tang of the salt.

The journey to the ports had been hard. The immigrants had learned to bribe the border guards and breathlessly race through the night, like Leon Solomon and so many others; to beware of robbers, like Steve Pakan; to cope with new experiences, new hazards every step of the way. But once in a port city, some of the fear evaporated. Suddenly it was legitimate to be an immigrant. Although there might still be bars to boarding the ship to America, and the whole voyage across the sea and the passage through Ellis Island lay before them, the midnight escapes and constant vigilance seemed things of the past.

AT THE PORTS

Immigration was a big business, involving millions of immigrants and hundreds of thousands of others who made their livings from the immigrants. These included immigration agents working as freelancers, as well as the proprietors and employees of the immigrant hostels run privately and by governments all over Europe and especially in the port cities; the railroad, ferry and steamship company people who transported them; the border guards, health officials and customs people who regulated and inspected them; the people who sold them food and other necessities en route; and even the thieves who preyed on them.

Many immigrants arrived at the port cities with steamship tickets in hand, having purchased them—or received them from relatives in America—as part of a package for transportation from their homes all the way to their destinations in America. Others purchased tickets on arrival in port.

The difficulties surrounding land transport often made it impossible for immigrants to schedule travel to meet specific ship sailings. Those arriving at a port city, therefore, sometimes made very quick connections with ships to America and sometimes had to wait for as long as a week or two for connections. Those arriving already ticketed were sent on as quickly as possible by the steamship companies from which they had purchased tickets, as the companies were by law in many countries made responsible for the care and feeding of immigrants awaiting passage on their ships. The companies usually put them up in private boarding houses, often run by their "landsmen." In some ports the governments ran hostelries for the immigrants and charged the ship companies for their keep, and some steamship companies built their own facilities. One model establishment just outside Hamburg, where Sarah Asher stayed, was built and run by the Hamburg-American Line, a major immigrant carrier.

From 1891 on, the American immigration law required that the shipping companies vaccinate, disinfect and examine their immigrant passengers and clear them before sailing; that they pay for the housing of detained passengers at Ellis Island and other American ports of entry; and that they ship rejected immigrants back to their ports of embarkation free of charge. The shipping companies complied, with cursory, quick and often remarkably ineffectual inspections, vaccinations and disinfection procedures, usu-

ally preferring to pass prospective immigrants and take their chances on the acceptance of most in America. Tens of thousands of immigrants who might have cured their physical problems and come to America a little later were instead sent on, only to be rejected and sent back to Europe from Ellis Island and other American inspection stations. Thousands of others, who had sold everything they owned and were accepted for passage, arrived in America to find that they had incurable conditions that barred them from the United States. All of these people were forced to go back to Europe, landless, jobless and infinitely worse off than they had been before they left their homes.

The sole major exception during some of the years before World War I was Italy. Fiorello H. La Guardia, as American consul in Fiume from 1903–1906, insisted on careful medical examination of all United States–bound immigrants, battled the shipping companies, and made his ruling stick, to the considerable benefit of those emigrating. The Italian government, seeing the success of La Guardia's experiment in Fiume, adopted his approach, and conducted careful medical examinations of emigrants after 1908, sharply cutting the number of those rejected in the United States and sent back to Italy penniless. Other governments, particularly those of northern Europe, conducted medical inspections of their departing emigrants after World War I. Then in 1924 the United States began requiring that immigrants' primary medical examinations be conducted before embarkation to America.

In addition, the American immigration law of 1893 required the shipping companies to get basic information about each immigrant before sailing, in the form of a ship's manifest—much like a description of any other cargo being carried—and to pass that manifest on to the American immigration authorities. Each immigrant was to be queried by a ship's officer, before sailing, on basic identification, origin, destination, ticketing, financial resources and sponsorship, as well as on medical, psychological, political, marital and other personal matters. Again, the work done by the shipping companies was often rushed and careless, and consistently skewed in the direction of getting the immigrant's passage money. In the early years, some manifests filed were simply false, with shipping companies fined only minor sums for submitting them to the American authorities. Inaccurate manifests caused many problems later, because these manifests served as a basis for examination by Immigration Service inspectors at Ellis Island and other ports of entry.

BREATHING SPACE

For some, the port cities meant long and difficult waits for papers, money and traveling companions. For others, a wait of a day or two, even a week or two, for the next boat meant a chance to break the trip to encounter a wide range of new and fascinating experiences. For these, the ports were a breathing space.

Celia Rypinski arrived in Rotterdam with a trainload of emigrants from Poland and other points east. Their two-day delay in Berlin had caused them to miss the boat they were headed for, but she wasn't at all upset. She was much too happy at getting away from her sister-in-law to worry about a short delay. Rotterdam welcomed her and provided a glorious experience for a thirteen-year-old traveler in peaceful 1908:

"We stayed there two weeks waiting for another boat in a big place . . . a beautiful place! We used to go to church every morning. It's a beautiful city, Rotterdam . . . on the ocean. I saw people living on the strip of land between the waters, with boats on either side. Cows were there. Oh, I had a ball!

"When we missed the boat, the whole mob was going to one place and they had people to take care of us greenhorns. We went to this great big house where we stayed two weeks waiting for the boat. Oh, the grand food! There were pickled herrings and that good butter, home-made bread that they were baking there. Boy, did I have a feast!

"Well, we were examined through the hair and through the body. But there were beautiful bathrooms and toilets. I had a double-decker bed and the others and I used to sing songs and if they sang Polish I sang with them. The time went by.

"I remember the great big horses pulling the great big kegs of beer. We used to have horses at home and I love them even now. If my father said for the boys to go and get the horses from the field, before they looked or finished eating I was in the field. So I admire those great big

horses with the wide feet. Four of them always pulled the beer in Rot-
terdam. In that building where we were there were a lot of halls for
young people that like to eat and drink and everything. It was pleasure,
till we came to New York."

Celia waited in Rotterdam, and her memories are those that
stayed in the mind of the child she was then—memories of new
and wonderful foods, of marvelous sights. And, almost by accident,
a stray recollection of the actual processing that all the immigrants
had to go through.

Fourteen years later, eighteen-year-old Rosa Martino—who later
married a fellow Sicilian, Frank Santoni—felt the same way, traveling to America with her brother in 1922:

"The trip, it was beautiful. I was young, you know. First we went to
Palermo. Then you have an overnight trip to go to Naples. The over-
night trip to Naples was quite uncomfortable, because there are a lot
of whirlpools in that part of the ocean . . .

"The three days in Naples were lovely. We walked around and at
that time on every corner was somebody with a guitar and a mandolin—
singing, singing. I thought Naples was the most beautiful city in the
world. There were a lot of young boys, young girls, that would come
to this country. So you can imagine the really wonderful time that I
had . . ."

But for Vera Gauditsa it was different. Even though she was
traveling second class, not steerage—in 1928, rather than in the
early immigration years—she found conditions at Le Havre almost
unbearable, quite apart from the fact that she was eight months
pregnant:

"When we came to France they put us in this place and I was
waiting there eight days for the boat to land. We came by train to the
harbor, to the dock. You should see where they put us—there were so
many people in such horrible scenery to look at while I was traveling
to that boat. They put us in some kind of storage room by the ocean
and you could hear the water at night.

"The toilet was in the floor, like an open sewer. We just went like
dogs and that was the toilet! I could not go there. Everybody, men and
women, were doing just that and you see them in this room. I just could
not go in a bathroom like that, and it started to work on me and I
started to be sick there.

"And at night it was so cold there! It was February and there was

no mattresses. It was straw on the floor and sheets on top. And we were there eight days, in that kind of place. You do not know the language, have no money."

Where you sailed from made a vast difference in your accommodations while you waited for a ship, as Vera found. If she had left from another port, she might have had a more pleasant wait. Catherine Bolinski went through Southampton in 1923 on her way from Poland. At age fourteen, she was traveling with her mother and younger sister to meet her father, who had gone to America eleven years before:

"We took a small ship to Southampton, England, and out there we stayed a whole week. The first thing I remember, because I'm a good eater, is the food. In Southampton, we had very good food.

"It would be about the middle of October. You needed a sweater or something, but it wasn't cold. We stayed in a large building, maybe fifteen, twenty, thirty beds in one big room. We kept to the group that we were with.

"When they say you come for breakfast at seven o'clock sharp, you look at the clock and you were there by the door at seven o'clock sharp. Because if you got there at seven-thirty or eight o'clock, there might not be enough food to give to you. You just lined up and the door opened. You cannot get in until a certain hour. You ate what they gave you. The food was different from what I was used to, mostly hard rolls, hard bread, sometimes a little soup, sometimes a small piece of meat, other times just vegetables. Whatever it was. But they always be sure that there's bread. If there was an extra roll, I put it in my pocket, saved it for later.

"My mother looked to be sure that we kept warm, not get sick, and so forth, because we had to go before doctors, with the eyes, full physical. And there was a lot of people that weren't so clean. Some were dirty and they had to see that you don't have any bugs, lice and that your hair was clean. There was like a community tub. Children and women were in one taking showers—the first time I was introduced to a shower. You have to take a shower, be sure that your clothes were clean. There were places that you can wash because we stayed there a whole week.

"My first shower, that was in England. Well, I was kind of self-conscious about it, because the children and grown-up ladies were together. So it was kind of bad, but they say you're going to do it, and that's it. There was a matron standing in the doorway to see that you're not cheating and, if you didn't want to take a bath, that you did. Otherwise they called you on it. Even if sometimes you don't understand the language, you could understand the signs, and the voice. They command you to do it, you do it."

BOARDING PROBLEMS

Especially after World War I, the United States began to close its doors to the "huddled masses yearning to be free" who had waited for the war to end and the door to reopen. This created some real problems at the ports of embarkation. For now whole shiploads of immigrants might go all the way to America, only to be turned back because quotas were full. Or individuals might be denied clearance to board ships bound for America because the quotas for their countries were full for the month or year.

When to travel to America became important. In the early 1920s, twenty percent of the quota allotment could be admitted in any month, but for some nationalities, that meant the year's quota was filled by November. No more quota immigrants from that area could be accepted until the next fiscal year beginning July first. This produced such hardship that the quota was later set as a monthly limit. Even so, immigrants often made a mad dash on any boat, no matter how unseaworthy it looked, that they thought would bring them in precisely on the first of the month— for if they arrived a day early or a day late, the quota might be filled and they would be sent back to Europe.

When Sarah Asher and her brother finally made their way to Hamburg in 1922, she was already twenty-two, highly educated and a veteran of much hardship. She would gladly have forsaken a stopover and sailed directly to America, but it was not to be so easy. Under America's new quota system, papers had to be in perfect order before an immigrant could embark; the whole process of screening and loading had become institutionalized. But after two years in transit, Sarah philosophically accepted her delay, knowing that it was only incidental to her trip to America. She was at least lucky to be staying in the Hamburg-American Line's "model village":

"When we came to Hamburg, we went outside the train. A huge man came. I remember he wore a gray coat and he was very nice, polite. He approached my brother—we were standing with our suitcases. He spoke German and we spoke very good German; we studied it in our schools. My brother was very worried, you know how it is, he is a man, and in this situation a woman is different.

"I ask this man what is the matter. He picked up his lapel. I remember right now I saw his button. He was a detective, like the FBI, and he said, 'You don't have to worry. I just wanted to tell you that you have to go into a farm house to be inoculated and washed. Do you have your passports?'

"I said, 'We have our papers.'

"Then he said, 'You don't have to worry, nobody will arrest you. You just go through that farm house and you wait until all the papers will be filled out and in order.' So he brought us to where the railroad was going and introduced us to a young man under whose supervision we were going—we couldn't go all alone. And he took us to that farm house.

"It wasn't a home, excuse me, it was a big village where all the farmers come from all over the world and they gave you room and food and baths and everything. This particular house was for farmers who were going to the United States. They had different houses for people that were going to South America and other countries. Then they had a special house where not everybody was let through, like that. They gave physical exams. If your papers were not right or if you were physically or mentally unfit, you were detained in those houses. They were like hospitals. We liked it very much there. It was beautiful. We were well, both of us. They treated us so nice.

"Naturally it took time until we got all the papers in order—about three or four months. In the meantime we volunteered to work in the office there. In fact, they were anxious we should remain in Germany, but we said, no, we wanted to go to the United States. Our brother had sent us papers and tickets and everything and we would just wait for them. We worked in the office. And then after three o'clock we used to take a walk. Certain days we didn't even work, so we went to Hamburg to see the city. It was beautiful; clean, spotless and very interesting. Very nice people were there in the office. Everything was in German language, naturally.

"Then it came the time, the day when all the papers were right and the tickets for the boat and everything and they told us a certain day we would board and start. We were in that place when New Year's came and all the doctors and nurses, about ten or twelve people, *came to our room and we celebrated the New Year. And it was so nice and friendly you can't imagine.*

"So then came the day when we had to go on the boat. A big ship came to Hamburg. Naturally, again a board of doctors were sitting in the boat, and you just pass by and they see if you are fit to go, physically and mentally. They asked us a few questions and then we went on the boat."

Very young children were not allowed to travel alone; some adult had to take responsibility for the child. For ten-year-old Paula Katz, that caused a problem. She was being sent alone by her grandfather to join her widowed mother in America and was ticketed second class from Galicia to New York, in 1913. Everything was all right until she got to Hamburg:

"I was traveling alone, and from Poland to Hamburg where I could get a boat, I was alone. That was okay, but when I got to Hamburg to get on the boat there was no one to go with in second-class passage, since there was no one who would take the responsibility of my being there. But the agent didn't want to just send me back to Poland. He tried to arrange for someone to look after me. He found a girl—I don't remember her name, I don't remember who she was—she was traveling steerage. So he refunded some of my money and tied it up in a little bag and gave it to me to guard. Then I went with her, instead of second-class passage, to steerage."

For people who traveled during the war, especially after the sinking of the *Lusitania* in 1915, there were additional problems. In 1916, Rachel Goldman, the one child in her family being sent to safety in America, notes the special checks conducted during wartime:

"In Rotterdam we were eleven days waiting for another contingent to come. There the sleeping quarters were closed for the day and we were all assembled in one large room which was noisy, smoky and not pleasant. On nice days when it wasn't raining we went around seeing sights in Rotterdam and were outdoors most all the time. The food for the Jewish immigrants was served not too far away and I believe it was paid for by the Joint Distribution Committee. I also understand that they contributed some money toward our food on the boat.

"We embarked on the steamship New Amsterdam in the evening, and I think it was in the dark. Being fall, the ocean was rough and everyone was seasick. Early in the morning they asked us to come up on

the deck to go through our documents. Most people were too sick to go, and those that came up were not fully dressed, including myself. The doctor came on the deck and suggested that everyone go to the dining room and eat breakfast and also stay on the deck and not go to the bunks. I took his advice and I felt fine the rest of the trip, which took 17 days—although most of the people were too seasick to come and eat in the dining room. Of the 250 or 300 people of third class where we were, less than 20 people ate in the dining room."

§ "Was there steerage on that ship?"

"I don't think so. It was a beautiful boat, the New Amsterdam. We stopped in England someplace, I do not know where, for Scotland Yard to go through the boat. They examined each passenger, and also everything that was on the boat. One of my friends who was seasick had been ticketed third class, but being that her brother had sent her money to come, she was transferred to the second class—and they gave her the third degree. They thought maybe she was a spy or something, you know. When we were in England, stationary, everybody felt fine. They were eating in the dining room and dancing and having a good time. And the minute we started out again on the ocean, they were seasick, and the same people were the only ones eating in the dining room."

Before boarding the ship, there was one final inspection, as Hans Bergner remembers. Hans, an orphan at nineteen, was leaving post–World War I Germany in 1924 for "the land of great opportunity where milk and honey flows, or so we thought in those days." He submitted to the usual health inspections before getting on the ship, but was taken aback when they were repeated right as he was boarding:

"As I walked onto the gangplank of the steamship Turingia in Hamburg—the gangplank, which lets passengers into the third-class compartments—two officials stood one on each side of the gangplank. As the passengers went by, most of them were carrying at least two light pieces of hand luggage and trunks if they had any. I had one steamer trunk that had entered the ship before and was already in my cabin, and I didn't have to carry that. But I was laden down with hand luggage. One of the officials immediately pushed my hat back, not so it was knocked off my head, but just away from my forehead. I asked, 'Why do you do that?'

"And he said, 'We do that to make sure there are no lice in the hair.'

"So this gives you a little feeling of how they, the steamship lines, felt about passengers that traveled third class. They weren't quite sure whether they had to take certain precautionary measures to protect the *ship against such individuals. This, however, did not stop some people from getting past this line."*

One way or another, most people eventually did get past that final preboarding check and settled in for the voyage from the old life to the new. It was a voyage that left a permanent imprint on nearly all who passed through it. As they boarded the gangplanks and scraped the European mud from their shoes, the immigrants knew that it was finally happening. America would be the next solid ground.

STORM-TOSSED WATERS

For people who lived in or near the port cities, the ship's departure was an event in its own right. The whole family turned out to say goodbye—and often to say "I'll meet you in America!" Irene Meladaki Zambelli, born in 1890, remembers just such a send-off. She was twenty-four when she left for America, and the trip is still sharp and fresh in her mind. Callers today find her alert, sharply observant and almost invariably hard at work at her museum-quality needlepoint and appliqué creations. With the eye for detail of the embroidery worker she now is and the dressmaker she once was, she gives a superb overview of the immigrant's sea voyage to America:

"February 10, 1914, was a chilly day, but not too cold. The sun was shining bright in the clear, arid Greek sky. The skiffs and small boats bobbed up and down in the choppy harbor waters of Piraeus, the seaport of Athens and the city where I was born. About fifty relatives and friends were there to tell me goodbye and wishing me good trip and good luck. Among them was my mother, who was not too beautiful, but when she was dressed up she made a rich appearance. My Aunt Evanthia who was telling me all what to tell my brother John, one of my twin brothers who she had raised and who was in Houston, Texas, five years. There were my two sisters. I don't remember what Calliopi had on, but Maria had a sea blue dress and a blue ribbon tied on her hair. Her eyes were the same color as the ribbon, her eyebrows black. Her hair chestnut brown, she was beautiful.

"My godfather was there, fat as a balloon. Looked just like Jackie Gleason, had dark skin and piercing blue eyes. When I was small he was good to me, bought clothes for me and my sisters and gave me money whenever I went to see him. He was a very good friend of Venizelos* and when there was a big parade they walked side by side. And I was proud of him, but when I grew up he wanted to sleep with me. He was a bachelor. When he was young he wanted to marry my Aunt Kristina, the youngest sister of my mother. But my father, who was his best friend, told her not to marry him because he was a scoundrel. So she did not marry him, and my father and he never spoke to one another the rest of their lives. So my aunt knew she was going to see him that day at the pier and had fixed herself beautifully. I could hardly get over it because as a rule she was sloppy and dirty and not like my other aunts and my mother who were very, very vain. But she was very pretty, had gorgeous brown eyes. She was married and had five children.

"At noon the call for all passengers to board the motor launch dimmed the excitement and gaiety. Tearful and sad we said our last goodbyes. As I embraced my mother and two sisters, we reviewed our plans: for them to leave our glorious but poor country as soon as I could arrange for their fares, and follow me to join our father and two brothers who had already migrated to the land of opportunity—America.

"A distant cousin, and a friend of his who I had never met before, were coming on the same trip. No one paid any attention to them. We boarded a small boat and went to Patras to board the ocean liner that was waiting there. The name was Austro-Americana. They said she was too big to anchor on the docks in Piraeus. But I am sure that they did not want any of the passengers to see her because no one would get in it. This ship was big but had no cabins, only a few on the top deck for the captain and a few select people. The rest was two floors with beds one next to the other, one floor for men and one floor for the women.

"As we sailed to Gibraltar everyone was feeling fine. The sea was good and we tried to make friends. I met a Jewish girl, Sarah, with her father who told me he was bringing her over to America so she could get married to somebody rich. They were from Salonika. She was beautiful, medium-sized, rather small, black hair and eyes, and white skin, sweet expression and manners. But her father was about four-and-a-half feet tall, skinny, and had a tremendous nose, but with all of that he had a kind face. They only spoke Greek, just like me. I was smaller than this girl. I was in perfect proportion, small feet, small hands, gray eyes, and light brown-reddish hair. We went around together and everybody told us we were the prettiest girls on the ship.

"After we passed Gibraltar the sea began to get rough and one by one the passengers started to get seasick and stayed in their beds. Sarah

* Prime Minister of Greece.

Advertisements like this one from Edward Tavcar's agency in Ljubljana, Slovenia, promised a five- to six-day trip on big ocean liners like the *Kaiser Wilhelm II*, but often immigrants ended up traveling two to four weeks in an unseaworthy bucket.

and I picked up courage and got up on the top deck. And there we met my cousin who told us that he met a friend of his who worked on the ship as a steward and who suggested to him to go to the hospital of the ship. He said if we went to the doctor on the ship he would give us something to feel better. He had gone and was coming back when we met him. He told us how to go to the hospital, but he was too sick to walk back with us. So we held to the railing, and went to the hospital. There was the doctor and the captain of the ship and the captain said to Sarah, 'Sit on my lap.' And as we did not know who was the captain and who was the doctor—they both wore uniforms—she sat on his lap, thinking that she was to be examined. He did examine her all right. He started feeling her breasts at the same time the doctor was feeling mine. But I fixed him. I vomited on him and he let me go. We both, Sarah and I, vomited our way back to our cabin.

"We sailed for twenty-two days in an awful, stormy sea . . ."

Irene Zambelli's ship was one of the hundreds that regularly crossed the Atlantic during the great days of steam. There were enormous ships, like the *Titanic* and *Lusitania*, *Mauretania* and *Rotterdam*. And a great many small ships, with names now long forgotten—*Austro-Americana*, *Lydia*, *Susquehanna*, *Batavia*.

Most of them carried both people and cargo. Voyagers traveled in three classes—first class, second or cabin class, and third class or steerage, where the people were treated much like the cargo carried in other airless, windowless compartments deep in the inner spaces of the ship.

Very few immigrants traveled first class. Some traveled second class, if they had the money, because the rigors of steerage were widely known and dreaded, and because second-class passengers were inspected and often cleared on board ship, with a chance of avoiding the more exacting inspection at Ellis Island. Many times a family would scrape together money for a second-class ticket for just one person, perhaps an elderly grandmother or a sickly son, while the rest of the family traveled down in the hole.

The overwhelming majority of the immigrants from southern and eastern Europe traveled in steerage, because it cost a great deal less than second class. Before World War I, steerage fare from Atlantic and Mediterranean ports cost as little as $10 to $15 in some periods and never more than $35. During and after the war, it went up, but still was by far the lowest priced way to travel to America.

And it was extraordinarily profitable for the steamship companies. In the early years, the only real differences in steerage between traveling on an old, slow boat and traveling on one of the superliners of the day was that the superliner went faster and was somewhat more stable. Not inconsiderable differences, but to the travelers, an upper cargo hold of a superliner was much like a cargo hold of a smaller ship. Some of the larger ships crossing the Atlantic jammed as many as 2,000 men, women and children into quarters unsuited for any habitation at all, fed them little and badly, and made enormous profits doing so.

Later in the period, just before and after World War I, some of the larger ships in the North Atlantic run provided somewhat better quarters for steerage passengers. And when the golden door to America was shut by restrictive immigration laws in the 1920s, the money went out of steerage, causing the shipping companies to convert steerage quarters into third-class "tourist" accommodations or into cargo holds.

Sarah Asher and her brother traveled across the stormy seas to

America, too, riding out the storms with all the composure and bravery they had shown every step of the way:

"We were given a stateroom, very nice for two people. Then we had to put our names and what kitchen. We didn't know they had two kitchens. Later we learned it said, 'Put your name for meals,' so my brother and I put our names. We were already settled in our room and had looked around the big boat and everything. So then came a gentleman and he said, 'I want to ask you, if you're Jewish, wouldn't you prefer to eat Jewish meals?'

"We said, 'To us it doesn't matter,' because we were so starved it didn't matter where we ate.

"So he said, 'I'll take your names from the Gentile list. They give you food, very good, but it's always ham in the morning and luncheon. I'll give you chickens and pot roast, you know, how the Jewish is.' He was a very nice gentleman. He introduced himself and he was a rabbi, but a reformed rabbi. He cooked, too. He was the cook and a rabbi. You know, on a boat they always have a few positions.

"There was altogether about 300 people on the boat and I would say about 50 people Jewish. But we didn't see them much. Some came in and out and then the boat started. We were very glad when the boat started. Then we said, 'Goodbye, Europe!' We said goodbye to our parents, sisters and everything. It was sad.

"So then it was almost suppertime and everything was served. After we went out from that spot, that was in the sea, until we reached the ocean it was nice and peaceful on the boat, and comfortable. We did not stop in England but we passed by it and that island was something unusual. It was purple. A big purple ball was on the ocean. It was interesting to watch everything.

"But when we reached the ocean, the Atlantic, the boat started to rock. We didn't care, it didn't bother us. So next morning we came to eat our breakfast with just a few people, maybe five people. We asked the rabbi, 'Where are they?'

" 'They are all sick. The boat was rocking and they all got seasick and they're way down in the bottom. How do you feel?'

" 'Very good.' Our breakfast was very good.

"He said, 'Would you like to eat more?' We said no. He said, 'Don't be bashful.' Both of us, we never was sick.

"For dinner, only my brother and I were in the dining room. The dining room was huge. They gave us soup in a big plate—we had to hold it in our hands to eat because it was shoving from one side to another side. And so we were eating.

"Well, for days and days conditions were just terrible. That boat was rocking so bad . . . it was a big boat. Instead of making our trip in seven days, we were seventeen days on that boat and all the time we never stopped rocking. The boat was simply terrible. The waves were thirty feet high. We were out on the ocean, who knows where. The whole boat had to be closed, all the stacks and everything, just locked, covered with special material because the waves were so high they were knocking everything off the boat and not to fill the boat more with water. Because through those old stacks the water was coming in.

"Usually in the morning we looked at the board to see what direction we were going and how far we were from New York. We were in such bad condition that one day we saw the captain didn't mark anything, the second day nothing. We were five days in one place. Of course the boat was moving, but in the same spot. We couldn't come out of that spot because the ocean was so rough, and he did not make any notations. So I was talking to my brother, 'Must be something bad.'

"Some of the stewards got so drunk, but one, ours, was a very nice man. He was worried that the boat was sinking because we took in so much water and were in the same spot. So he came and whispered to us that the boat is in very bad condition, we were sinking, so we should go to our room and pack our things. But we told him in German, 'Why should we trouble ourselves to pack our suitcases, if we are dying? Might as well let the fish have it.' We took such a different attitude, such a cheerful attitude towards sickness. We said, 'Look, we went through such a hell in our own country that nothing else mattered.' Yes, you go through a certain period in your life, nothing matters any more. Whatever situation you meet, you take it in a graceful way. So we said, 'We will dance.' So we danced. What can you do?

"And you know what happened? We were sitting in the middle of the boat, near the entertaining room where there is music or you can read books or do something. Very nice. So we were sitting there and eating what we had to eat. In Hamburg, we had a few cents so we bought chocolate for going on a trip, a big box of chocolate, about six or eight. And we had lemon. They said we should get lemon—herring the boat would give us—some schnapps, not wine or liquor. We bought a bottle in Hamburg, the cheapest. We never opened it, never ate the herring, but we ate the chocolate. One time the captain, a very nice young man, came in to see how was everybody. So he noted that my brother was reading an English book and I was sitting and embroidering alongside him and listening. We were studying English. When he saw the chocolate, and how we were eating, he got so upset physically that he actually started to vomit and rushed out. The chocolate. It was terrible. So he rushed into his room, and he was sick for three days. He was so yellow! And we were eating. We didn't know.

"It was wind and terrible fog that you couldn't see anything. Our captain sent an SOS all the time; some of the SOS's reached New York and they sent the battleship, Washington, to save us. That battleship never came near us, but was fifty miles away trying to find us. Can you imagine a battleship couldn't find us! It was terrible! They were looking and looking for I don't know how long, a day or so, and they couldn't find us. They returned to New York and we remained in that same bad spot. So one of the sailors came and we said, 'So what's the matter? Are we close to New York?'

" 'No, the weather's changed. We have a better wind and maybe we come out of that stormy spot.' Such a dense fog you couldn't see anything.

"For about eight or ten hours everybody started to breathe better. Those who were laying down in the bottom were still sick, very sick. We started to walk around, visit and talk, and then again after ten hours, again a different wind started to blow and rock the boat but not as bad as before. I remember I went way up on top where it was closed. It was a library. I sat down on a couch and was reading a book. So some sailors came upstairs. 'How do you feel?' they said.

"I said, 'I feel fine.'

"So they said, 'You're laying here so comfortable, everybody is so sick.'

"So I said, 'That's their privilege, to be sick. I feel fine.' And so we were talking with them, and the boat was rocking. Up on top was terrible—you know, the higher you go the worse you feel. And my brother was reading and studying and I was studying all the time. But we ate all the time. Maybe it was because we had starved before, something was conditioned. Yes, I suppose it was a physiological change in the body. It was my brother the same. Sick, no.

"About a day before we approached New York again we were in weather conditions and it was bad. Then it cleared. They started to paint the boat, and the captain put the mileage on the board . . ."

The stormy North Atlantic took a heavy toll on the well-being of most of the travelers. They were land creatures, temporarily uprooted from the earth and passing through a wholly alien environment. Many memories are indistinct, only flashes of fear and illness, like Mary Zuk's recollection:

"It was so rough! Oh God, it was so rough! I didn't see a thing. A lot of time you just lay in your bed when you don't feel so good. You don't get up and go because if you do you get dizzy and then you get worse sick, because the water was so rough. That was rough weather—in

November, winter starts. Oh, the waves! Oh God! I thought the ship would turn over, but it didn't . . ."

And her fears were not unjustified. Just six months before Mary Zuk's sea passage in 1912, the unsinkable *Titanic* had sunk after hitting an iceberg, and over 1,500 lives were lost. Especially during the winter months, when Atlantic storms continually scourged the ocean with their howling winds and waves, even the bravest voyagers had reason to wonder if they'd ever reach America.

For some reason, however, seasickness was the main scourge. Steve Pakan had got out from under the thumb of his cruel father in Czechoslovakia. He'd skillfully avoided robbers en route and survived hardships to get to the sea. Finally, he pulled into the port and prepared to leave:

"Bremerhaven is where the ship was—Kaiser Wilhelm der Grosse, a big ship. I had a ticket for third class. So anyway, I came into a fine hotel and I had to wait about five or six days until I got on the ship. Before I went on the ship, they checked us. They look at your eyes, they look at your throat, and they test your heart, too. That's about all.

"When I was third day on the ship, this big ship, I went to get food, just like the other people in line. It was sauerkraut and some sausage or frankfurters. I got it and I went on decks, near the sea. It was afternoon and the water started to get rough. Oh boy, it started churning my stomach and I got so sick! The seasickness came on me and it doubled me right up, right on the deck, on the floor and I throw up everything I ate three days ago. Somehow I got down the steps, down the stairway and to my quarters and slept. I laid there.

"I had people from my town, a girl and a boy. They used to go to school with me. The girl was a couple of years younger. She used to bring me water and she asked me if I wanted to eat. I couldn't. Finally she brought beer and beer tasted good to me after a while, a couple of glasses of beer.

"I couldn't lift my head for four days. On the ship I thought I would never see the United States. I thought I would die if I went on any longer. But as we came near the shore the seasickness left me."

Fear of sinking wasn't so bad if you weren't seasick. The waves could churn and frighten, but the amenities of a deserted ship offered some compensation. Irma Busch laughs now at the memories of the sorry, rocking Christmas that she spent on shipboard, pleasant memories compared to those of her childhood starvation in World War I. The pretty eighteen-year-old had a lot of attention to distract her:

"The trip was rough. I thought we would sink. The ship we sailed on was the Albert Balin. This was about the middle of December, the 16th or 17th of December, 1925. And we arrived here one day late. We weren't allowed on deck because the weather was so bad, and it was so stormy all the doors were not only locked, they were tied with rope so we couldn't get out. Because we would have been swept overboard. It was really wicked.

"I remember one day when there was supposed to be a dance. We tried, but you'd be in that corner, and all of a sudden you'd be in another corner, you know. And the dining room was empty. People were so seasick. I didn't get seasick. I ate like a horse. And what I had for breakfast! You know, the stewards used to laugh. There would be three of them waiting on me. I had come to the dining room, nobody was there, and they were happy that somebody came. They were wonderful to me. Well, anyway, it took thirteen days."

 "It must have been a pretty sorry Christmas on board."

"Oh, it was. I tell you, it was the saddest thing. Because they had tried to make it pleasant with a Christmas tree, you know, and everything, in the public rooms. And they had given us extra oranges, extra apples and all that, but it was sad. You were sort of homesick. As a child we had spent so many lovely Christmases, even if we didn't have very much. But all the same it was nice. So this was sad."

The waves of the North Atlantic kept Vera Gauditsa from feeling any better than she had in that reeking holding area in Le Havre. Traveling in 1928, her pregnancy added to her difficulties, and though at the time she was proud that she had fooled the doctors, today she shakes her head in astonishment at the folly of her youth. But she endured, and in the depths of her misery on board ship, she found a kind stranger to comfort her:

"I was pretty tough, but on the boat I was very sick. Oh, my Lord, I thought the child wanted to be born right then. I was so sick. Many times I said to my son, 'You were almost born on the boat.'

"I had a cabin, but in the cabin was nothing. You had to go through the whole boat on the other side to the showers and a toilet. So imagine when you are sick and you have to go to the bathroom and walk! When I was walking to that toilet, I saw everybody, even those working on the boat, they all had bandages on their heads. Everybody was sick. I tell you, I was walking through such a long hall and there was a railing all around so we was holding it because the ship was shaking. There was a very bad storm on the ocean. And when I came there, there were three people ahead of me. There was water in the cabin to wash but there was no toilet.

"The showers were far away from the toilets. But I did not get to them. I was there two weeks but I did not get to them, I was so sick. I did not eat for about ten days. And the boat was rocking and cracking at night. I could not sleep anyway, cracking or no cracking, but I had a window on the ocean and most of the time the window was covered with water, the waves were so high.

"The fellow who was taking care of the cabins, many times during the day he came and he wiped my perspiration. I was perspiring all over. He wiped my face and rubbed my arms. And then when he was finished wiping everything, he would lean down and kiss my cheek. He was an attendant of the ship, like a porter. He had so many cabins to prepare. But he came in all of the time and washed me and bathed me and he massaged my arms. But I could not talk with him and he did not understand me either. He was French, you know, and we could not talk to each other! I could not talk to anyone. The other people were not Czechs. If I wasn't so sick it would have been okay, but I was eight months pregnant."

But the raging sea bothered Hans Bergner not at all. So what if everybody else was sick and events seemed headed for a dramatic climax? When you're nineteen and unafraid, a howling storm can be most enjoyable:

"Another thing that is kind of interesting about the trip was that when you travel in the middle of the winter on a rather small ship, like the one that I was on, and you hit a storm in midocean, as we did, most passengers become very, very seasick. The smaller the ship, the more active the motion of the ship, when the waves are very large. I was very lucky, perhaps because I was born along the river Elbe, not far from the seashore and I was on small boats many times as a kid. It didn't bother me. But many of the other passengers were desperately ill during this voyage.

"This wasn't so bad. The worst thing was the captain announced one fine day that the steering mechanism was completely out of order and he could no longer steer the ship by means of the automatic controls from his bridge. He had to relay messages from the bridge to the stern of the ship where they had an old-fashioned large wheel that could operate a rudder by hand. This in a tremendous storm, where the sailors had to be lashed onto the steering wheel, three or four of them, and by means of several megaphones which carried the message from the captain's bridge to the men at the stern, they steered the ship by hand for several days.

"We had left Hamburg on the 12th of December and normally would have expected to reach New York ten days later. Well, we finally got here on the 26th. We had a four-day delay simply because of being like a cork on the ocean for several days until they got everything back in shape again. This was one of those extra little experiences that a young immigrant really looks back on with a tremendous amount of fun in retrospect."

And there were some whose faith turned aside the worst the sea had to offer. Little Anna Vacek had sent her dollies ahead of her on the voyage, promising that she'd see them in America. With her lucky star to guide her and firm word given, she had no doubt that she'd brave the storm:

"I was fifteen days on the ship. There was an accident—we hit an iceberg. Some said it was a rock. Three days they were calling for help, but in those days there weren't so many boats to Europe. For three days they were calling, whistling, whistling for help and nobody come. Then some small boats stopped and they fixed it and we went. They closed us up inside and nobody was allowed to come up.

"Before this happened there was a whale coming around the boat, and everybody said we were going to have hard luck . . . Even the sailors said, 'Oh, what is going to happen to us?'

"Some man said, 'Come on, kid, I show you the whale, come on.' So he picked me up, and I saw the whale was rolling around and I said, 'My goodness, what a big fish. It's just as long as our ship!'

"He said, 'Don't say much.' Then, all right, everything was all over and even the sailors said we would have trouble. Well, you could imagine how everybody worried that we would get here at all. But I wasn't afraid at all. I thought, 'I am going to America, I am going to get there. I'm going to see America and we won't drown.' "

STEERAGE

"Steerage" was quite literally near the ship's steering equipment, in one or more below-deck compartments of a ship, located fore and aft. Hans Bergner tells of the "old-fashioned large wheel" at the stern of the ship that had to be used when the automatic steering controls on the bridge became inoperable during a storm. That was the equipment that gave its name to "steerage."

A typical steerage compartment consisted of a compartment indistinguishable from any upper cargo hold, without portholes or any other effective ventilating mechanism, unpartitioned and six to eight feet high, crammed with two or more tiers of narrow metal bunks containing minimal mattresses. Men and women were separated, sometimes on separate decks, sometimes by nothing but a few blankets tossed over a line in the middle of a compartment. Children usually stayed with their mothers.

Toilet facilities were always inadequate; cleanup was almost nonexistent; and the combined smells from the ship's galleys and human excrement nauseating. The food was both monotonous and poorly prepared—if prepared at all—and fresh water was usually available only up on deck. The chief kind of food provided, described by many immigrants, was barrel after barrel of herring, the cheapest food available that might be relied on to keep the immigrants alive for voyages that lasted up to three or four weeks.

Under those conditions people got seasick and stayed seasick—they cried and kept on crying. Some people were even detained at Ellis Island later for suspected trachoma, when their eyes were simply red from continual crying all the way across the Atlantic.

Recollections of the sea voyage aren't all painful. Frank Santoni was only eight when the money finally arrived to bring him and the rest of his family across the ocean to America. For him, the voyage from Italy was a wonderful adventure; some memories still move him to laughter at the innocence and wonder of his youth, while some aspects of the passage in steerage bring back less happy memories:

"Oh, I remember quite a few things. We were two little youngsters. My brother, who was seven years older than me, had me by the hand all the time. We roamed the ship and a very funny thing was we came near the kitchen and we saw the goodies going on there. But a very important thing: we saw what we know in this country as a container, like three feet by two feet, used for the preserving of ice cream. You put the two tanks in and you surround that with ice and with the salt, and you preserve the ice cream. That's how ice cream was made—I believe it is even being done today in some ice cream parlors. We saw the

No deck chairs and stewards for these passengers,
but however ungracious these accommodations, the fresh air was better than
the unventilated steerage quarters below.

containers there and we took the cover from the containers. There were two latches and we opened both the latches. Lo and behold, we saw the ice and salt—and we saw something there that we didn't know. We didn't even taste it, for some reason or another. We did know the ice. We quickly got hold of a nice piece of ice, closed the thing and went about our business, not knowing what ice cream was. Now that's a very laughable story!

"Now I tell you another story which was not so laughable. We were steerage. I didn't know of any other class at the time. I know now. At the time I didn't know but we were down in the hole. I was allowed to sleep with my mother, but my brother was not, so I was the head of the family. My mother was sick one night and she moaned all night, practically. Sometime in the wee hours of the morning she asked me to please go upstairs and get some water for her, as you had to go up perhaps ten or twelve steps, in order to get up to the upper part of the boat, to get water, and that's what I did.

"It was just about dawn, and as I got to the last step, somehow or another the latched doors opened. It seemed to me I was just about to meet the water, the boat was heaving on that side and it felt to me as if I was just about able to reach the water. I was only seasick twice, that was one of the times. I got so sick, after that I don't remember whether I got the water."

Being seasick and in steerage was a trying experience. The foul odors and pounding of the engines and waves combined to knock most of the passengers into a state of muddled semiconsciousness, with only short flashes of painful clarity.

Like Frank Santoni, Arnold Weiss was another young boy caring for his mother—reluctant to leave Poland and then immobilized by seasickness. Arnold also braved the storm in search of that precious commodity, water, which wasn't easily available to those lying in steerage:

"We rode third class. I don't even recall the food I ate. Everything did not smell good to us because people were seasick. On the boat all the people were sick. Every one of them was sick, they used to throw their guts up. I wasn't sick, I used to see my mother—she was green. I used to bring them water; food they couldn't take. How did they live through it? They lived through it on water, actually, because in the meantime they were sick.

"I used to go up on the deck and the storm on the sea used to almost wash me off. One time I almost went over because I did not weigh

too much, I was just a kid. But that was why I was able to sustain everything that took place. I used to take care of all of them, bring them
this, bring them that. We slept in bunks. There were three or four in a
bunk and one next to the other. Not many other children were traveling
at that time."

Some passengers had to face possibilities even worse than debili-
tating bouts of seasickness. The voyage should have been a welcome rest for Fannie Kligerman and her family, after their flight
across Europe, escaping from Russia and the pogroms. It was the
last leg of their journey to America, to safety. Little did she know
that it was also destined to be the last voyage for a leaky disease-
ridden hulk of a ship:

"Batavia. Batavia was the boat. It never went back again. You know,
we got water in the boat on the way over. Water got in there, and they
had to take out the water, and we had to eat where we slept, because
we were that way in water. We left from Germany and we got water in
the boat and all the children got measles.

"Some of them died and they threw them into the water like cattle.
It was a pathetic thing that they couldn't ride with the bodies, they had
to throw them into the water. It was something that I will never forget.
And you can imagine how the women carried on. They took a child
away from them and they just tossed it in, nice and quiet. Into the
water. It was terrible. And my mother hid the baby, I remember, in a
big apron . . . She wouldn't let anybody see the baby. Maybe the baby
was going to catch it. So she had the baby in her apron and the baby
could hardly walk and was crying. We had to say, 'Sh, sh. Somebody's
coming, sh.' All the time, and that's how we struggled.

"On the boat they gave us food. They charged plenty—but we
didn't go in for nothing, they charged us. I still have the herring taste
in my mouth. Herring, herring, herring! And garlic, on bread. They say
you don't vomit when you have garlic on bread.

"But for Passover, we didn't go. We had bread, and you know what
it is, we had to have matzohs. And instead of fish, we had herring. But
we had food. We didn't like it, it wasn't tasty like you do it at home.
We had four boys among our children and they said, 'Oh, Momma, it's
bad, oh, Momma.'

"She said, 'I know. You're going to get good food. Right away,
right away.' Imagine how long we traveled."

Oh, those herrings! It's strange to see such a common, pedestrian
little fish grow into a truly memorable creature. So many people

remember their voyages in terms of herring—it's a remarkable link between nearly all of the third-class passengers who came to America. Their ships could be as different as night and day, their passage decades apart, but herrings were the great unifier.

Sister Wanda Mary Dombrowski left Poland in 1906. She was only a little girl of seven at the time and remembers just one fact about the voyage:

"We didn't come first class, we came third class, which meant there was a barrel of herring that you could eat. The food was delicious. I remember so well that great big barrel of herring. I didn't get sick. We could eat the herring any time we wanted to."

The shipping companies provided herring because it was cheap. But it was also nourishing and seemed to help combat seasickness. With herring, bread and little else, millions made it to America in steerage.

For some strictly religious Jews, herring was practically the only food that they were able to eat, even if other food was available. In later years, some boats had two kitchens, one of them for Jews, as Sarah Asher found. But most often, Jews who followed the prescribed kosher diet found their choice of food strictly limited. Traveling in 1901 from Lithuania, Leon Solomon's family observed kosher strictness with an unwavering faith, appropriate for the future rabbi:

"The name of the ship was Kensington. That ship took ten days to cross the ocean and arrive in the United States. We traveled third class, steerage in the bowels of the ship, and as religious Jews—especially my mother who was ultra pious—we could not partake of the food which the ship provided for us, except herring and potatoes, and hot water or tea. Otherwise we had to subsist on kosher food my mother prepared in advance, to supplement the food which the ocean-going steamer provided for us.

"It was a long journey, we suffered from seasickness. I remember how we listened with fear to the steam siren of the ship when it let loose long, powerful blasts, not knowing what the blasts were intended to convey. Whether it was a signal to other ocean-going liners or a warning of some kind, at any rate it was powerful and terrifying."

After the flood years in the first decade of this century, government regulation began to erase some of the worst abuses of steerage. The newer liners had third, or tourist-class decks, far different from the open, stinking holds that Frank Santoni remembers so vividly.

The immigrants still occupied the lowest decks of the ships, jammed into little cabins with the pounding of the engines for company, but the discomfort was more bearable—if you weren't too seasick. Some accommodations became fit for passengers, instead of cargo, and memories became more pleasant, like Adele Sinko's. And after wartime starvation, the cold cuts served on board ship in 1924 were like haute cuisine to Adele:

"We sailed from Bremerhaven, one of the harbors of Germany. It was on the Columbus. Sure, it was the biggest boat then. Well, we were so starved, you know! I think I told you that. They came with those piles of cold cuts or whatever. My friend, I called her sister-in-law, that I was traveling with on the boat, she took half of it. So the others got mad, you know. They had to wait until another platter come. So one lady sat across the table and she said, 'Don't you worry, dear. You can eat all you want. You pay five dollars a day for food.' Oh well, after that they couldn't stop us. It is awful when you're hungry and you get such good food—which I imagine wasn't so hot, but for us it was perfect. I only know at night was cold cuts. Dinners I don't remember. And all the long trays of cold cuts. So we had a very nice trip.

"But in those days those ships were built like traps. You know, you go down the steps, there is a little cabin just to fit two, one on top of the other, and boy, you could never get out if something happened. How many steps and how many floors you have to go down! All the way down is the luggage, but I came tourist, or third class. But I enjoyed the trip. It was something very new. We had a storm coming over. Then you feel trapped. They close up everything. You can't go out on the deck. But I didn't get seasick.

"And how long was that trip? I think nine days we were on the boat. Sure, that was swell, that trip. Can you imagine? We watched the flying fish, and the sun come up and the moon go down—it's so different."

Steerage was a world of its own, its inhabitants carefully segregated from the life of the first- and second-class decks by the ship's crew. In the world of the transatlantic luxury liner, the few first-class passengers ate, drank and danced their way across the Atlantic, while far below thousands of poor immigrants endured the journey shut away in hot, airless, crowded cargo compartments.

It is the stuff of a thousand novels; it is also the truth.

Leon Solomon remembered the segregation. When asked if he had met any of the wealthy people on the boat, he smiled, shook his head:

"We in steerage didn't meet any of the wealthy people. We only knew our fellow passengers in steerage, who suffered seasickness together with us, and met on board one of the decks together with us, and spoke Yiddish as we did. The wealthy ones—the first or second class—we didn't rub elbows with them. We weren't permitted to enter any cabins of people who weren't our social equals. We had to confine ourselves to steerage."

And Paula Katz, traveling in steerage, remembers the trouble she had trying to get a little chicken soup:

"We were on the boat for eleven days and the only thing I could possibly eat was sardines and rye bread. And that was just too much! By the eighth or ninth day I was just so fed up with the sardines that, when we were on deck walking around, I saw on the upper deck the steward running around calling people for afternoon tea. He had chicken soup! So I asked if I could buy some chicken soup. He chased me off the gangplank, off the steps. He said I couldn't stay there. At all events, somehow or other I got some chicken soup."

CHILD'S PLAY

The voyage wasn't all herring and seasickness. It was often a lot of fun, a pleasure-filled cruise, especially for the children. They seemed to be less afflicted with seasickness than their elders, so many youngsters, like Arnold Weiss and Frank Santoni, spent their trips caring for the seasick. But when there was free time, it was a child's paradise. A whole boat to explore! With most adults on board seasick and out of sight, the rest of the ship was wide open, full of surprises and adventure.

It certainly was fun when you were a spunky kid like Bessie Spylios, sailing from Greece in the spring of 1909 with her older brother:

"I remember the boat. We went to Athens and from there we took the boat and came sailing right through to New York. It took about twenty days on the boat. It was a slow boat to China, the Lydia, a Greek boat.

"We got food on the boat, paid for by the fare. Like we had to stay in Athens for two nights for the ship to come in, and they took care of us at no charge. There were about fifty people from the same village and they came at the same time. It was just like a family, we knew each other and all that. It was very nice. No, it didn't bother me at all. I swam, I ran up and down. We had the bottom of the boat for sleeping, but I never stayed there, just when it was bedtime. They had to chase me downstairs to go to sleep.

"I was upstairs on the deck where you watch the more rich people in first and second class. They had everything. I had it easy, because I wasn't bashful, I was forward. And there were Greek people on the boat—they talked my language and there was nothing to hold me back. I used to go with their food and everything. I used to get my lunch over there. Not what they gave us, but all the good things the other people ate. Fruit, and in May there were lots of cherries of which I ate plenty.

"They used to yell at me not to run up and down, but there was no fear. Like nowadays, you don't let your child run around. It was different then. It wasn't like now, to be afraid. I was as free as air going up and down stairs and swinging on the bottom of the boat, having a heck of a time. My brother got angry with me because they told me I shouldn't do those things, but I did. He was sick most of the time. He was seasick all the way through. To me, it didn't bother me. And after twenty days we were in the United States.'"

Oh, they had fun, those youthful sailors. Poking around the corners of the ship, carefree, too young to worry about the future, not understanding the uncertainties of the present. Catherine Bolinski picked up a sty in her eye during the voyage over—her mother must have worried herself sick, but it was just an incident to the excited fourteen year old. What a trip it was for her! There was the great food and the first showers in England, now a beautiful ship to explore. The Cunard liner's tourist accommodations were plain in 1923, but far removed from those terrible steerage quarters on older boats:

"We were out of England. We got on a large ship and that came to America, to New York. We had a cabin with a bunk bed, small one. Four beds, one on each side, with a little sink in the middle. Then you go and eat in the dining room.

"I scared my mother because I decided to follow somebody to see where it led to. I was the nosy kind, and so I followed some place and I went too low, went as far as the boilers. My mother was looking for me. They always put labels on a person: what cabin you are, what deck you are, your name. Then when somebody looks at you, they don't have to speak to you, they just know where you belong, so they lead you to it. So I didn't have my label with me. There was one lady from the first class, that was on the top deck. She looked at me. I'm walking around, walking around. I didn't know which way to go down again, so she came over. She looked at me so nicely and then she's speaking to me. I looked back at her, I didn't know what she was talking about. I believe she was talking English. So I just shrugged my shoulders and walked away. After that I found my place. My mother was worried because the ship was leaving and she didn't know if I was outside or inside.

"It was just a regular ship. It had a lot of immigrants, people coming over here. Yes, maybe a couple of hundred. The rest of it was people traveling first class. This one got sick, that one got sick, but I gained weight on the ship. The food was good. Mostly, I remember, they had delicious pickled herring. They served that a lot.

"It was exciting as a child for my part, I remember. We were out on the deck, we had to have drills on our ship, put life jackets on and they sounded the horn in case of emergency. We were in the middle of the ocean and the waves, you know, you cannot go out on deck. For fresh air, they made you go out whether you feel sick or not.

"And I had a sty in my eye. My mother got scared they might have to send me back. There was one young girl, she was born in America and had come to Poland for so many years and was going back. So my mother asked her to speak for us and she went to a ship doctor. So he put medicine in it and told me that I should stay in the dark and come back the next day and it went away before we docked in New York."

Ten years earlier, in 1913, another little Polish girl wasn't at all sure that she was going to like the voyage. Martha Konwicki's father, wanted by the Russian police for political activity, couldn't go home again, so his family followed him to America. But Martha wasn't happy about leaving and cried so much that she, too, had trouble with her eyes:

"Well, the doctor said that my eyes were bloodshot, and they wouldn't let me go among people. That was in Rotterdam—we had to miss one boat. Then my eyes got better. My mother was saying that I cried too much. I was crying night and day. I was scared. I didn't want to leave Poland, as much as I loved my father, I didn't want to leave. I heard so many stories that once you come you don't see nobody no more that you love and leave behind.

"And my sister Tina was so sick. She was only like six weeks old, and Mother didn't have no hope that she'd live. And she was afraid now if she would die, they would just bury her at sea. So my mother said to me, if anything happened to Clementina, that I shouldn't say nothing to nobody because she's going to carry her over and bury her in a cemetery. She'd not let them bury her in that sea."

Unlike Fannie Kligerman, Martha didn't have to witness the sea burial of a small corpse. Tina survived and the fearsome journey became something entirely different than Martha had anticipated:

"That trip, oh, I enjoyed it! Oh God, how I enjoyed it! We came on a third class, way at the bottom. And I was working on the boat, with the cooks, washing dishes, because third class, we weren't getting the same meals as the first class. But my mother was getting everything special because I brought it. She was sitting in the cabin alone . . . not me, I was all over. That I enjoyed.

"It was the Rotterdam, there was a lot of people, but we couldn't go to second or first class. We had to stay down. Oh I was busy! We had long tables and people had to come. My mother never had to come up. I was always sure to bring from the kitchen a plate special for her. I think fifteen days we were at sea."

GREAT EXPECTATIONS

While children like Bessie, Catherine and Martha roamed the ships having a ball, their parents and many of their fellow travelers occupied their time a different way. To them, the sea voyage was only a brief incident in their journey. It might be unbearably miserable because of seasickness, or it might be a leisurely cruise, but it wasn't an end in itself. America was just ahead over the ocean—America, and a new wide-open life.

The time spent shipboard was a time of enforced idleness. The immigrants' fates were temporarily out of their hands. There were days to pass the time, to wonder about the future, to anticipate—perhaps fear—the unknown.

Leon Solomon remembers the wondering:

"When we got together on a deck to which we were welcome, we would exchange impressions, reminiscences, compare notes—where we came from, where we were going to, our expectations, hopes in the golden land of Columbus.

"Well, each one was dreaming his own dreams. Some were dreaming of getting wealthy. There were legends that in America gold was available on the streets. This legend must have survived from the days of the so-called 'gold rush,' which brought thousands of people from all over the world to dig for gold. And that must have been the origin of the expression, 'In America, gold could be picked up from the ground.'"

Sometimes the ships sailing to America were lovely. By the 1920s many newer liners were plying the sealanes, and even the immigrants were treated as passengers, instead of cargo. Whatever the diversions available, though, there was still that big question, "What's going to happen to me?" Hedvig Nelson, a young Norwegian woman traveling on a boat full of her peers in 1925, had a great time, but that question still kept her close company:

"We all went on a big boat and it was filled with all Norwegian people, teenagers mostly. That was a big experience, coming to the United States. We were very anxious and excited, wondering what was our future. And on the boat it was very interesting. They had all kinds of games and everything, but we always had in mind what would be in store for us, in the United States.

"My sister was with me at that time, but she was not worried about the future like I was. She was a year older, but she took things more like day by day. I was more worried about the future, more than her. They had a lot of things going on at the boat and I remember they had a potato race, and somehow, I don't know why, I won the potato race. They gave me a bottle of champagne because I won the race. So then I thought, 'Oh yes, this bottle I will take to these people from Norway in the United States because I don't drink champagne.' And these people that we were together with, at the table in the dining room, they said, 'Oh no, you have to pour it, you can't take it over from the boat.' I felt so bad. Well, we had to pour it for these people because they said that was the only thing to do. I don't know, I was so much concerned about doing the right thing. I always had that in mind. I was kind of disappointed that I couldn't take it to these other people in the United States, because I thought, well, at least they would have this bottle. It would be nice to have something."

The waiting for arrival in America was filled with joy for Marta Forman. Leaving Czechoslovakia in 1922, Marta had borrowed money for her ticket from several people in her home town—and felt the debt very strongly. She was traveling to an uncle she had never seen, and was seasick from the first day out. So what! Each minute brought her that much closer to the land she had dreamed about for years, and the excitement and anticipation buoyed her spirits, from the day she arrived at the seashore:

"We came to Bremerhaven and the first time I saw the big boat, I could hardly believe it! And the ocean. I was going to run right into the ocean, I was so excited. The name of the ship was Susquehanna. It had only second and third class. It was a very slow boat and I got seasick right away. The first night I threw up. We had to go second class because they didn't have enough room in the third class; the boat was overcrowded. We had better food, we had a better cabin. There was only three in one cabin. In the third class, I don't know, maybe four or five. The boat was packed with immigrants from all nationalities and it was so interesting. Since I could speak German it wasn't so hard for me, and already I tried to speak English. I remembered words, and every day I mark it down, I repeat it, I repeat it. I was so excited, you know and then I was seasick the whole way, and they was so nice to me. We had very good food.

"I was dressed because I came from a city and I borrowed so much money I had to pay—oh my God, for a long time I had to pay all my debts because I wanted to be dressed a little bit decent. So I have a few nice things, really, thank God. Many people came from Slovakia and Moravia. Moravia belonged at that time to Austria. Czechoslovakia and Slovakia and Moravia used to belong to Austria before the First World War. And now, it is one country. So many came in their own costume and on the boat they were singing and dancing and playing harmonica and violin. Everybody had something. The captain from the second class, he came out on the bridge. He spoke to me in German and he said, 'What are they singing?'

"I said, 'Well, they are singing Czech songs so they won't feel lonely. They are young and they are willing to work. Nobody knows what's going to happen to us, but we are young and we are not afraid.' I explained it to him and he shook my hands. He started clapping hands. He didn't even understand the language, but the rhythm, it made him so happy."

They sang of their dreams and expectations, they sang to feel a little less lonely as they approached America. You didn't even

Like most stowaways, this Finnish boy, when found by the ship's officers, was probably put to work on the ship, held by the Immigration Service in port, and then deported on the ship's return trip, as "likely to become a public charge."

have to know the language—all you had to do was feel the hope, the anticipation of America. It drew millions of people across the ocean, seasick and poor, but anticipating a better life.

It even drew those who couldn't afford a ticket, but still had the dream. Almost every ship had its stowaways, and this March 28, 1907, headline from *The New York Times* might have appeared any time during the early part of this century:

> **SEVEN YOUTHS HIDE IN STEAMER'S HOLD**
> **DREAM OF ITALIAN LADS TO REACH FREE AMERICA**
> **SHATTERED BY IMMIGRATION BUREAU**
> **STOWED AWAY ON HAMBURG**
> **OFFICERS FIND BOYS PROVIDED WITH WATER AND BISCUIT**
> **AND VARYING MENU WITH RAW SPAGHETTI.**

Ship's officers became expert at finding stowaways' hiding places and the stowaways were put to work on the ship; on arrival in port, they were turned over to the Immigration Service, who almost invariably deported them on the vessel's return trip, as "likely to become a public charge." Sometimes the newspapers played up the stories of these stowaways so that someone came forth to put up a bond for them. Stories about Michael Gilhooley, a fourteen-year-old Belgian who stowed away to America five times in 1919, brought forth a shower of offers to support him in America. Adopted briefly by singing star Elsie Janis, "the Sweetheart of the American Expeditionary Forces," and later by a wealthy Cleveland family, Michael apparently stayed on and made his way in America. Most stowaways, however, saw America only from the sea; they were returned summarily, with their dreams of America unfulfilled.

THE LADY WITH THE TORCH

Finally, after braving the stormy seas, the misery of steerage—and far too much salty herring—the immigrants entered New York

Once past the Narrows, liner passengers could see the Statue of Liberty from anywhere in New York Harbor. This Hamburg-American liner, the *Imperator*, is steaming back to Europe for more immigrants, past Ellis Island, which lies off to the far right of the Statue. In the foreground is Castle Garden, the earlier immigration station.

Harbor. After all the years of talking and dreaming about her, they saw the lady with the torch—as millions before and millions after would see her. But first there was a stop in the lower harbor, out beyond what is now the Verrazano-Narrows Bridge.

Ships from abroad stopped in lower New York Harbor, where they were placed in quarantine pending clearance. While in quarantine, they were boarded by teams of medical and other inspection people from the Immigration Service.

Sometimes the inspectors found that whole ships were infested with lice or that epidemics were in progress on board. Those ships received very special treatment, with sterilization of everyone on board, often compulsory hair cutting and head shaving, even mass removal of passengers directly to hospitals.

But that was rare. Normally, first- and second-class passengers were examined on board, and those cleared, along with American citizens traveling in any class, were free to leave the ship when it docked at the pier. A few first- and second-class passengers were detained for medical and other reasons, and were often taken directly off the ships in quarantine and moved to Ellis Island.

For a short time in 1903, a group of women were employed as inspectors, boarding ships in quarantine with the special charge of searching for women being transported into the United States for purposes of prostitution, or "white slavery," as it was then called in the popular press and even in the legislative records of the time. Both admiringly and derisively dubbed the "Bloomer Girls," these women inspectors were employed with considerable fanfare but were soon fired, becoming victims of sexual discrimination on the part of Immigration Service administrators, who had opposed their hiring from the first.

After quarantine clearance, the ships moved into berths at Manhattan and New Jersey piers. American citizens and cleared first- and second-class passengers debarked. Third-class, or "steerage," passengers—the vast majority of all immigrants—were either held overnight on board for transfer to Ellis Island the next day or were immediately sent on to Ellis Island.

At the dock, they left the ship with their possessions and were transferred to barges for the trip across the harbor to Ellis Island.

Each person and his or her set of possessions was identified by a manifest number, and immigrants wore that number, prominently displayed, on the transfer barges and throughout the passage through Ellis Island.

For most people, the arrival in New York Harbor meant, first of all, calm waters and no more seasickness. Irene Meladaki Zambelli had had a long, long trip—"twenty-two days in an awful stormy sea"—and had been "deathly sick" all the way. But she prepared herself for a new experience with her customary verve:

"We finally arrived in New York and the Hudson River on March the third. There was no more seasickness and we got ready to get off the ship. We were all dressed up. Sarah not as much as I was. I had a very pretty suit and an embroidered blouse under it and a little hat to match the suit with a pretty bow on it custom made. My shoes were also custom made with high top buttons, the bottoms patent leather and the tops suede, the color of my suit rust brown. The rest of the women on the ship were mountain women with handkerchiefs on their heads. Everyone looked bad being seasick.

"The captain came and pulled me and Sarah by the sleeve and in an ugly way told us to be sure to stay in front of the line when the inspectors came. We did and they told my cousin to stay in front. He was a good-looking and happy boy but from being seasick, he was yellow as a lemon and smelled sour from the vomit. There was no place to take a bath and no place to eat. They would hand us a dish with sardines and bread and for a big treat they gave us bread pudding. I did not eat anything and when I tried to get dressed to get off the ship, my clothes fell off of me and I had to pin them with safety pins so to hold them up."

For many, the first memory was the "lady with the torch." Celia Rypinski prayed when she saw the Statue of Liberty; then endured a day of waiting in the harbor with that great love of life she still displays:

"I saw the Statue of Liberty. And we all ran out and I prayed because I heard so much in Poland about it—the Statue of Liberty. Then we pulled into the harbor and it was in the evening. We had to stay all day Sunday on the boat, until Monday morning. That was all right, but we were disappointed—not only me, but everybody. Because they didn't unload on Sunday; people didn't work on Sunday . . .

"We pulled in Saturday evening, and stayed the whole Sunday, and *were seeing the view. I admired Brooklyn—I saw such pretty streets, and the green hedges. Brooklyn is a beautiful city, so green, and the green hedges that you trim. That was something new to me . . ."*

One of those second-class passengers who took an unexpected trip to Ellis Island was Marta Forman. Although cleared at the inspection in quarantine, she was unable to identify the uncle who was to meet her, so she was not allowed to go ashore:

"Mr. Kovacs, the man who went with us, said, 'Now you have to watch when we land—I want to show you everything.' So we went on the first deck so we could have a nice view, and he said, 'You see, this is the Statue of Liberty.'

"That I will never forget. It was almost night, and you could see New York. Manhattan Island, all the lights!

"That was the year 1922. August 24th, we landed here. And I was so excited!

"After that we landed, but I couldn't recognize the uncle who was to meet me. He was there, but I couldn't recognize him. So everybody went home, and I was all by myself on the big boat.

"I said, 'What are you going to do with me? Why doesn't somebody call for me?' But I didn't panic.

"They said, 'You have to go to Ellis Island.'

"So the little boat that brings the people from the big boat to Ellis Island, it was waiting for me, and it was the last boat."

Hans Bergner's trip to Ellis Island was unexpected, too. He and other third-class passengers had been shocked to find that first- and second-class passengers did not have to go through Ellis Island. He remembers feeling indignant at the differing treatment accorded the more affluent passengers, and his indignation was still evident fifty years later:

"I must tell you right now that not all immigrants in the year 1924 had to go through Ellis Island. It was a shock to me as a youngster at the age of nineteen, after having passed the Statue of Liberty on the 26th of December, 1924, on a rather small passenger ship of the Hamburg-American Line. Its name was the Thuringia. On this ship were three classes. Tourist class in those days was an unknown entity, but there was a first class, a second class and a third class; altogether probably 300 to 400 people on board as passengers and about one-third were third-class passengers. I was one among those.

"The reason I didn't travel second class was very obvious. A friend

As the ship neared the coast, the waves died down—and so did
the seasickness. Then all the hundreds of passengers would come up on deck
for their first sight of the Statue of Liberty and America.

of mine had provided funds for the trip to the 'Land of Great Opportunity' where milk and honey flows—as we thought in those days—and he had bought me a second-class ticket. But when I received it in Hamburg, near where I was born, I decided that I needed $25 to show to the immigration officials upon arrival, because I had no funds to speak of. So I traveled third class and I was refunded the difference between second and third class, and this was just a very good idea. But it had its drawbacks.

"When we arrived on the 26th of December, on a very very cold winter day, and the passenger ship was fastened to the pier—Pier 84, I believe it was, at the foot of 44th Street in Manhattan—the first-class passengers were asked to leave the ship. The second-class passengers followed. Then the announcement went around all third-class passengers were please to remain on board overnight. They would be fed on the ship, be given a breakfast the following morning, at which time a lighter would come to take us over to Ellis Island. And so there was this slight feeling among many of us that, 'Isn't it strange that here we are coming to a country where there is complete equality, but not quite so for the newly arrived immigrants?'"

The extraordinary feelings of joy and relief at arrival in the safe haven of America are expressed by Sarah Asher and her brother. Their long journey away from war, revolution, civil war—the multiple murders of the innocent by those who claim to carry justice in the barrels of their guns—was coming to an end. The end of the storm at sea was for them the symbolic ending of the far greater storms they had endured all their lives:

"We looked outside and got fresh air. We were so happy and the music was playing and some were dancing. I remember one, a very tall man, middle-aged, maybe forty, he asked me to dance with him on deck. So I said all right and we danced waltzes. He was very nice. And some of the from-the-bottom people started to feel better and they came upstairs, too. So we were eating and it was very nice. You know, you make friends with all those who went. That boat was going to the United States, no other place.

"All those were not only immigrants. There were a few Americans who had traveled somewhere and were coming home. So we were all there. And then I remember my brother and I went on the deck, and it was nice, sunny and breezy, beautiful. Watching some fish jumping out of the water, here the breeze came. My brother had a cap, the cap flew off from his head and he made like he wanted to jump for it. I held him. I said, 'It is all right, you didn't lose your head, but the cap is gone.'

"So he said, 'You're right. It was just as easy to lose your head in the old country.' Because through the Revolution they were killing people 600 to 800 a day in Kiev.

"About twenty-four hours later, we started to approach New York. The water was nice and mild in comparison to what we went through, and so we arrived at the harbor in New York at night. It was beautiful, all those electric lights. You could see the New Jersey shore. And our boat stopped, because we had to have an escort boat which would take us to the spot where we would have to get off. At night escort boats don't work so we had to wait until six o'clock in the morning.

"So we stayed, looked round and around and about four or five o'clock in the morning we all got up. The whole boat. Everybody came out after such a trip, came out on the boat and facing the shore. Waiting for the boat at six o'clock. The sunshine started, and what do we see? The Statue of Liberty!

"Well, she was beautiful with the early morning light. Everybody was crying. The whole boat bent toward her because everybody went out, everybody, everybody was in the same spot. We had been sinking and we survived and now we were looking at the Statue of Liberty. She was beautiful with the sunshine so bright. Beautiful colors, the greenish-like water—and so big, and everybody was crying. The captain came and said, 'Please, everybody, we should move a little bit to the center. You will see everything,' but nobody would move. He was pleading. Finally he said, 'All right.'

"Then the little boat came out to us and escorted us to the port where you have to go out. It started to move the boat a little bit and we moved past the Statue of Liberty. We could see New York already, with the big buildings and everything and we came to South Ferry. There was a house where the boat stopped, but only the Americans were able to go out. The captain looked over their papers and everything and let them out, but we foreigners had to remain on board. We remained. It was morning, about ten o'clock, and our boat moved further, and that was when we were going to Ellis Island."

The original Ellis Island formed only a small part of the upper island
in this picture, taken around 1921. The main building, with its characteristic
arched windows and canopy, held the Great Hall, while sections to the rear
and side held dormitories and other special purpose rooms. The two islands
below, filled in later, held the hospitals.

V

THE ISLAND
OF HOPE
AND TEARS

"What was Ellis Island like? It was hell and it was good. For one who passed by, everything was all right. For one who was detained or sent back, oh, that was awful."

❧❧❧

THEODORE LUBIK
Ukrainian, from Austro-Hungary
Arrived 1913
Worked at Ellis Island 1914–1917

AND FINALLY—Ellis Island! Journey's end, the last hurdle. Island of hope and gateway to a new world for the overwhelming majority of those who came. And truly an island of tears, of lives destroyed and hope denied, for those who were turned away.

Journey's end—and a new beginning. Behind them a world of police, borders, visas, permits and all the multiple oppressions only the poor and the outsider know. Ahead, a whole continent, and the taste and touch of freedom.

Of course, the streets were not paved with gold. Certainly the new world exhibited many of the worst features of the old and added crass materialism and new bigotries of its own. But for the vast majority of the tens of millions who came, Ellis Island was literally and symbolically the end of a long, often extraordinarily difficult journey to freedom.

It was a nexus, a whirlpool of forces, people, contending ideas. A place where the long-growing, deeply felt idea of a free and open America came into sharp and irreconcilable conflict with an equally old and strong tradition of bigotry in America; where industry's desire for an unending supply of cheap labor clashed head-on with organized labor's attempts to protect the jobs of its members; where earlier immigrants tried to help the new arrivals, often their own relatives and neighbors from the old countries— and where tens of millions of people from all over the world came to the America of their hopes and dreams, knowing little or nothing of the maelstrom they would enter at the gateway, the island of hope and tears.

THE PLACE

Ellis Island is little more than a sandbar—a small, flat, low island in upper New York Harbor, one of a group known as the Oyster Islands, after the oyster beds found there in the early days of the American colonies. The island was originally about three acres in area, and at high tide the water threatened to cover it.

It had been called Gibbet Island in the eighteenth century, apparently after a pirate named Anderson had been hanged there in 1765. Other hangings followed, and the name became firmly established. Late in the century, it was renamed after its then-current owner, Samuel Ellis.

Shortly before the turn of the century, the new nation fortified the island against the wars then raging in Europe. First New York State, then the federal government, took over the island, and it was Fort Gibson for most of the nineteenth century. During the Civil War, the fort was expanded and modernized, with substantial ammunition storage facilities. After the war, it became an ammunition dump.

In fact, Ellis Island was far from the first choice of those who sought an isolated island in the harbor on which to build the first federal immigration station. First choice was Bedloe's, now Liberty Island, the site of the Statue of Liberty, and another of the Oyster Islands; second choice, Governor's Island, the site of a substantial Army installation. The Immigration Service lost out on both and wound up with Ellis Island, which nobody wanted, and which required substantial channel widening and deepening before it could be used as an immigration station.

Before 1875, the federal government had very little to do with the regulation of immigration, leaving that to the states. Then, between 1875 and 1890, a series of federal laws and regulations began to place the entire immigration process in federal hands and to restrict immigration, a process that ended with the rigidly restrictive laws and regulations of the 1920s.

The main United States port of arrival for immigrants during the nineteenth and twentieth centuries was New York. From 1855 until the opening of the federal immigration station at Ellis Island in 1892, the arrival center was Castle Garden, at the Battery at the foot of Manhattan Island.

People all over the world knew of Castle Garden. It meant arriving in America. In some languages, it was simply "Castle Garden," in others "Kesselgarden," "The Castlegarden," or perhaps "Kasselgarda." Even in the 1970s, many people who arrived at Ellis Island in the twentieth century, long after the closing of Castle Garden, still insist that they came to America through "the Castlegarden."

Castle Garden's terrible reputation seems justified—it was shot through with corruption. Inspectors, service personnel and outsiders all preyed on the new arrivals, taking advantage of exhaustion, language difficulties and culture shock to rob tens of thousands of immigrants of their money and other possessions. In fact, much of the rationale for bringing immigration under federal control and isolating the immigration station from the mainland was an attempt to fight corruption and to provide protection and fair treatment for immigrants. At the same time, the plain truth is that federal control of immigration coincided with the beginning of a series of exclusionary laws and regulations, reflecting antiforeign influences that were far more successful on the federal level than they had ever been under the states.

The Ellis Island immigration station was still unfinished when it opened on January 1, 1892, the first immigrant being Annie Moore, from County Cork, Ireland.

The main station then was a large two-story wooden building, 400 feet by 150 feet, with a large baggage handling area occupying the first floor. On the second floor were the main processing and handling facilities, including the inspection areas, holding enclosures for those who had passed inspection, railroad ticket offices, money exchange counters, food stands and several administrative office areas. The Island, by then substantially enlarged, also included a dormitory for those detained, a hospital, bathhouses, a restaurant and other service and staff residence buildings.

The entire installation was said to be capable of handling 10,000 immigrants a day, and during the period 1892 to 1897 seemed entirely adequate. More restrictive immigration policies and the United States depression of the mid-1890s combined to dampen immigration, and the "old immigration" from northern and western Europe, while still substantial, seemed to be leveling off. But the "new immigration" from southern and eastern Europe was just beginning to accelerate, and the massive arrivals of the first two decades of the twentieth century were neither anticipated nor prepared for.

The people who came through that first Ellis Island station were as diverse a set of immigrants as at any other period of immigration to America. In addition to the young Irving Berlin and his family, they included: from Austria, Felix Frankfurter, who became a U.S. Supreme Court Justice; from Poland, Samuel Goldwyn, whose own film production company ended up as the "Goldwyn" in the Metro-Goldwyn-Mayer; from Russia, Samuel Chotzinoff, piano accompanist and voice of the famed NBC Symphony radio broadcasts under Toscanini; and from Norway, Knute Rockne, legendary football coach at Notre Dame University.

All during the immigration of the mid-1890s, the work on the Ellis Island station continued and was officially completed on June 13, 1897. On June 14, the next day, shortly before midnight, fire broke out. Within an hour, every wooden building—the entire station—had burned to the ground. Of the many people on the Island when the installation burned down, no one was seriously hurt. However, the old ammunition vaults, which had held the Castle Garden immigration records, buckled, destroying records going back to 1855.

The immigration station buildings were a total loss, and it was back to the mainland into temporary quarters at the Barge Office on the Battery for almost three years. Through these constricted quarters, immigrants continued to flow, among them the Danish William Knudsen, who later became President of the General Motors Corporation.

Lying low in the water, this is how Ellis Island looked to the millions brought to it, with ferries and barges lined up in the ferry basin, and the New Jersey docks in the background. This photograph was taken by Augustus Sherman, Chief Clerk at Ellis Island during its early years.

The new, fireproof, Federal Immigration Station on Ellis Island opened in December 1900. Much changed and expanded over the years, it stands to this day, and is now in the process of restoration as a national landmark.

The main building was nearly the same size as the one that had burned down in 1897, almost 400 feet long, 165 feet wide and over 60 feet high, with four corner towers 100 feet high. The first floor held baggage handling facilities, railroad ticket offices, food sales counters and a waiting room for those traveling beyond New York.

The second floor held the Great Hall, a room 200 feet by 100 feet by 56 feet high, which was the main immigrant registration and examination hall on the Island. A mezzanine floor in the early years held observation areas, and later administrative offices. The second floor also held detention areas, administrative offices, waiting areas and special inspection rooms.

Completing the installation were a restaurant, bathhouse, laundry, powerhouse and dormitory, along with a hospital which was finished in 1902. In later years, as the original three acres became twenty-seven, a hospital for contagious diseases was added, other buildings were expanded and somewhat modernized, and other service buildings were added. The entire facility was able to handle several thousand immigrants a day; to hold, feed and house hundreds of detainees; and to treat hundreds more in hospital. During the peak immigration years of 1900 to 1914 and 1919 to 1921, it did that and much, much more.

For many immigrants, the necessity of passing through Ellis Island was a rude shock. Arrival in New York Harbor meant safe haven and the Statue of Liberty. Despite the millions of people who had come before them and sent back word of golden America —and the hazards of "The Castlegarden"—few were really prepared for the process that awaited them. Some, like Hans Bergner, were sharply indignant at learning they would have to go to Ellis Island for special immigration inspection, from which most first- and second-class passengers were exempted.

For the Immigration Service, arrival at New York Harbor meant the beginning of their inspection process. Helen Barth, who worked at Ellis Island for the Hebrew Immigrant Aid Society (HIAS) from 1914 to 1917, describes the process from the time the Immigration Service picked up responsibility for the immigrants at quarantine in the lower harbor until their arrival at Ellis Island:

"I tell you what we did. As quickly as possible, the little doctor, who was working for the Public Health Service would climb up and down the ladder on those ships that came in—he worked very, very hard. Sometimes they had to meet a ship at two or three o'clock in the morning, and they would start their work at that time. I remember one of the doctors asking me on an Italian ship, I don't remember the name of it now, to have dinner with him. The ship came in at six o'clock in the morning and there were lamb chops, which were such a novelty and such a wonderful meal in those days, you know.

"The big boats came in to all places, like Boston, New York, and so on. They each had a place where the immigrants went. Now, when I was on Ellis Island, the New York and New Jersey boats sent their immigrants, the third-class passengers—or worse than that, steerage,

This Italian family, brought from their ocean liner on this "little boat," is waiting to get off the ferry at Ellis Island, to start the immigration clearance process that they hope will lead to a new life in America.

they called them—to Ellis Island. The doctor went along—they would sometimes have pretty sick people. We had a hospital on Ellis Island.

"The boats they took the immigrants in were not very good boats, but they were big enough to carry hundreds at a time. They were like ferries, but stronger—they were flat-bottom boats. The immigrants were very fearful, terribly afraid.

"The relatives would try to come in with them, but they weren't allowed on the boat that took the immigrants across. The relatives came on the Ellis Island ferry—like the Hudson River boats, that style that goes up and down the river, they have three tiers. We employees used the upper part of the Ellis Island boat. Later, when the immigrants were discharged, they were allowed to go on this boat with their relatives."

The entrance to Ellis Island on this day in 1926, after severe immigration restriction, was very different than it was in the peak years, when people had to wait hours in barges before they could debark and form into lines under the canopy.

The transfer barges that brought the immigrants to Ellis Island were crowded, often with little protection from the elements, and without seats for most people. Once moored at the Island, immigrants waited on the barges, sometimes for hours, while others ahead of them were being processed. If the barges were needed elsewhere, immigrants were unloaded and stood in line waiting to enter the main building.

Theodore Lubik, who came through Ellis Island as an immigrant in 1913, then returned to work in a food concession there from 1914 to 1917, describes how the immigrants were transferred and cared for until they entered the main building at the Island:

"They brought you to Ellis Island with that small boat—it might take a couple of hundred or even a thousand people. The regular ship would pull up at the pier, but the little one moved somehow next to the ship and transferred the people over there. The immigrants were brought there and landed on Ellis Island. They made lines of four, like soldiers. Then the small boat went again and took more, if the big boat had more people. If not, it would take from another ship. It was coming every day. The boat that ran between the big ship and Ellis Island took only immigrants.

"Sometimes when that little boat came into the shore—it's not little, but next to the big boat it is—when it came in at twelve o'clock, everybody went for dinner, doctors and watchmen and everything. Maybe the immigrants would have to wait until two o'clock or four o'clock—they would have no chance to get into the building because it was full. You can't keep them waiting, so we fed them there. We took two, four, five cans of milk, coffee, some brown bread cut up into fancy slices, boxes of sardines or herring, different kinds of food, whatever was ready—we put it into the wagon we had. Then we went to that little boat and we gave food to anybody who wanted it."

Once landed at Ellis Island, the immigrants were formed into groups by ship and manifest number. A canopy outside offered some protection against snow and rain as they stood in line—the first of many such lines—wondering what was in store for them inside.

PASSING THROUGH

Eventually the immigrants were led up the main stairway by an interpreter, to the Great Hall, the central examining area on the second floor. At the top of the stairs, the first step of a two-step medical examination took place. Immigrants, spaced so that the doctors could study them as they approached, moved in single file past a team of two doctors, placed some distance apart.

The doctors examined as many as 5,000 immigrants a day, checking for a wide range of abnormalities and diseases (some treatable), which might cause an immigrant to be excluded from America. They checked for all kinds of "mental" problems, both specific and general; for such disabilities as very poor eyesight and

Carrying straw baskets and other hand luggage, this group of Slavic immigrants edged their way up the stairs as room cleared for them in the Great Hall above, in one of the peak immigration years—1905.

partial blindness, senility, lameness, deafness, general weakness and physical deformity; and for many specific illnesses, especially trachoma (a kind of conjunctivitis that causes eventual blindness), favus (a scalp disease) and tuberculosis, all causes for summary rejection.

Especially in those peak years, the two doctors spent no more than two minutes with each immigrant and often much less. The resulting examination was therefore, to put it gently, rather minimal. They looked generally at the people as they approached and then more closely at hands, face and throat. If they saw any basis at all for further examination, they put chalk marks on the immigrant's back or chest, in a rudimentary code indicating the nature of the suspected condition. Given the wide range of possible medical exclusions and the brevity of this primary medical examination, it is not surprising that hundreds of thousands of people were chalkmarked and held aside for further examination during the peak immigration years.

Once past the first team of doctors, the immigrants encountered another team at the end of the examining aisle. These doctors, using glove buttonhooks, turned the immigrant's eyelids inside out. This second step of the medical inspection, mainly directed at discovering trachoma, was a painful and frightening experience. Immigrants had no preparation for it except stories of pain and damage told by earlier immigrants—and the very real pain they saw as others ahead of them in line experienced the procedure.

Those detained were held in screened detention areas, clearly visible to other immigrants moving through. Later they were moved into special inspection areas for further examination, dormitories for detention, bathhouses for disinfecting and delousing, and sometimes directly into hospitals, as thought necessary by the examining doctors.

If not detained for medical reasons, the immigrants were moved, still in groups by ship manifest number, to benches between the medical examination area and the main inspection area. When their group was called, they were moved onto another series of benches arranged in long, narrow aisles. There they waited until, one by one, they were called for examination by one of the immigration inspectors, who sat at the end of each inspection aisle at a raised desk, as does a judge in a courtroom; an interpreter was usually present also.

The immigration inspector had before him the ship's manifest, listing the basic information about each passenger, that had been filled out by the ship's officer in the port of origin. The basic questions contained in the manifest were set by the immigration law of 1903, and focused on identification, marital status, skills, personal history, financial responsibility and prospective employment.

If no problems arose during this review of the manifest information, immigrants who passed were free to join their relatives on the boat to the Battery or were taken by numbered groups to make railroad connections for the balance of the journey inland. Those not examined before nightfall were held overnight at the Island and inspected the next morning, because immigration policy precluded nighttime inspection and clearance. Cleared immigrants might also be held overnight if the inspection concluded in early evening.

Immigrants detained because of problems at any point in the inspection were held for further examination, often waiting arrival of the American sponsors. Some eventually were sent back to Europe; the majority ultimately passed for entry into the United States and were free to leave Ellis Island.

During the peak immigration years before World War I, an average of about a million immigrants a year came through Ellis Island. On many occasions, the Island's staff handled well over ten thousand immigrants in a single day.

Immigration fell sharply during World War I, but later picked up to nearly prewar levels. But by then the Island was no longer able to process immigrants so quickly, because in 1917 the United States Congress, over President Wilson's veto, had passed a far more restrictive immigration law requiring closer checks on each immigrant. This 1917 law for the first time instituted a literacy test for immigrants, as well as requiring that inspectors ask a good many more questions than before. The quick line inspection, with one inspector handling several hundred immigrants a day, was a thing of the past. The Island became able to handle only 2,000 or 3,000 immigrants a day, at best. Because of this reduced capacity, large numbers of people were detained and for considerably longer periods than before the war.

These conditions of overcrowding and long periods of detention continued until the 1921 and 1924 quota laws, which sharply cut "new immigration" and transferred responsibility for the primary inspection abroad, changed Ellis Island from a general processing point to a place for examining only those immigrants with special problems.

This, then, was the general procedure that immigrants went through at Ellis Island during the first quarter of this century. What it felt like to the immigrants themselves is a very different matter, and what they remember of their experience there is very much affected by their own fears and problems.

One sharp-eyed observer was Irene Meladaki Zambelli. Moved to the head of the line by the captain as she was getting off the ship, she was still in front when she entered the main building at Ellis Island. So she passed through the various aisles, which she calls "gates," first and was able to watch others behind her:

"We got off on Ellis Island, Castle Garden, and there were police officers and lawyers and judges to inspect us and question us. There were little gates the same as you go to the subways, only you did not have to drop the fare, of course. Being in front, my cousin and I passed first. The first gate we passed they asked what we were to one another. The inspector put one hand on the back and one in front of my cousin's chest and tried to straighten him out—he had a bad habit to stoop over. When he asked me if I was in America before, I bent back my head and raised my eyebrows, and clucked my tongue on my palate, as the Greeks do, meaning, 'No.' He smiled and said, 'Go ahead!'

"Then we came to the next gate and they asked us how much was two and two, and four and four. We answered and went to the next gate. They asked us how much money we had. We had between us $30 in gold money. We proudly showed off the money and they hung a plaque with a number around our neck* and told us to keep going.

"Because we were the first to get out, we stayed and watched the rest of them. One man when they asked how much is two and two, he did not know and my cousin kept nudging him and repeating, 'Four, four, four.' Finally the man said, 'Four,' and they let him go. Then I

* To indicate the group they would join for the proper train connection.

161

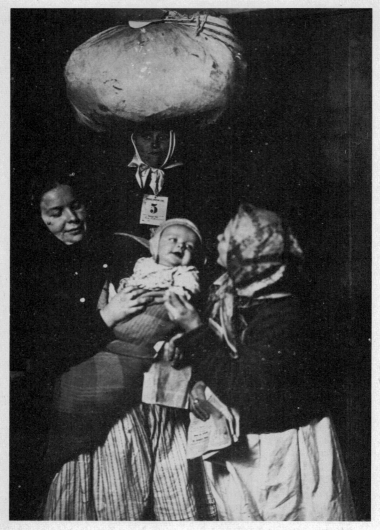

A study in old-country styles, these Slavic immigrants await entry at Ellis Island. The woman carrying the bundle on her head prominently displays her ship's manifest tag which, besides her name, indicates that she is listed as number 10 on ship's manifest number 5, from the Hamburg-American Line.

heard screams and a woman crying, saying, 'Yes, she is my daughter! She is my daughter!' I went near to see what was the trouble and she had given her age to be younger than her daughter's. They were both crying for fear they would be sent back. I said to the daughter, Tell your mother to try to remember her age because she could not be your mother if she is younger than you. I do not know what they did because I could not stay any longer, but they let them pass."

Another view of the general process is given by Hans Bergner. Coming through in 1924, he indicates some of the additional kinds of checks added to the inspection process since those early years of mass processing of thousands of immigrants a day:

"Third-class passengers had to come to Ellis Island, and none of us knew exactly what this would mean. What it did mean was that, first of all, the immigration officials would make sure that we knew where we were going when we arrived. We had, of course, been sponsored by someone in the United States in order to get here in the first place, but there had to be some proof shown that someone was going to pick us up or that we had some destination that we were going to go to.

"The other thing they wanted to know was whether we had $25, and the third thing they wanted to know was could we read the English language,* so each of us was asked to read a small paragraph from a book that the official would show us.

"And then came the last step, and of course, the most familiar to people who have served in the armed forces, namely that there was a physical inspection awaiting us, the women on one side and men on the other. Then came the great moment when we stood in front of the immigration official, who was a doctor, who examined us for venereal diseases. And if there was one who had a venereal disease, that particular person would not be allowed on land. There again I had my peculiar feeling of the strange separation—that venereal disease among first- and second-class passengers was apparently acceptable and for third-class passengers venereal diseases were not. Well, this was one of those introductions one never forgets, but I must say that it has long, long ago been completely erased by the tremendous opportunities the United States has offered . . ."

THERE HE IS!

Most immigrants had a quick passage through Ellis Island. And for some, it was a marvelously sunny experience—after all,

* Literacy in German would have been acceptable.

they had made it to America! Marta Forman's visit to Ellis Island was unanticipated, because she hadn't recognized her uncle at the pier, but coming out of postwar starvation in Czechoslovakia in 1922, even Ellis Island was a dream come true. Her voice quickened with remembered excitement as she described it over fifty years later:

"So when I came to Ellis Island, my gosh, there was something I'll never forget. The first impression—all kinds of nationalities. And the first meal we got—fish and milk, big pitchers of milk and white bread, the first time I saw white bread and butter. There was so much milk, and I drank it because we didn't have enough milk in my country. And I said, 'My God, we're going to have a good time here. We're going to have plenty to eat.'

"So then everybody was waiting for somebody to call for them. Now, after fifty-one years, I can imagine what a job they had spelling all those names, all different nationalities—it's not so easy. Some of the names were so long, so hard to pronounce and hard to spell, and so I was always waiting to hear when they were going to call my name, if they could only spell it. I stayed near the man so he wouldn't miss me. Everybody was going. After a lot of them went, I said, 'My gosh, what are they going to do with me now? I'll have to sleep here overnight. But that's nothing, you know.'

"One lady who was waiting came in Czech costume, and she said, 'My gosh, my boy friend is supposed to pick me up and we are supposed to get married on Ellis Island.' All of a sudden she saw him and they hugged and kissed and cried. Right away she gave me her address, so after I settled down I should come and see her so she won't be so lonely.

"After that, I thought, 'Boy, I'm going to sleep here.' Then one, two, three—one man was calling my name. My gosh, he got my name!

"I hollered, 'Here I am, here I am!' and there was my uncle . . ."

For the proud, independent Greek girl Bessie Spylios was in 1909, the passage through Ellis Island was simply an extension of her wonderful ocean voyage. Even waiting for her father, who came to claim her a day late, failed to dampen her enthusiasm. Eleven years old, with her older brother still in tow, she roamed the Great Hall much as she had roamed the ship to America, and sixty-nine years later her eyes sparkled as she told of it:

ಆ§ "Were people pretty happy at Ellis Island?"

"Yes. Happy! They waited for the people to get them. You got to have somebody to receive you when you get there. You can't walk in and out. Where are you going to go? If you speak English, it's all right and you might go, but with another language it is very hard . . .

"We waited to see when my father would come. And another girl was with me. Her father was a neighbor in the old country. Her father and my father were coming together. So we waited and stayed overnight."

◆§ "How did you feel when your father didn't show up that first day?"

"Well, I wasn't concerned. I was young and I didn't care. I knew he was going to come. And a special woman talked to us in Greek and we felt more secure. We knew we were in the right place and that our father was going to come. And she told us, 'Don't worry or cry. Your father is going to come—if not tonight, he will be here tomorrow. And when he comes, there will still be many people ahead of you, as we go by numbers and call everybody's name.' "

◆§ "Did you get a meal while you were there?"

"Yes. They had a big table set up with everything. Of course, everything was new to me, but I ate just the same. I wasn't going to go hungry. My brother didn't want to eat because he didn't know what it was. But I said, 'It won't kill everybody else, so it can't kill us!'

"It was some kind of meat, and bread, and I had a banana. I had a few cherries in little baskets. We had a pretty good meal. The only thing was that I was anxious to get out of there . . .

"What a place that was! Beautiful. It wasn't like now, that place. Balconies on top, you know, all the way around and people who had to wait a long time could go upstairs and watch the people downstairs. And they had cots where I slept. They had quite a few cots in a big room and a lot of people. You slept with your boots and the way you came was the way you went to bed. There was no place there to get undressed to go to bed. Just lie down and sleep. And get up in the morning ready to travel."

◆§ "No place to wash up?"

"Oh, yes. They had bathrooms, yes. A nice, clean place. I can't forget how clean that place was.

"The next day we got up and went downstairs in line where they called so many names at a time. So when they called my name, I said to my brother, 'Come on!' And I took him by the hand.

"He said, 'Where are we going?'

"I said, 'They called our name. Let's go. Don't wait!'

"So we went into a room, and they had guards there. And there was a woman at the desk who talked Greek. She said, 'Where are you going?'

" 'To my father.'

" 'Do you know your father? Is he here?'

"And I looked around. 'No, he is not here. But he will be,' I said.

"She said, 'You got money? To pay for your fares wherever you go?'

"We had ten dollars between the two of us, which was a lot of money then. Because they told us you have to have some money for your fares after you finish with Ellis Island, and are on your own. And pretty soon the guard stood in front of me and my brother. I tried to push him away because, you see, I didn't want to miss anything and I was anxious to see my father. So then I saw my father come in. And I started to get up and the guard said, 'Sit down.' He made me sit down, and the lady said to me, 'You better sit down until I am ready, until after you answer the questions I want to ask you.'

"So I did, I sat down nicely and I was waiting and I said to the lady, 'What are you keeping me here for? My father is here. That's my father.' And I got up and went to my father and put my arms around him."

BUT THOSE CAGES!

Many of those coming through Ellis Island had very little trouble themselves, yet saw the place as truly an "island of tears," of bars, cages and callous brutality.

They saw iron railings covering most of the floor of the Great Hall. The bars were there to create aisles for orderly movement within the Hall; they saw them as the iron bars of a prison. They saw wired detention areas, which they identified as cages.

They saw people detained, heard people crying. Crying and laughing are both contagious, and there was good reason for calling Ellis Island the "Island of Tears." The crying epidemic there started the day it opened, was fed by exhaustion, fear, confusion and tragedy observed—and by the Island's personnel. Many were no worse than bureaucrats everywhere, some a great deal better than they had any reason to be, themselves exhausted by an enormous and never-ending workload under conditions of extreme crowding and tension—and by the crying that never stopped.

Even Anna Vacek, following her dollies and her dream to America, was affected. And it was only 1901, shortly after the opening of the rebuilt Ellis Island immigration station, and long before immigration reached its peak:

In the early years, when Anna Vacek, Frank Santoni and Leon Solomon
arrived, the entrance stairway was in the center of the Great Hall, and
people emerged into this maze of railings and benches, surrounded
by high wire fences and caged areas.

"I came here in 1901, the day President McKinley was buried, and my sister took me from Ellis Island. I was there in a cage, like, for the immigrants in those days.

"And when she looked at me, she said, 'My goodness, child, you are so small. I thought when I saw your picture that you were much bigger.'

"I said, 'Well, that's all right, Lisa, I'm going to be a little servant girl here.'

"She said, 'You need one yourself, you're so small. I don't know what I'm going to do with you.'

"I said, 'Don't worry. I will be all right. I will listen to you and everything will be all right.'"

For those fleeing the tyrannies of eastern and southern Europe, the encounter with American bureaucracy at Ellis Island was particularly upsetting. Millions of Russian Jews had illegally crossed borders, fled Europe and crossed an ocean to find safe haven in America—land of the free. But when they came face to face with immigration service people in uniform, they could not help but identify them with the hated and feared soldiery of Czar, Kaiser, Emperor and Sultan.

Almost three quarters of a century later Fannie Kligerman, traveling with the seven families that fled the pogroms together, still remembers Ellis Island (she calls it Castle Gardens) as if it were a prison run by Czarist soldiers:

"We came here to Castle Gardens, and we had those, what you call it, guards. It was just like a prison. They threw us around. You know that children don't know anything. They would say, 'Stay here. Stay there.' And you live through it, you just don't fight back. And when it came to food we never had fresh bread, the bread was always stale. Where they got it, we don't know.

"One of my brothers had something wrong with him. It was a sty. He had wiped it and rubbed it and he went to play marbles, more dirt came in, you know. You know how young children are. He had a sty, and he tore it off. It left a funny thing, and they put him aside. And they told us that if there was anything wrong with him, he'd have to go back to Europe.

"Oh, it was frightening. My father said, 'I'm not going on without the children. We will all go back.' You can imagine!

"They said they would take him away to try to cure him, and my mother had to sign that she was willing. So in a few days it was cured.

"This I remember well—the eye exam. It was such a fright, such a

This young Jewish girl might have been Fannie Kligerman, arriving at Ellis Island in 1905, fleeing the Russian pogroms.

fright. And who examined us? A soldier. This I remember, too. But except for that little eye trouble we were all healthy."

Fannie Kligerman wasn't examined by a soldier. The painful eye examination was done by a doctor. The nearest soldier was at Governor's Island, across New York Harbor. But she did see uniformed guards, immigration service personnel, doctors and nurses, all in some kind of uniform. And just as much to the point, she saw hundreds of people behaving as officials and bureaucrats do everywhere, all in a place of bars, cages and regimentation. Small wonder, then, that for so many immigrants Ellis Island, their first substantial experience of America, was truly an Island of Tears, as Fannie describes:

"The worst thing was, you wouldn't guess! Every morning they came around to delouse us. You know what that means? Our things were taken off, we were naked to be deloused.

"We didn't have a bath or anything. All they knew how to do was delouse us, you should excuse me. They took all our clothes, nice dresses, and made rags out of them. As soon as we entered America we had to put them into the garbage.

"I was a very small thirteen year old and they pushed me. Some children at thirteen are a nice size. I wasn't—in America I grew up. But you live through, you can't fight back.

"All of a sudden my father decided to see where he was, to look around and have a chair to sit down on someplace. And we got lost. There was no father. He knew where he was. He wanted to see what kind of people they were, and I started to cry because I love my father and I thought they did something to him. So I stole away from my mother and the oldest daughter and went out to look for my father. Before I got thirty feet, I heard my father calling me, 'Fannie, Fannie.'

"I found him. I felt as if I had found a million dollars! 'Father, what did you do?'

"He said, 'I just wanted to see where we're going. I'll come back.'

" 'So why didn't you tell us that you were going to see?'

" 'I forgot . . .'

"Everybody was sad there. There was not a smile on anybody's face. Here they thought maybe they wouldn't go through. There they thought maybe my child won't go through. There was such a sadness, no smile any place. You could see . . . That's when I came here in 1905. The people had such terrible sad faces. Such a sad place there.

"Oh, did I cry. Terribly. When you cry and I can see how you cry, I cry, too. All my sisters and brothers cried. So I cried. You don't know why you cry. Just so much sadness there that you have to cry. But there's more tears in Ellis Island to ten people than, say, to a hundred people elsewhere. There is all of these tears, everybody has tears."

The air of sadness lingered on Ellis Island, far past the time of enormous overcrowding and the tensions it produced. By the 1920s the reputation of Ellis Island as the "Island of Tears" had been long-established all over the immigrant's world.

For Irma Busch, too, it was "a sad place." She came through Ellis Island twice, in 1925 and 1933. Both trips through were well past the time of peak immigration, and the Island was therefore relatively uncrowded. In addition, she was German, one of the northern Europeans very much favored by both the quota laws and the Immigration Service staff. And she spoke English. Even so, this is how Ellis Island felt to Irma coming through in 1925, young, fresh, full of hope, only seventeen, and seeking the America of the Wild West novels:

"When we arrived, this was a Friday morning, we arrived in New York, and this was, oh, so amazing when we got into the harbor! It doesn't matter whether you are on a ferry, or a big ship, or whatever, when you see Manhattan appear with all these tall buildings, you know, it looks as if it's just a lot of tall buildings on a pancake, swimming on the water. I mean, it's so amazing. And it's beautiful, and of course, seeing all these different islands as you approach the harbor, like Staten Island, and all these other islands; it's fascinating. And every time I go somewhere, and go by ship and go under the Verrazano Bridge now, I tell you, really, the skyline is gorgeous. It is beautiful. But then, of course, it was just a little bit scary—you were so new and strange, and so young, and never been away from home. So, well, we docked, I think it was Pier 44, which was on 46th Street and the Hudson River. And then, of course, we had to get on the ferry for Ellis Island.

"I traveled third class, and I remember it cost $75, which I had to pay back to my uncle, and he had to give me $25 more to hold. I had to show that I had some money, that I would not become a public charge.

"So then, we were taken by ferry to Ellis Island. And, of course, that alone was disappointing, not to be able to get off the ship, be met by someone and leave."

◆§ "Ellis was your first actual step on dry land?"

"Right. To me it was a sad place, because the people, they were all anxious, worried, and you didn't know what was going to happen. I know I felt very blue.

"I followed the crowd in and we all sat down. Then we had to line up and they looked over our papers and checked our shots—I had four shots given to me before we left Hamburg. I remember at Ellis Island they looked at the fingernails, you know, cuticles. They can determine certain diseases by looking at your cuticles. I wasn't examined any other way at all."

◆§ "They didn't check your eyes and scalp?"

"I think the eyes they did check. Nothing else. Nothing else that I remember. But they looked you over as you went along. Well, maybe I looked all right, I don't know.

"Then we were told to sit down. I sat there for hours. I would say maybe three hours. But you see, I was heartsick. I really was heartsick. I had no ambition to wander around and look it over at all. I didn't. It would just be quick impressions I had. Like the cots, and I thought, 'Well, how do you get up there? Climb up?'

"By this time it was around lunch time and they were serving fish. I don't know, it looked like everybody was enjoying their meal. There were long tables and benches, and everything was on the table, fish and vegetables, whatever, water, water pitchers. These people, they really looked pathetic, most of them, but they seemed to enjoy their food, and they sat there and said, 'Come on, come on.' They kept saying to me,

'Come on, eat something. It is good.' But, oh, no, I didn't sit down; I knew I couldn't eat."

&§ "Did these people come over on the same ship with you?"

"Well, some. There were people, I guess, who came over on that ship. Some may have come over on another ship, because after all, they all had to congregate on Ellis Island. And you know, some of them had to stay there—they wouldn't let them go for one reason or another. If they weren't well, or they had something wrong with them, or they did not have a reliable person to vouch for them, and it had to be a very reliable person, then they had no way of leaving Ellis Island."

&§ "Did you see people going through the doctors' inspection who were put aside?"

"Sure. Yes, definitely. People were put aside, because I saw people that had not arrived with us or come later or anything, people who seemed to have been living there, for I don't know how long. You know, they were used to all this. They were wandering around. They didn't have suitcases. They appeared to have room and board, because they couldn't get out for one reason or another. The inspection was really very strict in those days. That's why you had so many good people coming here, all nationalities. Of course, I don't know when it started, but before that, before they had the quota numbers, anybody could come and they would let them in. And that was all right, too, because of lot of these people were adventuresome and some of them were the kind that went out west and helped build this country.

"They came with such high hopes, so much expectation. No suit-cases, just a bundle of something. You saw all kinds of people, babies, all the way up. Old people. The people that had arrived from somewhere on some ship were so kind—they tried to help each other. You would see people so exhausted and worrying, for they didn't know if they would have trouble getting out, whether someone would come to meet them, and all that.

"Well, I didn't pay much attention to anything else; all that counted now was to get out of there. You know, officials sitting there, and we were waiting on benches, waiting to be called."

As it turned out, Irma had a special problem—her American sponsor was unable to pick her up and sent a friend in his place. The Immigration Service did not let immigrants leave the Island with people who were not relatives or bona fide sponsors—they were especially careful not to let young women go with unknown men. So Irma met with further delay:

The Great Hall after 1911 was organized by benches and railings into sections, each leading to an inspector's desk at the end of the line (middle of photo) where an interpreter also sat. Running around the second floor of the Great Hall were the balconies where Bessie Spylios played—and where notable visitors came to watch the immigration processing first hand.

"When they called my name, my uncle wasn't able to get there to pick me up. He arrived the next day on another ship, and he was my guardian. So he had told a friend of his to pick me up. This friend talked to the authorities and I was called.

"He was a man, I guess in his thirties. I was meeting him for the first time. He had a wife and children, but they weren't with him, of course, so they told him, 'No, she can't go with you.' You know, he couldn't pick me up. Well, that was it, that was it! I was wishing to be back home with my mother."

❧ "Were you up there when they were talking about this?"

173

"Well, no. I was sitting there, and they were over by a desk talking and talking. And he, I don't know whether he gave them an argument because my uncle couldn't come until the next day. I kept looking around and I saw these tiers of bunks, you know.* It seems to me there was three, one on top of the other—and I thought, 'Oh, my God, do I have to stay here, and sleep here maybe? I can't eat—impossible!' I mean, all the way across my appetite had been good, but then it left me. Well, so there was nothing else to be done. This man had to leave, and he told me he would be back.

"It took about an hour and a half or two hours, and he came back with two nuns. His wife couldn't come with him because they had small children. So he had gone to his church, and he came back with these two nuns. When they talked to the authorities, they came to me and they said it was all right. I could leave now. And that had me worried because my parents had tried to put me in a convent when I was eighteen—I wanted to come to America and not go into a convent. So here, to leave with two nuns! But I had to leave with them because otherwise I couldn't get out."

Irma went back to Germany in 1932, and came home to America within six months, and went through Ellis Island the second time much more easily:

"I had to go to Ellis Island again. Why this was I don't really know. And again all these questions, you know, what was I going to do here, and I said, 'Work.' I did secretarial work, and they wanted to know where I had worked before and I told them. I told them I had had typewriting and shorthand and all of that, and they wanted to see my shorthand. I wrote English and German shorthand, so they just let me go with my friend, and that was that."

⋙ "What did you feel like going through Ellis Island a second time?"

"It looked different to me somehow. Maybe it was because I had more experience and knew more about the surroundings and New York. It didn't frighten me like it did the first time. And it looked clean; it looked scrubbed and very disinfected."

⋙ "Were you back in the Great Hall again the second time?"

"I don't think so, because this took no time at all. These friends of mine, they talked to the officials, and they didn't examine me or even look at my fingernails, and I was out. So we went home."

---

* The dormitories were elsewhere, but after a trip across the ocean and a storm at sea, for her there were bunks there.

THE DOCTORS HAD TRICKS

Helen Barth, as HIAS representative at Ellis Island, was one of those extraordinarily dedicated social service workers who made the passage through so much easier for millions of immigrants. She has a fine eye for detail and an almost total recall of every aspect of her experience at Ellis Island. She remembers the doctors trying hard to make some kind of meaningful medical examination, with an average of something under two minutes available for each immigrant:

"As they got off the boat at Ellis Island, the immigrants walked in a parade up those stairs into the building and there they were put on line. They were put into sections and aisles. The doctor would be standing by his platform and had various little tricks he played—the doctor would have them put their hands down on the desk and if they showed pink, he passed them as not suffering from a heart condition. But when the nails were very blue we put them aside as a heart case.

"When a man came in with a very thin, stringy beard, they thought there was some lack of physical development, for whatever reason.

"When someone walked and hesitated and constantly looked down on the ground to see where he was, they knew that he had trouble with his eyes.

"When a woman was pregnant, for some reason she always had disheveled hair. We all wore our hair neat in those days, with braids, you know, and very carefully done. But these little women—their hair seemed more what they look like today, cut short and very pale and very dirty. They knew there was something wrong with those women.

"The tuberculars all had, not hunchbacks, but a little curvature of the spine. They showed the tuberculosis that way, and were not admitted either."

People remember the very brief medical examinations at Ellis Island quite selectively. For those who passed through easily and quickly, it was a long time ago. The examination took place just a few minutes after going up the stairs into the Great Hall, before they had any chance to adjust to their new situation.

People remembered that their eyes were checked, but with very few exceptions seemed to have blocked out the precise nature of the examination. In fact, the examination was quite painful, and often left the eyes hurting and sensitive for days or even weeks

Seeing the uniform worn by this immigration inspector conducting an
eye examination at Ellis Island, it is easy to see why many people,
like Fannie Kligerman, said that a soldier examined their eyes. The towels
on which the inspectors wiped their hands are a far cry from the trays of
antiseptic solution described in the official reports.

afterward, as attested by contemporary accounts. Yet of all the hundreds of personal accounts of Ellis Island procedures secured for this book, only Catherine Bolinski sharply remembered the eye examination. Of course, Catherine had had a sty in one eye on the boat; although it had responded to treatment prescribed by the ship's doctor, she and her mother still worried about being sent back to Poland. Here is her recollection of the very brief medical examination:

"They turned your eye over—I had to blink a couple of times that way. I'll never forget it.

"They looked at your throat, and to see if you had any rashes on your body. I wasn't unbuttoning fast enough, so they shoved me out of sight. My mother got scared; she thought they were going to send me back. But then they said, 'If you're unbuttoned, come on out,' so I came out, and was with my mother again.

"They found things wrong with some people. Some of the big girls were ·pregnant. They wanted to come here, but they sent them back, after they had sold everything to come here, so they were crying, they felt very bad. The ones that passed were put someplace else and were given box lunches."

THERE'S A MAN GOIN' 'ROUND CHANGING NAMES

At least seventy-five percent of those passing through Ellis Island came through unchallenged—but not necessarily unscathed.

After passing through the medical examination, immigrants waited for the main line inspection, conducted by Immigration Service inspectors. The first question asked, in haste and under conditions of mutual exhaustion and overcrowding, later caused a good deal of trouble to immigrants seeking citizenship, and today makes it difficult for thousands to get past the barrier of Ellis Island on the way back to trace the centuries-long histories of their families in the old country.

That question was simply: "What is your name?"

Some immigrants wanted their names changed, and accomplished that at Ellis Island, simply by responding with shortened and altered versions of their original names. Tens of thousands

Ellis Island is indeed an Island of Hope to this mother and two children awaiting entry into the New World.

of others had their names changed for them by the immigration inspectors, or by the ship's officer who had filled out the manifest, often in ways that were objectionable to them. Most didn't object, feeling they could not object to anything the inspector did. The inspector seemed to have unlimited power over their futures, and in fact did have an enormous discretion as to acceptance or rejection of an immigrant. Other immigrants didn't know what was happening, especially the approximately twenty percent who were illiterate in the years before the literacy law of 1917.

Many immigration inspectors were careful and conscientious in the matter of getting names right. Some leaned heavily on the interpreters normally present during main line inspections, who tried to get names correctly pronounced and spelled.

But some immigration inspectors were casual and uncaring on the matter of names. These inspectors misunderstood replies to the "what is your name" question, misspelled, and often "helped" with suggestions for "Americanized" names. Some even capriciously changed names, with little or no concern for the feelings of those they were mishandling.

Helen Barth saw it this way:

&§ "How do you explain the fact that so many people had their names changed at Ellis Island?"

"They had to. They spoke very badly, were very nervous. The inspector would say, 'Where do you come from?' And they would say 'Berlin.' The inspector would put the name down 'Berliner.' The name was not 'Berliner.' That's no name.

"All the 'witz's,' and 'ski's' got their names from their fathers. For example, Myerson is the son of Myer. We knew that, and changed the names here because they were spelled so badly. For instance, a Polish name would be Skyzertski, and they didn't even know how to spell it, so it would be changed to Sanda, to names like that. It was a much easier way.

"Then there were names like 'Vladimir.' That would be Walter in American, or Willie, some name like that. Vladimir was strictly a Russian name, you know, and they often were very anxious to Americanize quickly.

"And sometimes the children and parents would use first names, and they would call the father 'Adam,' and it became 'Mr. Adam,' and that was the way they went through.

"It was also my work to get verification of their landing when they later applied for citizenship. We had the statistical division there on the Island, and terrifically big books that were too heavy for me to carry.

"I would have to look up this man's landing in order for him to become a citizen. Now many times when they came through the Island in a hurry, the clerk would say, 'What is your name?' The man's name might be Goldenburg or Goldenburger, and the clerk would put down Goldberg. Then I would have a great deal of trouble getting verification of the landing, and the statistical division would have to give me a lot of information—the ship, how many children there were, what the names were of every one of them, and so on. It was very important in order for them to become citizens."

PLENTY TO EAT!

People sharply recall their reactions to the food served at Ellis Island. It is variously described as wonderful and terrible, as interestingly diverse and institutional slop. The dining and food service facilities are called immaculately clean and unutterably filthy.

One thing everyone agreed on was that their first experience in the land of plenty indicated that at least there was plenty of food. Another was that new foods and some new ways of serving familiar foods would take some getting used to.

Their first experience of food at the Island was while waiting in line for the various steps of the inspection process, as Frank Santoni recalls:

"*I remember that as we got off the boat at Ellis Island we were given bread, which I relished very much, Italian bread, about twelve inches long, intermingled, twisted. I enjoyed it. And we were given wine, even at that age, we were given wine to drink.*"

⋦§ "Did you like it?"

"*It was a very heavy wine. It was pretty muddy. I didn't like it. I didn't drink very much. I liked the bread.*"

Frank had probably been given the bread and wine by a social service worker, someone like Helen Barth, but working for an Italian organization, such as the Italian Welfare League. That was in 1901. Later on he wouldn't have had to consider the question of the wine, as alcoholic beverages, other than beer, were prohibited at Ellis Island, to the considerable annoyance of those to whom wine was a major life-supporting substance.

Helen Barth remembers how it was working for the Hebrew Immigrant Aid Society:

"*I was a young girl at the time, and I was dressed in long dresses with a little black apron, white blouse.*"

⋦§ "Why did you wear an apron?"

"*Everybody wore an apron. It was the style in the office. We had white celluloid cuffs to keep our sleeves clean and every afternoon at three o'clock I had to go among the immigrants with a big basket with crackers and milk to feed the children. The food was given to them gratis.*"

⋦§ "Was this just the Jewish immigrants?"

"*Among the Jewish immigrants. The other agencies did other things.*"

"*We had a great deal of sadness. I was always very tearful. They called me 'the angel of mercy' or some name like that, when I came along to give the children their milk and their crackers. We had Uneeda biscuits, and I would take a great big basket like the butchers use, and put it on my arm and go among them. They weren't even used to drinking milk, but I would force it on them, give them a little cup and give them milk.*"

Immigrants detained for any reason, even for a few hours, were usually given a meal. Here they encountered sandwiches and ba-

This is part of a dining hall at Ellis Island, where people held over—those who weren't still sick from the boat trip or too put off by new kinds of foods —found, like Marta Forman, that America did indeed have plenty to eat.

nanas, often for the first time. After passing through the Ellis Island examination process, immigrants traveling beyond New York bought or were given boxes of food for the train journey to their destination.

Steve Pakan was one of those who bought food for the journey, after passing inspection, and found himself defeated by his first banana:

> "I was waiting in this place, and there was a guy with a pushcart, a Jewish man. He had sandwiches in boxes. He was advertising, 'You're going to take a long trip. You better buy a box.'
>
> "I thought to myself, 'You better buy one.' So I bought a box for one dollar. It had one small sandwich in it, and two green bananas, just as green as grass, and I never saw bananas before. So I started eating a banana, biting it, and it was hard. And I thought, 'It can't be they eat it like this.' So I opened it up and started eating the inside and it was worse. There was one piece of bologna in the sandwich and there was three, big, big cookies. Very big. The whole thing wasn't worth 10 cents, maybe 12 cents. He was making big money, though. I had with me in my baggage some nice cheese, hard cheese, and that's what I ate. I didn't buy anything else."

Vera Gauditsa had other problems later at Ellis Island, but first, still sick after her sea voyage, she was introduced to bananas and sandwiches:

> "They gave us lunch—I never had a lunch like that before. It was a sandwich. We never had the style in Europe to eat sandwiches. That was ham between rye, I think. And somehow I did not feel like eating; I was still sick. I never saw a banana in my life, and they served a banana. I was just looking at it.
>
> "And they ate the banana with the skin on! Some of them were Hungarians, some of them were Polish—and I understood what they were saying, because the language is similar. Some of them never had a banana before. So when the Czech lady came a couple of hours later, I asked her what it was—the banana—and she showed me how to peel it and eat it."

Even a little thing like how to handle sugar in coffee stirs a vivid recollection, over fifty years later. Hedvig Nelson was twenty years old when she came through Ellis Island from Norway in 1925. She best remembered meeting a new language and a new way of having coffee.

"It was some experience to come to Ellis Island where everybody was speaking English. We didn't know too much about English, and then we said, 'Oh, my. They are serving coffee here.' That was the first thing they served and we understood about coffee. But then after they gave us the coffee, they put sugar in it and we all hollered, like a choir, 'Oh, we can't have coffee with sugar!'

"So all these other people were thinking, 'What's the matter with them? They don't put sugar in their coffee?' In Norway, they don't have sugar in the coffee. But at the end of the coffee we had like a sugar lump in our mouths, and some of us said, 'What's the difference?' Well, it's just mind over matter, I guess. It's what you're used to . . ."

Food at Ellis Island was supplied by concessionaires, working under government contracts. Two sets of kitchens were maintained; one for all immigrants other than Jews, the other a kosher kitchen. The steamship companies paid for food consumed during the examination period and periods of longer detention. Food for their further journey was bought by the immigrants themselves, or provided by the social service organization.

Helen Barth remembers it this way:

"When it was dinner time, they sat down at these big tables. The Jews went into one section, the others went into another. There was a special cook for the Jewish immigrants; they wouldn't eat otherwise.

"I never could stand the odor when I went near those kitchens. It was awful. A lot of food. The food was all right—we had a nice kosher cook—but the place wasn't clean, and the odors were just awful.

"If the immigrants had places to go, like to the West or Middle West, they waited in the railroad room. We would give them a box of food, quite a nice, tall box, about a foot wide. And in those boxes, if they were Jewish immigrants, they would get cheese sandwiches. If they were Christian immigrants, they would get ham. And they were very happy and thankful for a can of sardines and bread. They were very happy and thankful to get those boxes.

"But I was very sick when I saw those boxes, because we had a dining room where people came from outside to make those sandwiches. The food was spread out on the table with cheese and big mounds of ham and when the four o'clock whistle blew, everybody stopped working. They didn't clear the tables and put the food back in the icebox where it belonged, but left it on the tables . . .

"We had so many rats there, on Ellis Island. If you took a walk on the boardwalk, you could see them playing on the piers. It was really awful. But nobody seemed to mind. In fact, if someone was eating a sandwich, it would be nothing to throw a piece of it down to feed the rats."

✍ "People fed the rats?"

"Yes, they treated them like little animals that came near the pier . . .

"By the way, we had a beautiful dining room on Ellis Island for visitors and people who could afford it. There were tablecloths and napkins, a nice silver service, and they served nice meals there. The employers, or the visitors, or lawyers or doctors that came, that part was very nice . . . But the rest of the Island was very strong with disinfectant . . ."

Theodore Lubik worked at Ellis Island at the same time Helen Barth did, helping to prepare the food she describes. Here is how Theodore remembers distributing food to waiting immigrants and making up box lunches for the further journey.

"I never expected to have a political job. Three of us, Ukrainians, were working on the boat that came to Ellis Island from New York; they called it the Ellis Island ferry. It carried people, carried food, because we used to feed a lot of people over there; 1,000, 3,000 people sometimes in one night, coming in all kinds of ships.

"We came on the same boat as the people who met the immigrants. The wagons were loaded on the New York side, pushed on the boat to Ellis Island, and there we picked them up. Then we sent the empty wagons back, they filled them up again and sent them back. We fed only the immigrants.

"The section where I worked, when the tide was down, was the worst for us, because we—two or three men—had to pull a hand truck from the ferry. When the tide was high, it was easy. And that was our job.

"All the produce came from New York City—flour and everything that came to the table. We took it to the bakery, where they were making those boxes for the immigrants. The people there would take a piece of cardboard, fold it to make a box, and put in two or three sandwiches, an orange, some salami. One would put in something, then the next one would put in something else—everyone made an assembly line."

✍ "Did they make up different boxes for different nationalities?"

"No, everyone the same thing. Except for the Jewish people; they were kosher.

"So I was working there; pulling this little truck behind me, distributing bakery flour and stuff like that—they were making the food boxes for the immigrants.

"The immigrant would pay a dollar and take the box with him. In the box, there was a loaf of bread, one orange, a piece of salami; just about enough for a meal or two, when he went out on the train to Chicago or somewhere.

"They had to take the boxes whether they liked it or not, because they didn't know what was waiting for them. So they came, formed a line with a dollar in their hands, and everybody got a box. Then, maybe two or three hours later, they would take off for the train to their destination.

"Immigrants who were going to local people, to New York to their family, or brother or sister or friends who lived nearby—they stayed in the rooms they had on the Island for a couple of hundred people to sleep overnight. They would notify the families to come and pick them up, and the families would come."

〜§ "What were the sanitary conditions like? Were there a lot of rats? A lot of dirt? How were the kitchens kept?"

"They kept everything in pretty good shape. They threw the garbage in big barrels and took it away. Different boats took it away. Everything was organized, and they didn't throw the garbage away in the water or any place around us, but took it to New York."

〜§ "Oh, so by the time you were there, they were keeping it pretty well?"

"Oh, yes. I believe they kept it well. Government places, they really take good care of. They knew if they're going to keep somebody there, it had to be a nice place. They tried to feed them good food, check the bedding for lice, and so on. The people can't run away . . ."

Theodore had been hired by a man he knew from Europe, who managed a food concession at Ellis Island—and who had come back for a visit "dressed fine, like a governor." As Theodore later found, this man made his money bilking immigrants on change for their lunch boxes. With reform-minded immigration commissioners, inspection limited such practices, but didn't eliminate them completely, as Theodore notes:

"People there had the concessions, selling candy, apples, and so on. They're the ones who made the most money. There was an Italiano sitting there, doing nothing. He had two, three special boys who knew already how to make change from the dollar. But still they watched themselves because they don't know if an inspector approaches them sometimes.

This Slavic family was clearly happy to be in America—although the girl rubbing her eyes might well have had trouble getting past the eye inspection.

"If you knew the language, they couldn't take advantage of you. But if you don't know the language, they can do whatever they want. How do you know the difference?

"That Ukrainian friend of mine, he took a lot of Ukrainian fellows that went over into Ellis Island; that's one good thing he did. There was room for anybody who knew him, because the dining room was such a big place. A couple of hundred people would eat there at once. There my brother and my cousin worked nights. They gave the immigrants supper, cleaned up, then set the tables for breakfast. I was working days outside. When we came in, they went out. ,

"Myself, when I was already here, working at Ellis Island, I met lots and lots of people. In fact, I met girls and boys I knew from where I was living in my country. There I was, working to feed them, and there I saw them coming through. They came in. They didn't expect to find me there. I didn't expect to ever see them again, either.

"And when they saw me in my white coat, nice and stiff, they thought I was an officer! Everybody had a uniform there, you know."

Theodore worked at Ellis Island until America entered World War I. Then he was fired as an enemy alien, a Ukrainian who was a citizen of Austro-Hungary, even though he had left Europe largely to avoid serving in the hated imperial army.

BROUGHT FROM HOME

Many people brought their most prized possessions to America. The harsh necessities of the trip precluded any large or heavy mementos of a life about to become a memory. A few hand-embroidered clothes and a down quilt to bring warmth to recollections, a bottle of rye whiskey and home-cured sausage to preserve the flavor of a former life, a few treasured dolls and books, perhaps a present from a mother to a son or daughter she might never see again. These few things became a large bundle to be dragged and carried to America.

Young Hans Bergner, arriving in 1924 from Germany, remembered some of the extraordinary things people, including himself, brought all the way across Europe and the Atlantic:

"When they arrive as immigrants, people of the poorer classes are very much attached to their feather beds when they come from certain parts of Europe. As they had to open some of these bags in order to show to the customs officials what they were bringing in, I noticed that there were a number of people who had half their steamer trunks filled with feather bedding, which of course made for pretty difficult spacing for the other things that had to go into the trunks.

"In addition to that there were certain people who were fond of certain types of food, especially people from farming stock, who were used to eating smoked things, especially if the smoking of the pork was done in their home farms. So nothing would be a better remembrance of home life than to bring along smoked sausages or smoked ham. The customs officials in those days were not as strict as they are now, so that people were allowed to bring in these things. Since I traveled on a German ship, the interest was largely in sausages and things of that sort, and I'm sure many of them later on, who stayed in New York, discovered that there were places in Yorkville—where the German element has located over many, many years—where you can find half a dozen pork stores with exactly that type of food for sale that people had brought from Europe.

"I remember only one thing that I brought along and that was smoking tobacco. I had a certain kind that I was very, very fond of—I was only nineteen but I was smoking in those days; I have given it up since. This was a Turkish, very mild tobacco. I had it in a large tin can, and when the customs official saw the can he wanted to know what was inside and I said, 'Help yourself.' He opened the can that held this light fluffy Turkish tobacco, and spilled it all over my shirts and everything else. He was a little apologetic, but nevertheless he was convinced."

Steve Pakan was one of those who brought a feather bed—in his instance four feather beds—all the way from Czechoslovakia in 1908, at the age of eighteen. He vividly remembers his encounter with the immigration official:

"I had baggage. I had such baggage of stuff. My two sisters got married, and two brothers, and our mother sent a bottle of rye whiskey to each one of them. And feather beds, and it made me such a big package like, hey, I didn't want to take it!

"They said, 'You have to take it.'

"But I said, 'Good Lord, how am I going to carry it?' Well, finally I got over here with it. The inspector came and he had a long rod with needles in it. And as people lined up with baggage, standing in front of them he shoved the big rod in everybody's luggage."

⋐§ "Right through the feather beds?"

"No matter what you had. If it was a suitcase, you opened it up. But this was like burlap, you know. So then, as he was coming to inspect me, he just made a mark with chalk that he had already inspected me and then was called away to the other end of the line. Then he came back and saw there was a chalk mark on my baggage already and didn't go any further. He went on to the next guy. He missed me. Boy! He was going to surely find those bottles. The baggage came to Little Falls, and they said whiskey was a stupid thing to send, because over here whiskey was selling for a quarter a pint. But the people over there wanted to send something."

Helen Barth saw hundreds of thousands of people bringing those bundles to America, many of them wearing all the clothes they had:

"Many of them came through with all their bedding and belongings and pieces of silver wrapped in a bundle. These were the last possessions they owned. Most of the children I saw were pretty shabby, clothing torn, and the mother would wear four or five petticoats because that was her baggage, you know; they wore everything they owned. They

Carrying all her possessions with her, this Slavic woman prepares to enter America. The bundle on her back may well contain one of the many thousands of feather beds brought over from Europe by immigrants.

didn't accumulate too much. They had a lot of crocheted things, cro-cheted coats for the babies, for the children . . .

"We had the Greek immigrant that came through wearing Greek costumes, with the white fluffy skirt and so on. The Germans came through—all of them with pink cheeks; I remember their pink cheeks for some reason, and their shiny eyes. All their garments were knitted and crocheted. They didn't wear coats in those days. Some of these peo-ple looked very nice. But most of them just wore shawls, the mothers."

Irma Busch didn't have to "meet her dollies in America." She brought them and books with her:

"I remember, I didn't have a suitcase. I had a little basket, like a trunk. And I didn't have too many clothes to pack and I had some dolls with me that I have had forever and ever. I still have books that were given to me as a child, German fairy tales and things like that—Ander-sen. I still have them.

"When we finally arrived and I went through customs, they opened up that little basket, they saw the dolls, they closed it again immedi-ately. Well, I mean, I was just a kid, really, seventeen."

HOW MUCH MONEY YOU GOT?

From the early 1900s on, immigrants all over Europe understood that one of the main hurdles to admission into the United States was the matter of money—$25, to be precise.

The information as to the $25 rule came from agents working the cities and countryside, searching out prospective immigrants; from steamship companies; from returning emigrants; from newspaper and magazine articles; in letters from family and friends in America. The message was unmistakable: America is the land of the free, home for the homeless—but only if you can show $25 a head at Ellis Island.

And their own experience during the journey to America verified that information: the ship's officer filling out the manifest required by American law asked about money. So immigrants reasonably assumed that America required a show of money before opening its doors.

Oddly enough, it was only partially true. What was entirely true was that an administrative regulation was unevenly applied, resulting in intentional gross discrimination against poor immigrants from southern and eastern Europe.

Commissioner of Immigration William Williams, an outspoken and implacable foe of what he called "low grade immigrants" from southern and eastern Europe, required as early as 1904 that all immigrants show $10 and tickets to their destinations, if they were going beyond New York. When he left office in 1905, his successor, Robert Watchorn, formally repealed his $10 regulation. Four years later, Williams returned as Commissoner of Immigration, and immediately instituted a new regulation, in no way supported by the immigration laws, requiring that all immigrants show $25, plus tickets.

The resulting storm of protest from outraged immigrant organizations, coupled with court challenges, forced him to pull down the notices he had posted at Ellis Island, announcing the new regulation, and two years later to eliminate reference in the regulation to the specific $25 amount.

But his retreat was simply sham—the regulation was not re-

Not gold to be picked up from
the streets, perhaps, but this
Italian child has just found
her first penny at Ellis Island.

pealed. In fact, the regulation stayed fully in force until he left
office in 1914. The new commissioner, reformer Frederic C. Howe,
repealed the $25 rule, but many immigration inspectors continued
informally to use $25 and other money amounts as "means tests"
long afterward.

And immigrant fathers, older sisters and brothers continued to
work in New York sweatshops, on railroad gangs and as hod car-
riers to produce that extra $25 a head to bring the rest of their
families to America. Twenty-five dollars may not sound like much
today, but during the immigrant years it was a good deal of money,
often representing months of painful penny-by-penny saving, de-
nial and continued separation from family still in Europe.

For in 1909, when Commissioner Williams imposed the $25
rule, children like Fannie Kligerman were making $2 a week turn-
ing collars, and recent immigrants were earning $3, $4 and perhaps
$5 per week as full-time unskilled sweatshop workers, hod carriers
and domestic workers. Rentals in New York's terrible tenements
were relatively high—$8 to $10 a month for a three-room apartment
or a few dollars a month for a room or just a bed in someone else's
crowded apartment. And although you could buy a herring for two

cents and might walk to work, it was still very hard to save anything at all on seasonal sweatshop wages.

For immigrants with families still in the old country, that $25, for each of perhaps six members of a family, meant a dollar a week saved for 150 weeks—if they were working steadily. Often that $25 was the difference between bringing a family over this year or next; two older children or one; the reuniting of a family in 1914 or of the survivors almost a decade later, after the storms of war and revolution had swept Europe.

And yet, while the whole world knew you had to have $25 to get into the United States, administration of the rule was inconsistent and capricious, sometimes even as to the very southern and eastern Europeans Williams and others were trying to keep out of the United States.

Bessie Spylios was asked to show money, and showed $10 in 1909, even though her father was coming to pick her up.

In 1908, when no regulation was on the books at all, Steve Pakan came to the "Tower of Babel" and remembers one question better than all the rest:

"When you came to Castle Garden,* they put you in some sort of cage and then you wait for an inspector to come and question you.

"It was just like the Tower of Babel, all the different languages. There were Swedes, there were Russians, there were Poles, there were Hungarians, there were what have you, anything. A lot of Jews.

"And I waited two or three hours, and they asked me, 'How much money you got?' I said I had $25."

Stanley Roszak came from Poznan, in German-held Poland, with his whole family in 1914, just two months before the outbreak of World War I. His father had the money—without it, perhaps seventeen-year-old Stanley might have fought in the German army instead of finding safe haven in America. Yet he never got to show his money:

"I thought we were sent to a concentration camp because they didn't land us in New York, but landed us on Ellis Island.

"There you had to sit, and they called you and pushed you. There

* Actually Ellis Island.

This ferry carried cleared immigrants, people who came to meet them, employees and supplies. Immigrants not yet cleared were ferried from the ships to Ellis Island separately. To the left is the earlier immigration station, Castle Garden.

was a barricade so that you could walk in a row. You walked up, they asked you your name and they asked you this and they asked you that, and they asked you if you had any money so that you could take care of yourself. We said 'Yes,' and my father wanted to show it, but they said, 'Oh, no, no, you don't have to show.' They believed him; and they made a white cross on a yellow card and we went on a small boat there and the small boat took us to New York . . ."

Theodore Lubik, arriving in 1913, was very clear on the need for $25—and working at Ellis Island did not change his view:

"You were not allowed to come in without any money. You had to show $25."

Esther Almgren and her husband encountered one set of officials who let them come in with only $1.50 between them. They were lucky—as it turned out, other immigration officials on duty later the same day would have turned them back. She and her husband were young, healthy Swedish citizens, arriving in a boatload of Scandinavian immigrants in 1923. She remembers how frightened they were about the $25 rule when they arrived at Ellis Island.

"They looked at me and at my husband and said, 'Let them go through. They are young, they will make it. Don't worry about them.'"

Sarah Asher and her brother reached America at about the same time, after the long journey that started in Kiev during World War I and the Russian Revolution, and they, too, encountered the $25 rule:

"Well, twenty-four hours before we came to New York, a young man came to us on the boat and asked if we wanted to send a cablegram to Buffalo to our brother. We asked him how much it would cost—$3— and we had $3.20 in our pockets.

"We said, 'No, it's not necessary. Our brother knows.'

"He said, 'Your brother knows that you are coming?' We were on the boat and he didn't really know whether we were alive or not. But we didn't send the cablegram.

"We decided we would tell the truth because we didn't have the money, only $3.20. Maybe we would have to remain in Ellis Island until our brother would send for us.

"At Ellis Island, clerks started to ask our names and put our papers in front of the commissioner.* The commissioner—he was appointed by the government—had a big desk and we were there. He looked at our papers and greeted us very nicely. He said, 'Well, you won't have to stay on Ellis Island. I see you are going to your brother in Buffalo. While your papers are in order and things are right, you know the rules of the United States are that each of you has to have $25. Everybody has to show it.'

"But the commissioner didn't ask us to show it, so we didn't have to answer. He was so delighted with our papers, our diplomas, everything. He said, 'I'm sure that you both will succeed in this country.' He shook our hands and said, 'Such immigrants we greet, and we are happy to admit them into the United States.' He was very nice."

There was no question at all about the $25 rule in Hans Bergner's mind. After all, he'd cashed in his second-class ticket to be sure he would have that $25 to show on reaching America. And just as clearly, there was no such question in the minds of the other people on his boat. Hans describes how they helped some of those who were short of the necessary cash:

"Another little sidelight on how an immigrant got through the lines here. Not all of it was done exactly the way the officials would like it to be, because $25 was not available to everybody as they arrived. I can assure you that certain $25's were passed along from one passenger to another to help out those that didn't have it, and this had to be done

* The immigration inspector.

with a quick motion of the hand so no one would get caught doing this, but I do know that this was part of the whole procedure. Immigrants help each other in these trying moments, as all want to get off Ellis Island and get to the United States, so I recall this well."

REUNION

Some of the tears at Ellis Island were tears of joy, for it was a place of joyful reunion for husbands and wives, parents and children, brothers and sisters, separated often for years. Until the immigrants had completed the inspection process, they were held in the cages Anna Vacek described. Relatives and friends were kept separated from the main inspection area by fencing. As Theodore Lubik put it, "You think you're in a zoo!"

Then immigrant and sponsor had to identify each other, as Bessie Spylios identified her father for the inspectors, before the immigrant would be released. This identification wasn't always so easy, given the changes that years apart can bring. Helen Barth describes some of the problems involved:

"Immigrants came to this country and we would be notified. We would tell their relatives here, 'Your family is coming over today' and they would get a pass to go on the boat to Ellis Island. There they would be—just as the plane companies today have them—by fences looking in, they too would stand there. But they did not always recognize each other, because sometimes the children were changed, too.

"The inspectors would ask the father, 'Who are you waiting for?'

" 'I am waiting for my wife and six children.'

" 'Give me the names of every child.' If he made a mistake with one name, that maybe the mother all of a sudden had changed, they wouldn't allow the family in. A simple thing like that. They went through a great deal of struggle."

It was in just such situations that the social service organizations were so very helpful, in sorting out the multiple confusions caused by time, distance, language difficulties and culture shock.

Identification was even more difficult when the immigrants were young children traveling alone, sometimes to relatives they had never seen or had not seen since infancy. Vera Gauditsa passes on the story her Uncle Milos told her many times, about his arrival in 1902:

"Milos came here, he was nine years old. They sent him here because his uncle was here. And he had no passport, nothing, just a piece of paper from the town where he came from. And when he came to Ellis Island, he said they were behind iron gates like animals, to be kept there all day. He said they had no seats or nothing, they just stood there and were kept there until somebody came to pick them up. When the relatives came, they were just in a line behind the wire, talking through the gates, going from one to another.

"His uncle, Joe, had never seen him so Milos had a picture in his hands. When Joe came to him in the line, Milos said to him, 'Are you Joe?'

"And his uncle said, 'Yes.'

"'Are you my uncle?' 'Yes,' so right away they found each other and he took Milos home. About two weeks later, he started to work in Pennsylvania, making two dollars a month in the pencil factory."

Starting hard work at age nine, Milos grew to be a millionaire by the 1920s, lost everything in the Crash, but rebounded to live a full life until his death in 1970.

Some children, even though separated from their fathers for years, had no problem recognizing them. Seven-year-old Frank Santoni describes his first meeting with his father in 1900, after a separation of over two years:

"There was plenty of bars at Ellis Island to keep the immigrants from the other part, but bars did not keep me from my father. I saw him about fifteen or twenty feet away, standing there waiting for us. I ducked underneath the bars and finally got to his side, and that's how it was."

Sometimes identification was anything but difficult. Childhood sweethearts, who thought they might never see each other again, had no trouble identifying each other—even when they met by surprise. Theodore Lubik had left quickly and quietly one day in 1913 to avoid the Emperor's army. He next saw his childhood sweetheart at Ellis Island, while he was working there:

"I met Nina, my wife, first here. She had to stay there for three days or four."

ᴇ§ "Oh, was that when you first met her?"

"No, not the first time. I met her in Europe. Oh yes, that was a childhood love. After hours at Ellis Island, we would sit in the yard between the buildings where they had the old ambulance truck. We had a good time."

❧ "Did you come in at the same time or was that when you were working there?"

"When I was working there. I was about a year and a half ahead of her. She brought a pillow for herself—as if there would be no pillow in America! Crazy! These pillows, so big and soft and filled with feathers, people carried them all the way from Europe just to do a favor for a mother, sending something for her daughter."

Nina was claimed by friends living in New York, as Theodore explains:

"They wouldn't give a girl to a man or a boy like I was. She must go to somebody who is a woman, married. She had, not exactly family, but friends, neighbors from the other side. They had been here two, three years already—they were not in a hurry to pick her up. But they came for her. I went with them on the elevated to Astoria, Long Island, to see where she would live."

Theodore and Nina married later and started their new life in America together. For them, as for most immigrants, Ellis Island was indeed an island of hope—the end of a long journey and the beginning of a better life in America.

VI

PROBLEMS
AT THE
DOOR

"There was an inscription on the wall.
"It said, 'Why should I fear the fires of Hell? I
have been through Ellis Island.' This inscription was in
English for everyone to see and read."
ᴇ§ "Who put it there?"
"An immigrant."

ᴇ§§ᴇ

IDA MOURADJIAN
Armenian, from Turkey
Arrived 1922

PEOPLE attempting to emigrate to the United States during the Ellis Island years ran the risk of leaving jobs, selling property, using all their meager resources to get to the United States, and then being refused entry and returned for any of a substantial number of reasons, some mandated by law and some at the discretion of the Immigration Service.

Most immigrants' problems centered around these areas:

- Certain specific diseases that we have mentioned, such as trachoma, favus and other scalp diseases, and tuberculosis.
- Mental illness—a matter of widely differing diagnoses at different times by different people with exclusion ultimately a discretionary matter for the Immigration Service.
- The literacy test—inability to read, in English or in one's native language, was, after 1917, also a mandatory cause for exclusion.
- A wide range of other physical deficiencies and weaknesses with exclusion up to the Immigration Service's discretion, in all but those very few cases in which people and organizations in the United States could intervene on the part of arriving immigrants.
- Criminal records of any kind.

This Russian Jew, arriving in 1905, has been marked for special examination, the "K" chalked on his coat indicating a suspected hernia condition. Like many immigrants, he wears several coats—wearing being easier than carrying them—and has the identification label pinned on the outer one.

- Likelihood of becoming a public charge. This was the genesis of Commissioner Williams' $25 regulation, and the reason that so many of those arriving had to have some kind of sponsorship.
- The possibility of being imported for or subsequently impressed into "white slavery." Poor and unaccompanied women had extraordinary difficulty securing admittance into the United States without sponsorship, no matter how well-educated, healthy and clearly capable of self-support.
- Being a "contract laborer," someone imported to work, with a job promised on arrival.

Immigrants had their first indication of trouble right on the medical inspection line, when doctors put strange marks on people's jackets. Rachel Goldman, who arrived during the war, when European immigration had slowed to just a trickle, describes what it looked like:

"When we arrived at Ellis Island everyone was very nervous and we passed through the lines and there were men on either side, and on some of the people those men put chalk marks on their backs. The peo-

*ple themselves did not know it. People in back of them could see it
and were worried and wondering what it was all about. Only later we
learned that those men noticed something unusual, either physical or
something else, and wanted to examine those people more thoroughly."*

These marks, sometimes on the back and sometimes on the
front where the immigrant could see them, were a crude code: E
for indications of eye trouble, H for suspected heart trouble, X
for possible mental defects and so on. Immigrants so marked were
detained in a large caged area and experienced a kind of processing
and checking unknown to those who breezed through with no difficulty.

A DIABOLICAL ARRANGEMENT

Statistics on the detention and exclusion of immigrants, like
most statistics, are subject to a wide range of interpretation. One
way of putting these statistics is to point out that 80 out of 100
immigrants passing through Ellis Island went through quickly and
easily; that 20 of each 100 were held, usually for a short while,
under clean, sanitary conditions, and were humanely treated; and
that only about 2 were eventually refused admission and sent back
to Europe.

Another way of putting the same statistics is that 20 of each
100 were detained, often in wire cages clearly visible to all other
immigrants; that they were held in detention quarters that were
cramped, often unsanitary and poorly ventilated, with heat often
over 100 degrees during the summer period of maximum immigration and therefore maximum overcrowding; that ultimately 2 in
100 were deported, far poorer than when they came and often
homeless; and that 2 in 100 means that close to 250,000 people
were turned back during the Ellis Island years, with deportations
in the peak years averaging over 1,000 per month.

However you choose to put it, there isn't the slightest doubt
that Anna Vacek's perception of "Ellis Island, which was a cage,
like, for the immigrants in those days," was entirely justified by the
Ellis Island she saw in 1901, and that the physical facts she saw

were essentially the same all during the first quarter of the twentieth century.

As late as 1922, Sir Auckland Geddes, British Ambassador to the United States, who visited the Island after vigorous complaints from British immigrants and the British press, spoke of it as a "diabolical arrangement," a place of locked doors, wire cages and conditions that seemed to him worse than those at Sing Sing.

And in truth, in some physical respects it was worse than Sing Sing. The four main dormitories held about four hundred wire cages each, in three-tiered steel bunks, set in long rows with narrow aisles between them. Each steel bunk had a blanket, but when he visited Ellis Island and for most of the previous two decades there were no mattresses, pillows or sheets. The space between the tiers was about two feet high, ventilation was minimal, and New York summer nights can be very hot indeed. In some physical respects, then, it must certainly have been worse than Sing Sing.

Not only that, but despite Ellis Island's rough-and-ready delousing procedures, such as Fannie Kligerman described, the main building and the dormitories were, for much of the main period of immigration, lice-infested. Mary Zuk, who spent the night and then passed through quickly in 1912, had just one recollection of Ellis Island: "It was lousy." When she realized her interviewer didn't understand her, she laughed and explained: "Lousy. Bugs all over!"

Celia Rypinski, having spent weeks in transit from Poland to Rotterdam to America without encountering bugs, remembers the same thing at Ellis Island:

"And I'll never forget. People went early to lay down and they ran away. There were louses all over. I sat on my grip and yet I got a few of 'em!"

In August 1923, Baroness Mara de Lilier-Steinheil, a Russian woman who had spent some time in Soviet jails and three midsummer days in detention at Ellis Island, expressed her view of the Island:

"The prisons conducted by the Soviet government are not more dirty or more favorable for disease than the hall on Ellis Island where I *was confined with a thousand men and women. I have been through worse things than Ellis Island's Tower of Babel, but I have never been forced to live in such filth and under such unhygienic conditions."*

Her outrage was widely viewed as "overstatement" by an immediately defensive American press and government, just as similar criticisms had been treated for the previous quarter century. But the many such comments during the peak immigration years, and the experiences of the people in this book, essentially bear out Ambassador Geddes' observations and Baroness Lilier-Steinheil's outraged cry.

Ida Mouradjian gives a strong, articulate view of Ellis Island as she experienced it in 1922 after the multiple impacts of the Armenian holocaust and World War I. Held for weeks, she focuses on the thousand daily encounters with an entrenched bureaucracy; she bitterly remembers being herded, handled, pushed—and most of all the constant fear of being sent back:

"We were pushed around. Now with my knowledge of what a patronage job means, I can explain it. They were a bunch of patronage job holders, who were ignorant. What's more, they didn't have hearts, they didn't have minds, they had no education. They were very crude. Many were foreigners, who delighted in the fact that they could lord over the new entries, the new immigrants. They had accents as thick as molasses, every kind of accent, but they acted the way small people become because they had a little power. They pushed everybody around, actually, literally pushed.

"You are afraid that maybe they can do you harm; therefore you close your month, until you can't close it any more. So one day I said, 'Look, if you can't read English, I can.' The sign said, 'Employees are required to be civil to immigrants. Employees are required to be helpful to immigrants.' Yes! Don't you see those signs? Didn't anybody ever photograph those signs?

"I'm not saying that Ellis Island or the organization was responsible. It was the petty employees. Employees who sat behind desks and felt like Mr. Wilson, sitting behind the White House desk.

"When I was in Ellis Island, my English teacher was working for her Ph.D. at Columbia. She came to visit me and very defiantly I said to her, 'Miss Arkanian, is the language you taught us English—or is English the language spoken in this hell-hole?' Can I swear on tape? I did. Wipe it off if you don't want it.

"She said, very sadly, 'Ida, what I taught you is Shakespeare's Eng-

lish, the king's language, not this brogue.'

"And they pushed you around. They pushed you into showers—burning hot water, the cold water control was outside. They had to control the mixture. It was either too hot or too cold, they didn't care. So you got out and they pushed two blankets into your arms and they pushed you into a room, bare cots, one blanket under you, one blanket on top of you, and that was your bed. And maybe 150 in one dormitory.

"I can't describe the food. It must have been inedible. I can't describe it because I don't think I ever ate it. Maybe a piece of bread. And I thought to myself, 'You know, cruelty is not the privilege of one nation or one group of people or another. God Almighty, it can happen here.' It happened there* and I thought it was unique but it can happen here, given the same set of circumstances. It can happen here, too.

"One of my students was a sixteen-year-old boy, who had relatives in America. In the meantime he was traveling with me, on the same boat. And the poor boy was 'God damned' a hundred times a day. He came one day to me and said, 'What does "God damn" mean? It must be a good word because God is included in the sentence, and I thought this was a Christian world and the name of God is not supposed to be used in vain. What's going on here? "God damn, God damn"—all day long.' And I had the sad duty to tell my student, who was coming to America with big dreams, too, that that was the worst kind of swearing that one can wish upon somebody else.

"I stayed at Ellis Island three and a half weeks. I was frightened to be sent back where I came from, where I did not have a job, I did not have a family. I did not have a home, I had spent every last cent of my money. Before I left my job even, I was replaced, and where would I go?"

Ida did finally pass through to America with the help of some friends, but not before the Ellis Island experience had been seared into her memory.

EYES RED FROM CRYING

During the peak years, between 150,000 and 200,000 people were detained each year at Ellis Island. Most were detained for a short time; a few hours until family or husband-to-be arrived; overnight until train tickets or money arrived; for a few hours to a few days while suspected medical problems were observed and treated. Most

* In Turkey.

of those detained were ultimately admitted. Family arrived; so did money; medical problems turned out to be minor.

Judith Cohen Weiss's experience is typical. After terrible starvation during the war, she and her family were finally coming to join her father in America, but the doctors thought her mother might have trachoma:

"We went straight to Ellis Island. I remember we got in during the night and we had to walk through a breezeway into the Island when the boat landed. It is like when you go into a plane. You go through a certain spot where your plane is and you get on there. That was the same with us, like we had a breezeway where everybody walked off. I remember they had lights on. And of course they right away got you into a room—nobody was put separate. It was more or less that every boatload had a room. I think that they didn't want to separate the people for the simple reason that they felt all the people that were on one boat—if they had any germs or disease, they had passed it already among themselves. I think they did not want to put all the people together to give others the same thing, if they had anything wrong with them, so they kept the boatloads together.

"The next day I remember that they put all the women in a room. My sister and I were with my mother; the boys were in a separate room. They took off all our clothes and deloused them, and they gave us showers to take with certain medication, I guess a disinfectant or something.

"Then we went before the inspectors—you could not get off without the doctor's examination. The only thing is that my mother had trouble with her eyes. You see, my sister took sick on the way—she had some kind of childhood sickness, measles or something. My mother was very concerned and here we were on the boat. She said, 'I left Europe with five children, I promised your father five children, and I am going to bring him five children!' She was only worried that my sister would die. You know, you get into such a depressive mood. She was very worried, so every night she would sit and cry. My sister got better on the boat, but when we got off, my mother's eyes were very red from crying. So when she got to the doctor at Ellis Island, he wouldn't pass her. They thought she had some trouble with the eyes.

"So when my father came, they told him he would have to wait. I did not even know him. When he embraced me, I got very frightened because he had a little beard and a mustache—I had never seen this. So I was frightened and started to cry. My sister came over to me and said, 'What are you crying about? It's Papa.' We were all fine except my mother with the red eyes and that is what kept us three more days . . ."

For some immigrants, there was legitimate cause for concern. Adele Sinko came through World War I, but not without damage. She was ten years old when the war started, went through the terrible starvation of those years living just outside Vienna, and along the way wound up with a lung scarred by tuberculosis and somewhat impaired vision.

Arriving at age seventeen, she was sponsored by her brother, who as an Austrian soldier had been shell-shocked and gassed in Italy during the war. She still feels the impact of being held aside at Ellis Island, having to strip during the special medical examinations, and fearing she would be turned back:

"Then my brother came over here. He met a girl who had an aunt over here, and he wanted to get away from Austria. So they got married and they came here. And he is the one who took me over.

"He came in 1921. He was just twenty-one years old. Now look, my brother was shell-shocked and gas-poisoned and he went through customs here easily. No trouble. The only thing is, they cut off all his hair. He had beautiful hair. They just shaved everybody's hair."

� "When he came through?"

"Before he could land. Everybody."*

⋧ "Women, too?"

"No, no. Some of those Polish Jews—not that I have anything against them—but they had these long beards and they shaved them off. They were crying, some of them. You know, they were so disfigured, all their lives they'd had them. Yes, they did that to them. The women, no.

"Well, when I arrived, they wouldn't let us get off the boat. My brother was there, I could see him down there, but they wouldn't let us off, because we had to go to Ellis Island in the morning.

"Then I went through all those examinations. I don't know how many times we had to go through inspections. At Ellis Island you had to stand in line, you know. And while standing in line I had to strip. This was so embarrassing for me. I wasn't even twenty-one, very bashful, and there was these big kids running around, but you had to do it.* The examination was done by women, but the kids were there. That I resented, when you had to strip to the waistline. Nowadays it is nothing, but in those days—and I never forgot that.

---

* Probably part of a delousing and disinfecting procedure.
** Adolescents were allowed to stay with the mother when the sexes were separated for special examinations.

Like Adele Sinko and Catherine Bolinski, these women had to strip to
the waist as part of the more extensive medical examination conducted on
people detained, and on most people in the postwar years, before clearance
inspection was shifted abroad.

"*There was a young girl there, too. And she wore glasses. She didn't pass. She had to go back. Why did they pass her over there before she got on the boat? She had to make that whole trip back. Oh, she was crying. And then there were some people who were held back. I don't know if they just kept them for a few days and let them go.*

Women like Adele were not the only ones embarrassed by the public stripping, often in front of adolescent children who had stayed with their parents. Arnold Weiss, too, was embarrassed. He had talked his reluctant widowed mother into coming to America and she had been violently ill during the whole sea voyage. She wasn't about to let her son out of her sight after all that, so thirteen-year-old Arnold stayed with her during the whole disinfecting process:

"*When we got to that island, I remember that they took all of the women in one place.*"

&ऽ "Were the men separated from the women?"

"*Yes. My mother did not let me go. She wanted me to stay with her all of the time. So I was more or less with her. I was a kid, and they left me. It was open. I could see my mother—the women were getting washed and bathed, taking showers. They took off all their clothing. The clothes were being put through machines and what not— they were sterilized. They did not bother with me much because I was a kid.*"

Fifty-seven years later Arnold is still uneasy at the memory, feeling that he should not have been left there.

Most immigrants, like Adele Sinko and Martha Konwicki, had medical problems that turned out to be minor. Others, like the girl Adele describes, were not so lucky. Sometimes the seeming trachoma, favus or tuberculosis was real—and exclusion was mandatory, with no possible appeal. Many observers questioned, as Adele did, why they couldn't spot such diseases at inspections on the other side. The questioning grew so strong that eventually medical examinations were carried out entirely abroad, except for those who showed signs of illness on arrival in America.

After working as American consul in Italy, Fiorello La Guardia worked as an interpreter for the Immigration Service at Ellis Island, between 1910 and 1912. Always a man of extraordinary depth and compassion, he describes some of the terrible scenes that resulted in the long years before his advice was adopted. Among the special problems was that an adult had to accompany any child returned, creating terrible decisions for the family:

"The immigration laws were rigidly enforced, and there were many heartbreaking scenes on Ellis Island. I never managed during the three years I worked there to become callous to the mental anguish, the disappointment and the despair I witnessed almost daily. Some of the employees did become callous to the suffering after a while, but on the whole they were a hardworking lot, conscientious and loyal . . .

"Several hundred immigrants daily were found to be suffering from trachoma, and their exclusion was mandatory. It was harrowing to see families separated because the precaution had not been taken of giving them prior examinations on the other side. Sometimes, if it was a young child who suffered from trachoma, one of the parents had to return to the native country with the rejected member of the family. When they learned their fate, they were stunned. They had never felt ill. They had never heard the word trachoma. They could see all right, and they had no homes to return to. I suffered because I felt so powerless to help these poor people, and I did what I could by writing letters to Senators and Representatives telling them of my experiences at Fiume, and urging legislation to remedy the situation. Everyone seemed to agree that the law should require a physical examination at the port of embarkation. But nothing was done about it officially until 1919, when such a law was passed.

"The physical requirements for immigrants were very high, and a large percentage were excluded for medical reasons. In addition to trachoma, cases of favus and other scalp diseases were common. I always suffered greatly when I was assigned to interpret for mental cases in the Ellis Island hospital. I felt then, and I feel the same today, that over fifty per cent of the deportations for alleged mental disease were unjustified. Many of those classified as mental cases were so classified because of ignorance on the part of the immigrants or the doctors and the inability of the doctors to understand the particular immigrant's norm, or standard.

"One case haunted me for years. A young girl in her teens from the mountains of northern Italy turned up at Ellis Island. No one understood her particular dialect very well, and because of her hesitancy in replying to questions she did not understand, she was sent to the hospital for observation. I could imagine the effect on this girl, who had always been carefully sheltered and had never been permitted to be in the company of a man alone, when a doctor suddenly rapped her on the knees, looked into her eyes, turned her on her back and tickled her

This family of Serbian gypsies is thought to be part of a whole boatload of gypsies sent back to Europe. For them—with New York so near, yet so far in the background—Ellis Island was surely an Island of Tears.

spine to ascertain her reflexes. *The child rebelled—and how! It was the cruelest case I ever witnessed on the Island. In two weeks' time that child was a raving maniac, although she had been sound and normal when she arrived at Ellis Island."*

GOING BEFORE THE BOARD

Immigrants held aside at the discretion of the Immigration Service inspectors were almost immediately brought before one of the several Boards of Special Inquiry usually functioning at Ellis Island. There were, for example, immigrants detained and placed in jeopardy of deportation because their sponsors and money hadn't arrived, or they had no sponsor and seemed likely to become a public charge. Or they might have been held aside because they were suspected contract laborers, brought to America with the promise of a job; because they had a criminal record; or because they were thought to be prostitutes or "anarchists" entering the United States for criminal purposes.

A Board of Special Inquiry consisted of three Immigration Service officers, who heard each such case privately. The immigrant had no right to counsel, usually had no time to prepare a defense, and seldom could speak English. An Immigration Service interpreter was usually present, however, and sometimes immigrants were able to call witnesses on their behalf.

Adverse rulings could be appealed to the Commissioner of Immigration and to the Commissioner-General of Immigration in Washington. However, since most immigrants appearing before the Boards of Special Inquiry were penniless, friendless or both, in practice the Boards often served as classic "star chambers." There were no right to counsel, no court-appointed counsel, no jury trial, no procedural guarantees. Only the immigrant—and three government officials acting as judge and jury.

Small wonder that Theodore Lubik said that "For one who was detained, that was awful."

Ida Mouradjian was detained at Ellis Island for weeks while her case was sorted out. Even so, she was lucky she had someone influential to support her appeal to be entered as a professional person, and thus not be counted in the normal quota for the month:

"Third-class passengers had to go to Ellis Island. Well, I thought, what's the difference? I am traveling by the express consent of the ambassador of America. I am a school teacher, therefore a professional person, which is not subject to the common rules and regulations of immigration laws. What a disillusionment! If you travel third class, nothing helps.

"First of all the quota for the month was filled. I said, 'I'm not coming by quota. I am traveling as a professional.'

"They said, 'No, no, school teachers aren't professionals.' First they had to find out whether school teachers were considered professionals or not. And they had to find out whether my diploma, the school I graduated from, was the equivalent of American schools. How could it be equivalent to American schools? They had killed every professor, every man of letters, and when I returned to school, it had been reduced to a common ordinary high school. I wasn't bragging that I was the equivalent of an American college graduate. Of course not. But still, in my own country, I was a school teacher."

❧ "They actually threatened to send you back?"

"Yes. Because the quota was full and you were not acceptable if you had not come through the regular channels. And if you did not have somebody here to back you financially, you could be a public charge. A healthy, educated twenty-two-year old, who spoke four languages, could be a public charge here in America. Well, tell me, is that possible? But they thought I could be a public charge and I was threatened to be sent back.

"So finally I had to swallow my pride and send word to the family that ran the school where I had taught. I sent word that I was one of their school teachers and I regretted very much that I had to leave my job and that I was suffering difficulties here and would they help me out, and they did.

"If that family had not sent their lawyer to Washington to intercede for me, I would have been sent back. My oldest friend's parents were sent back, all the way to Greece where they had to again apply for re-entry and spend all that money, and the anxiety and the time to come back. They didn't hesitate to put you on a cattle boat and send you back. That was not becoming to a country like America.

"When I left Ellis Island, it was one happy day."

Other immigrants had to rely on relatives—and on their own ingenuity—to pass by the Board. Thirteen-year-old Arnold Weiss had persuaded his mother to come to America in 1921. The problem was that his father had died in the great flu pandemic of 1919, and his mother had no skills, nor could she read. Arnold describes how they surmounted these obstacles in that place of turmoil he calls "Kesselgarden":

"So then they took us to Ellis Island. Now on Ellis Island they scrutinized you. They wanted to know everything about you, as to where, what and when. Who was going to support you?

"Their main questions were in reference to health. What you had contracted in Europe, what sicknesses you had, if you had any of this and that. They were questions of interest because, come to think of it, it was logical. They did not let people in just like that, you know. But in spite of it, people used to come in bringing some sorts of diseases that they brought from the other side—as careful as they were. But they were careful, I tell you that. They were careful in my time, when I was there.

"Ellis Island was like what they call a Kesselgarden—an influx of a lot of people, one was running this way and one was running the other way. It was turmoil. Everybody and anybody, they were all waiting for their relatives to come and get them. All the people were there behind gates.

"We encountered trouble for the reason that we did not come here to anybody who could guarantee our support. They asked if we were bringing money with us. We didn't have any money. In order that we shouldn't have to go on charity, who is responsible? So we had a relative who was a pharmacist. They asked him to come down. He was an uncle—I don't know—a fifth wheel to the wagon—but he came down to guarantee us. He had to sign for us—a pharmacist had status. Well, anyway, we never gave him any trouble.

"Then again, they also questioned people on literacy. It did not make any difference whether they were Jewish, Hebrew, whatever. You had to know how to read and write. My mother was a complete illiterate. My uncle called me aside, when he came to take us off. He said, 'She doesn't know how to read.'

"I said, 'That's all right.'

"For the reading you faced what they called the commissioners—like judges on a bench, they sit there, you know. I was surrounded by my aunt and uncle and this other uncle who's a pharmacist—my mother was in the center. They said she would have to take a test of reading. So one man said, 'She can't speak English.'

"Another man said, 'We know that. We will give her a seder.' You know what a seder is? It's a Jewish book. The night they said this, I knew she couldn't do that and we would be in trouble. And I wanted to be here in the worst way.

"Well, they opened up a seder. There was a certain passage there they had you read. I looked at it and I seen right away what it was. I quickly studied it—I knew the whole paragraph. Then I got underneath the two of them there—I was very small—and I told her the words in Yiddish very softly. I had memorized the lines and I said them quietly and she said them louder so the commissioner could hear it. And that served the purpose. She looked at it and it sounded as if she was reading it, but I was doing the talking underneath. I was Charlie McCarthy!"

Others were lucky enough to encounter a little benevolent blindness from the officials. One Armenian family tells how their mother, who could not read, passed the literacy test. When the inspector asked her to read from an Armenian book, she put her finger on the page and recited the Lord's Prayer. He asked her to read again, and again she recited, "Our Father, who art in heaven . . ." in Armenian. Finally he looked at the family and said, "Bono," and let them pass.

After her long trip away from that wicked sister-in-law, Celia Rypinski was held at Ellis Island for two weeks in 1909. Like so many other poor immigrants, she was thought likely to become a public charge, even though she had four brothers in America, one of whom had paid her way. The problem was that they were all poor, she was only thirteen, and the immigration officials required a substantial bond before they would admit her. A promised bond arranged through a priest had not come through, and Celia's brothers had a hard time finding someone else to guarantee her:

᷎§ "Why did you have to stay in Ellis Island for two weeks?"

"I was waiting to be called. Until that man put a bond on me, because I was a minor, they were going to ship me back."

᷎§ "How did you finally get out of the building?"

"I got out of the building because one man—God bless that man—put up the bond. He had a saloon and hall, and my brother Stanley was married in that hall. And Stanley went and told him the story about me sitting in New York, and the priest refusing to sign the paper. I was a minor. Three of my brothers had all little children; one was single. But they were all poor.

"So Stanley told the story to the man; he had to go to the saloon. That man had nineteen children. And he put up the bond on me."

᷎§ "How much was the bond? Do you know?"

"Eighteen hundred dollars. And until I was eighteen years old, they would watch me. If I didn't behave myself, if I was a bad girl, they would ship me back because I was a minor."

This young Slavic woman is—surely not for the first time—sleeping on the bundle she has carried all the way from Europe. Her dress, of a heavy brocade fabric, is probably her very best, put on for arrival in America.

BELOW

Some people detained at Ellis Island provided their own entertainment, while others watched. The sign in the background says, "No charge for food here" in several languages, as does the sign in the dining room shown on page 181.

ಈ "In other words, he had to put up $1,800 for five years because you were thirteen years old at the time."

"Yes."

ಈ "Did he get any interest on the money?"

"*I think he did.*

"*My first job was right across the street from him. The people I worked for had a feed store. I was supposed to take care of the children, help her out. My sister-in-law got me the job because she knew the people.*

"*And he used to call me and give me a dime or a quarter, and say in Polish, 'My little girl. My little girl. I was her sponsor.' Of course, in Polish it sounds different. And I did not know at that age now to appreciate what he had done for me or anything. But God give him heaven! And his family, too. Otherwise I would have been sent back to Poland to that cruel sister-in-law . . .*"

Three years later, in 1912, Sophia Belkowski ran into precisely the same kind of problem. She was held for a week, even though she had three brothers and two sisters in the United States, but was eventually released to join her relatives in Chicago.

Paula Katz, sent by her grandfather to join her widowed mother, ran into what could have been a very large problem at Ellis Island. Some fairly complicated family receiving arrangements broke down, and for a while it looked as if she would be shipped back, after her first appearance before a Board of Special Inquiry. And a young woman who had been asked by the shipping company to travel with Paula (because she was only ten years old) was in jeopardy of being returned, too:

"*When we eventually got to Ellis Island, I was supposedly coming to see an uncle. But after the hearing at Ellis Island, when no one came to pick me up, it proved that this man was not my uncle, because both my father and his sister were dead. This uncle was married to my aunt, so the court felt I was no relation.*"

ಈ "Where was your mother? Was she in New York at that time?"

"*According to my grandfather's instructions, I was not to say I was coming to my mother, but just to this uncle. It seems that my mother did not expect to be in town. She was trying to earn enough money to return to Poland, so she went as a housekeeper-cook into the summer area, the Catskills. She did not know if she would be back in time. At all events, I didn't know anything about that. I followed instructions.*

I was told that I was coming to see my uncle, and he did not pick me up. Therefore, this girl, who was looking after me, was also stuck to have to go back to Hamburg with me. I was on Ellis Island for five days ready to go back!"

◄§ "What were your impressions of Ellis Island?"

"Kind people, meant well. They were very conscientious about not allowing an unattached child, not related to anyone, to land. They didn't want any part of that, and they were going to send me back after the hearing.

"The translator asked me who I was going to see and I said, 'My uncle.'

"And he said, 'How is he your uncle?'

"I said, 'He was married to my aunt.'

" 'Is your aunt living?'

" 'No.'

" 'How is she your aunt?'

" 'She was my father's sister.'

" 'Well, he has remarried. He is no blood relation. He is no uncle of yours.'

"And when they found out my father was dead, they asked me me about my mother. But my instructions were to say nothing about my mother, so I kept quiet. They assumed that my mother was also dead."

◄§ "Why weren't you permitted to talk about your mother?"

"Because my grandfather didn't know whether my mother would be in the city to receive me when I arrived here. So the arrangement was that my uncle would pick me up—but he never showed up! So for five days I was ready to go back . . .

"As to my first impression—that first day when we got off the boat and we were traveling across the river to Ellis Island—the bridges, they looked like pearls. With the lights on them, they were like a string of pearls going around your neck, a beautiful sight."

◄§ "Where did you sleep on Ellis Island?"

"I don't remember, probably on one of the cots, you know, one of the public places.

"I don't know whether the girl that I was with, the people who were expecting her, got in touch with somebody, because she would have had to go back with me, but then they found my mother.

"Then we had another hearing in this little court. My mother spoke first. Then they asked me why did I say my mother was dead, and I didn't say anything. It was funny, I just didn't say anything. That was my experience on Ellis Island.

One classic "Catch-22" each immigrant had to face was the question about contract labor. Earlier in the nineteenth century, American business had actively advertised for labor from Europe, but by 1885 workers protecting their own jobs and higher rates of pay pushed through passage of a bill outlawing the importation of "contract labor"—immigrants who had been promised jobs by American companies.

The problem faced by immigrants was this: if they said they *had* a job, they might be sent back home as "contract laborers"; if they said they had no prospects for a job, they might be sent back as likely to become public charges. Wary and forewarned immigrants had to thread the needle—as well as they could through interpreters, since most knew no English—by conveying that they had "good prospects of a job." In fact, that was usually the truth, but that didn't make it any easier for the immigrant. Fiorello La Guardia describes that and some of the other problems that came before the Boards of Special Inquiry:

"It is a puzzling fact that one provision of the Immigration Law excludes any immigrant who has no job and classifies him as likely to become a public charge, while another provision excludes an immigrant if he has a job! Common sense suggested that any immigrant who came into the United States in those days to settle here permanently surely came here to work. However, under the law, he could not have any more than a vague hope of a job. In answering the inspectors' questions, immigrants had to be very careful, because if their expectations were too enthusiastic, they might be held as coming in violation of the contract labor provision. Yet, if they were too indefinite, if they knew nobody, had no idea where they were going to get jobs, they might be excluded as likely to become public charges. Most of the inspectors were conscientious and fair. Sometimes, I felt, large batches of those held and deported as violating the contract labor provision were, perhaps, only borderline cases and had no more than the assurance from relatives or former townsmen of jobs on their arrival . . .

"Persons convicted of offenses involving moral turpitude were excluded from the country. Immigrants were required to present certificates showing them free from penal offenses. Some did not have them, and others would not present them. That created a presumption of guilt, and then the immigrants were questioned very closely. I discovered that many were being deported for minor offenses or because of incorrect interpretation of their answers or inaccurate translations of their penal certificates. I got the translators together, and we brought about some uniformity in the translation of these crimes, and that prevented a lot of injustice.

"There were rare cases of husbands who had sent for their wives after two or three years of hard working and saving from their small wages, only to learn for the first time that a child had been born in the meantime. We also witnessed scenes of great generosity, understanding and forgiveness . . .

"On the whole, the personnel of the Immigration Service was kindly and considerate. At best, the work was an ordeal. Our compensation, besides our salaries, for the heartbreaking scenes we witnessed, was the realization that a large percentage of these people pouring into Ellis Island would probably make good and enjoy a better life than they had been accustomed to where they came from. . ."

WOMEN ALONE

Women traveling alone had a particularly difficult time getting through Ellis Island. Partly, there was legitimate concern over possible harm to unprotected, often young, naïve and resourceless women from the farms and small towns of Europe, most of whom could not even speak English. But there was also sharp discrimination against women in every aspect of United States life during the first quarter of the twentieth century, and Ellis Island was no exception to the general rule.

A strong national women's rights movement existed before World War I, and many of its finest leaders were working women, some of whom had come through Castle Garden and Ellis Island. Some women's rights advocates and leading reformers were active in immigration work, and their influence was felt on the Island especially through the social welfare organizations.

For most of the period of peak immigration, however, the Immigration Service itself and the main portion of the Island's staff were little touched by the women's rights movement. Helen Barth speaks of being one of very few women among hundreds of men working on the Island. The attempt to add women inspectors, the "Bloomer Girls," to the boarding staff in 1903 was very quickly killed by Commissioner Williams. And Commissioner Howe, a reformer, speaks bitterly of his experience in securing a woman commissioner to handle the cases of women and children, late in the period of peak immigration. When he finally did convince Grace Abbott, an outstanding social activist from Chicago's Hull House, to take the job, he found himself unable to hire her, having to take instead a political appointee.

Beyond all that was the "white slavery" hysteria. From the late nineteenth century right through the 1920s, the United States—provincial and puritanical—experienced a long, lurid, media-fanned "white slavery" scare. The Mann Act of 1910, which prohibited the transportation of women across state lines for immoral purposes, was the result of a nationwide campaign, and its passage served only to fuel the hysteria.

Many of the young women who came to America to be married were thought to be imported for prostitution. So Immigration Service regulations were very strict on the handling of young women, especially brides-to-be. Fiancées arriving at Ellis Island almost always had to be met by the husbands-to-be personally and married, before the Immigration Service relinquished control of them. Otherwise, young women alone had to be met by family or vouched for by recognized social service organizations after inquiry at their intended destinations. If neither married, met, nor sponsored, these young women were sent back to Europe.

There were some reasons for the care taken. In those years, women alone and unable to speak English were in some danger from those who preyed on immigrants. And surely some women were imported for purposes of prostitution, but most women so imported were actually transported in second-class cabins and usually avoided the Ellis Island experience. Sometimes they were picked up and questioned during the inspections conducted during the period of quarantine in the harbor; more often they were not—so the legal net cast to pick up the big fish usually caught only minnows.

Fiorello La Guardia remembers accompanying couples from Ellis Island to New York City to be married—and being appalled at what he saw:

"Often we interpreters at Ellis Island had to accompany couples to the city to be married. These were cases of young men who had sent for their fiancées. The men would arrive at Ellis Island all prepared to marry before admission had been granted to the young ladies. We would take them to the City Hall in New York, where marriages were performed in those days by aldermen. The aldermen took turns performing the ceremonies and getting the fees. Some of the aldermen were not averse to getting a little extra, above the two dollars prescribed by the law. I know that most of the Immigration Service personnel protected the immigrants and were not parties to these overcharges.

"I was assigned to only a few of these cases, but a few were plenty. I would escort the bridegroom and his bride and their witness to the City Hall to see that they were properly married and then give the bride clearance for admission to the country. In the few instances I attended the aldermen were drunk. Some of the aldermen would insert into their reading of the marriage ceremony remarks they considered funny and sometimes lewd language, much to the amusement of the red-faced, cheap "tinhorn" politicians who hung around them to watch the so-called fun. I was happy when years later the law granting aldermen authority to perform marriages was repealed. Later, as Mayor, I had occasion to improve conditions in the City Clerk's office, where systematized graft in marriage fees and licenses had been going on, and my early experience with this contemptible petty thievery made me all the more eager to improve those conditions."

Not all the couples he and others brought to be married were childhood sweethearts. In the long-established tradition of frontier communities everywhere, many were "mail order" brides. In those years, southern and eastern Europe housed a group of very active, profitable immigration-related industries, including immigration agencies, labor contractors, false document providers—and marriage brokers. These marriage brokers conducted a high-volume business, finding marriageable young women who wanted to go to America for young European men who had settled in America, made some money, and wanted to "marry a girl from the old country."

Because the women supplied pictures of themselves to their prospective husbands (the men usually did not reciprocate), the media called them "picture brides." A New York Times headline for August 3, 1922, for example, said: "200 Picture Brides Come Here to Wed, Greek and Armenian Girls Met at Pier by Their Prospective Husbands." Two days later the follow-up headline read: "16 Picture Brides Married, 195 Left, 45 More Arrive and

Join Those Now in Care of Travelers' Aid Society, Soon All Will Be Wed." Of course, it didn't always turn out that way—sometimes the husbands failed to claim their brides-to-be and sometimes the young women didn't like the looks of the men, regarding the marriage as too high a price to pay, even for entry to America. In those cases, the young women would be returned, unless some other acceptable person or agency took responsibility for them.

Married women, too, faced stringent requirements, and pregnant women, even more so, because with a confinement coming and then a young child to care for, officials feared that both mother and child would become public charges. So the Immigration Service checked very carefully to see that someone was in fact ready to receive and support the pregnant woman.

One person who went through very rigorous checks as a pregnant woman coming to her husband was Vera Gauditsa. Her husband had been born in America of immigrant parents, and had returned to their home town for a wife—Vera. For a few years, he spent part of his time working in America and part of the time with Vera in Czechoslovakia. But when she found she was pregnant, she decided that the child should be born in America and off she went to join her husband. Leaving home seven months pregnant, she managed to convince the doctors in Prague that she was only five months along. By law she should not have been allowed to emigrate so close to term, but as Vera says, "I was a pretty good liar."

Although immigration had been sharply restricted by 1928, Vera saw the same diversity of people, costumes and languages that struck everyone who passed through that Tower of Babel. But her husband wasn't there to meet her, and her fascination at the "scenery" before her turned to fear of being sent back:

"We came in very early in the morning to Ellis Island. When I was getting off the boat a man took my passport—he spoke the Czech language and told me I was stepping on the United States land and he wished me good luck. That I liked. He was nice.

"You should see all the kinds of people on that Ellis Island. The boat was full. Oh, my Lord! I grew up on a farm in Europe and I wasn't used to this—but there you saw all kinds. Some of them looked like beggars—they were dressed in patches. Some of the men had big beards and their hair; some of the Jewish people had braids. There were a lot of people, all kinds, and all of them seemed to me poorer looking and poorer dressed than I was. Some of them were very tragic, with patches one on top of another and the coats and suits. People looked ruined, as if they were coming from some kind of great poverty.

"So when we came to New York, my husband did not show up. Maybe they didn't let him know. I was there the whole day until six o'clock. And you cannot speak when you don't know the language—you are deaf and dumb. This Czech lady came to me and said, 'Your husband is supposed to come and he didn't show up. We are going to send you back.'

" 'Oh, my Lord, send me back! Two more weeks on the ocean?'

" 'Well, he has to come and sign the papers and he has to get you out.'

"They took us to a pretty big room there. We were all in a row, and one by one they were calling us to the office and asking us questions. I could not talk to them, only to this Czech lady who translated. Each one had an interpreter. They asked me all kinds of questions, as if they didn't already know the answers. They knew already. They had the papers saying where I came from, telling them how old I am, if I have been sick, why I came into this country and all kinds of other things. They asked questions that were answered in the papers to see if I was lying or not. It wasn't easy to get out. I was coming to my husband, but these other people must have been through hell sometimes.

"They took two or three hours for the line to finish. Then we came back to the same room, but on the other side. The ones who passed were on one side and the others who weren't finished were on the other side.

"And some of them didn't pass at all. They kept them right there somewhere. I did ask about that because I didn't understand. I saw a lot of people and they were coming from that room. They were crying and then I did not see them any more in the big room. Probably they were sent someplace or sent back to hospitals. Most of them were sad. I was sad myself and I felt like crying.

"Some of them were sick and they had to be put in a hospital. In Czechoslovakia, they had a little bit better system. The best examination was in Prague. The doctor there examined the people coming here. That is why I did not have a medical examination at Ellis Island; he gave me the papers in Prague, telling what kind of condition I was in. But some people from other countries had to go to the doctor's examination on Ellis Island.

"They gave me a dictionary. On the same page, they had English and Czechoslovakian. First was English and the second line was Czechoslovakian. You read English like Czechoslovakian and it sounds terrible

—it sounds like nothing. I knew how to read, but not in English. So they said, 'Try again.'

"The Czech lady told me afterward, 'You will be all right.'

"Then other men and this Czech lady came—they could not talk to me but they questioned me nicely and she helped me. She took me to this room, like an office. They had big books opened up and the names of each of us translated. Then they looked for my husband, searched all over for him, sent a telegram, and tried to find him.

"This Czech lady was talking to me about I am going to have a baby. I said yes, that I was pregnant five months. And at that time I was afraid I was going to mix up everything and say eight months. Maybe they would ship me back or something like that! It was against the law in those days to immigrate more than five months pregnant. But I was a pretty good liar, so all of the time I did not get myself confused and was telling them 'five months!'

"Then she told me again and again that the trouble was because my husband did not come on time. Many times during the day one fellow came and asked me questions, another fellow came. Maybe they questioned me so much because they thought my husband didn't want me, you know. And that is probably why she told me that in case he didn't come, they were going to ship me back. But she told me that they still were going to wait another two or three days for him to come.

"They were calling him and he was not at home. Finally they reached him. At six o'clock they were closing and he just came in at the last minute. He told me he went to look for work, and that he didn't know I was coming that day. It wasn't too bad on the Island if my husband had come on time. But I suffered the whole day because I was worried."

So Vera passed through Ellis Island and got her wish—to have her child in America:

"Exactly one month later, my son was born, the 22nd of March. I came on the 22nd of February. I said to my husband, friends and relatives that I was coming to have the baby here. They all said I was crazy, that I didn't know what I was talking about. I weighed 134 pounds when my baby was born! And my son is so healthy—he's 50 years old and he's never been sick. Many times I thought to myself, 'They always say a sea voyage is good for you . . .'"

Many young women came to America not to get married, but to work. Greta Wagner was no stranger to work. She had worked in Switzerland and Holland, as well as in her native Germany, to save up enough money to come to America. A long illness used up all the money she had saved, so she started again, working and borrowing and scraping together enough money for the passage. But the steamship ticket took every cent she had, and she arrived at Ellis Island in 1923 with no money and no sponsor. Prepared to work hard and pay her own way—which in fact she did, all her life— Greta was, like Ida Mouradjian, thought likely to become a public charge. She would certainly have been sent back to Germany save for the ultimate intervention of a social service organization:

"When I came here, naturally we were shipped first to Ellis Island, and that was not very pleasant. It was rough, very rough. Years ago, they called it a cattle farm. Oh, it was just like a barn. Millions of people standing around with their bundles. You were with a big herd. And they fed us with a wagon full of that cattle food. They slapped it on the plates.

"You were just like a number. Over 5,000 a day were arriving from all over—Russia, Rumania, Poland, from Germany, from France, and naturally I couldn't speak one word of English. I couldn't find one of the legal aid societies or the sisters from the girls' home. They had some of these assist people, but you couldn't expect they would listen to everybody, that they could help out in all the languages.

"I was detained for two weeks. I talked with the directors every day but I couldn't explain anything. But they wouldn't let me go. They wanted to send me back to Germany. Oh, believe me, I never thought I would live long enough to stay healthy and go back from that Island . . ."

*§ "Why were you detained for two weeks?"

"Because nobody got off Ellis Island unless they were called for by someone who would stand good for them. Somebody had to come up and sign.

"But after two weeks, they took me to the girls' home—I'm Catholic, you see. They said that whatever happened they would take over the money until I had a job. Then I would pay them back.

"So I lived through it, and it's a part of history."

ANGELS OF MERCY

Greta Wagner's experience points up the enormous importance of the many social welfare organizations functioning on Ellis Is-

Missionaries, like these in 1908, also worked at Ellis Island,
aiding people of their own faith, holding services for those detained,
and also handing out religious tracts,
which can be seen clutched in the hands
of many immigrants.

land. But for the "helping hands" organizations and their selfless,
tireless people, Ellis Island would have been a much colder, harder
place than it was—and tens of thousands of American families
would not exist today, their grandparents and parents having been
sent back to Europe.

Organizations for every nationality, organizations that cut
across nationalities, organizations of Americans of all kinds worked
to make the world's homeless and oppressed truly welcome in
America. Helen Barth worked for the Hebrew Immigrant Aid
Society (HIAS). Other organizations such as the Italian Welfare
League, the Polish Society, the Travelers' Aid Society, the Immigrants' Protective League, the Catholic Welfare Council, the National Council of Jewish Women, the Daughters of the American
Revoluton, and scores of others worked at Ellis Island on behalf
of arriving immigrants.

The work Helen Barth did for HIAS between 1914 and 1918 is representative of the kind of work done by these organizations and people:

"At Ellis Island, we had to do so many things. It was social service work during the heavy immigration. When the terrifically heavy immigration came, we worked overtime. My hours were from nine in the morning, the nine o'clock boat, until four-thirty. It took twenty minutes to come over. Many times we worked until seven or eight o'clock. There was no such thing as extra pay.

"I did secretarial work. We had the briefs to make out when the immigrant was detained, couldn't come in on account of illness of some member of the family or might become a public charge. These briefs had to be sent to Washington, and I had a lawyer as my employer at the time. He would dictate right on the machine, no such thing as shorthand; we had no time for anything like that."

✍§ "Where was your office?"

"On Ellis Island, on the ground floor. And we didn't have walls— we had like metal fences dividing the rooms and everything was open. The other social service agencies were there, too. I was with the Hebrew, and we had Italian, Polish, Russian and well—all the countries were represented. But they all had just the one desk and they spoke the language of the immigrants. Jewish immigration was heaviest at the time on account of the pogroms that took place in Russia.

"When I started work at Ellis Island, I was about fifteen and a half. I was taken out of high school and given this job. At fourteen you were allowed to go to work. And then I went to night school and made up my courses at the high school. That's the way we handled it then. We didn't go to high school, all through, or college—it was an expensive thing. That's the way children got their education. Very few of them had even as much education as I had. When they were through with public school, they thought they had a real fine education.

"I must tell you that we were only 6 women working among 400 men on Ellis Island. They didn't like women. Well, women weren't employed. They were just women and didn't belong in any field."

✍§ "How did they treat you?"

"Beautiful. Everyone just loved me to death . . .

"At the time another Jewish organization was formed and called The Council of Jewish Women. Sadie American was the representative on Ellis Island, and they had only to do with wayward girls. When the immigrant girls came over, they had a terrible time keeping right. The work was bad, they worked in shops, they worked in private homes, they would be taken advantage of by the men. Many men were without their families—they came here before they took their children over—and so many of the girls became pregnant. And this Council of Jewish Women would help these girls through, either see them through their confinement and then send them home, or send them home right away. They just picked up the girls who were wayward and helped them. Our organization never bothered with the wayward girls."

↝§ "How did they know they were wayward?"

"We all knew, because they would be arrested, and if they were arrested and they weren't citizens, they would be sent right away back to Ellis Island.

"And any man who was found stealing or begging would also right away become a public charge, who had no one to take care of him. We saw these people through by helping them. We took care of their health, we gave them food, we gave them clothing, we gave them homes, and we had representatives going all up and down the East Coast, speaking to all kinds of groups to employ these thousands of people, who were without funds.

"If a woman was pregnant, she could not come in, unless they posted a separate bond for her, because she might become a public charge. Who's going to care for her? The father has no money; they came in without money. Who's going to confine her? Where's she going to have the baby? Now these people were accustomed to having their babies at home, and it was no problem to them. But in our country, conditions were not favorable for that, and we also knew she couldn't go to work because then she couldn't take care of her children."

↝§ "What happened if a baby was born on Ellis Island?"

"She took it along as an additional child.

"If a family or a child was to be deported because of sickness, we would take them to Ellis Island and there would be a charge for the hospitalization. HIAS stood a great deal of that money. We would plead to have them stay, and to have the government or the shipping company pay for the hospitalization. We said it was their fault, because they allowed this family or child to come in sick.

"Supposing we had a child in such a condition. We would have to file a bond with the government and file a brief, and ask the government's permission to have this child treated on Ellis Island. A lawyer would have to come in from outside, and he would be paid for his services. We had many good men, and they would come there and place a $300 or $500 bond for the period. But they would never have to lose their bond—we would stand good for it."

↝§ "What happened to a child, if it went back without its family?"

"That was very sad. It couldn't go back alone, so we would keep the family here and make the mother go back, or an older brother or sister, and that was why we took it so to heart—that this little child, a five- or six-year-old, a little immigrant, just because he is sick, developed a fever, he had to go back to be treated on the other side . . ."

◄§ "Did the family have to pay for another ticket?"

"They did not have to pay for the ticket that took them to Europe, but they had to pay for a ticket to bring them back here. They were deported, as we recorded, 'free,' because the shipping company was responsible. But they were not responsible to bring them back here to this country, so the poor father had to again struggle and save and put penny to penny."

◄§ "When you were there, do you remember any instances when that would happen?"

"Often. Often. We were making briefs out all the time. I was typing and typing to make these briefs out and they were on long legal paper, giving the government reasons why the family should stay and that the little child should be allowed to be treated at Ellis Island. Such reasons as that it was a hardship for the family because the mother was pregnant at the time, the father just had a small job, giving all sorts of sad reasons. The government let them slip through very often, very often, but we had to have it done legally. . . .

"Every one of them wore a ship's card, you know, President Lincoln, President Grant, whatever the boat happened to be, and they would just put a cross for special examination.

"I learned a little about the various languages. For instance, I didn't know how to speak Dutch, but I would say to the immigrant the Dutch words that meant 'What ship did you come in with?' They would show me their card. Sometimes they had to wait a long time at the railroad room to be shipped on trains out west to go to their destination."

◄§ "Did you have a hard time sometimes telling where they were going?"

"Oh, yes. But we always had that little card with the string so they didn't get lost, and so that the families stayed together. The card gave us the story: 'OK, passed' or 'Held for Special Inquiry.' "

◄§ "In general, how did they treat the immigrants on Ellis Island?"

"Very nicely. There was no abuse, that's sure. We didn't do anything that wasn't right. There were so many thousands that we had to clear them out as quickly as possible . . ."

Rachel Goldman arrived at Ellis Island, sixteen years old and alone, during the war, when few immigrants were traveling. Her passage through Ellis Island was smooth and easy, with the help

During the late years of World War I, immigration was almost completely shut off. This Sunday afternoon Ukrainian concert shows how much less crowded Ellis Island was in 1916, when Rachel Goldman came through.

of the Travelers' Aid Society and probably some careful checking by social welfare people:

"Being that my address was to go to my cousin's in Evanston, Illinois, one of the Travelers' Aid Society persons came over and helped me purchase a ticket to go to Evanston and also suggested sending a telegram to my cousin.

"Ellis Island was a large place. It wasn't too crowded, and was spacious. And being that I was being helped by everyone, I didn't have to look for anything and found it very convenient. I didn't find it at all oppressive and I had no trouble at all because I was in perfect health, young, and as I say, the Travelers' Aid Society was a great help, and I was only a few hours at Ellis Island."

I BECAME A JAILER

"The whole country was swept by emotional excesses that followed one another with confusing swiftness from 1916 to 1920." That is the way Immigration Commissioner Frederic C. Howe described the antialien hysteria that preceded the virtually complete closing of the golden door to southern and eastern European immigrants in the early 1920s, a period that came to a climax with the trial and execution of Sacco and Vanzetti.

Starting early in the war, and climaxing in 1916, the number of arrests of aliens for alleged prostitution and related offenses sharply increased, as "white slavery" was thought to be an alien importation. Hundreds were shipped to Ellis Island for deportation, and had to be held there indefinitely, as it was impossible to ship them back across the Atlantic because of the war.

When the United States entered the war in 1917, 1,800 German citizens were interned at Ellis Island, following the seizure of all German ships in New York Harbor. Thousands more "enemy aliens" were seized all over the United States, accused of a wide variety of "crimes," and sent to Ellis Island and other detention centers to await deportation. As Howe put it: "I became a jailer instead of a commissioner of immigration."

The feeling against enemy aliens was further sharpened by the Black Tom explosion of 1916, in which German agents blew up munitions stored on Black Tom Island, part of Jersey City, causing considerable loss of life and enormous damage to many installations in New York Harbor. The Ellis Island Immigration Station suffered massive damage and some minor casualties, but astonishingly, no one was killed. By the time full-scale immigration resumed in 1919, the station was fully repaired.

Then just after the war, the United States experienced its first bout of anti-Communist hysteria, in the aftermath of the Russian Revolution and during the growth of powerful new nativist, antiblack, antialien movements. Thousands of accused anarchists, communists and other radicals were seized and prosecuted with little or no regard for due process of law. The aliens among them were sent to Ellis Island and hundreds were deported, including the

Emma Goldman, who immigrated through Castle Garden in 1886 and worked
in a Rochester, New York, clothing factory, was deported as an anarchist
during the Red Scare of 1919. When the hysteria died down, she returned—
disenchanted with Russia—and stayed until her death in Toronto, in 1940.

anarchists Emma Goldman and Alexander Berkman. The majority
of them were ultimately saved from deportation by the energetic
resistance mounted by Frederic Howe and a handful of other
defenders of due process.

Howe himself fell victim to the hysteria and was forced from office early in 1919. Later that year, the Palmer Raids brought mass arrests of aliens, substantial numbers of internments and some deportations. For a time, Attorney General Mitchell Palmer and his assistant, J. Edgar Hoover, were able to run roughshod over the Bill of Rights, and especially over the very minimal rights enjoyed by aliens under American law.

Eventually, others came forward to occupy the ground Howe and a few others had held in 1918 and 1919. By late 1920, the Red scare had waned, the Republic was seen to be relatively safe, and most of those held at Ellis Island had been released.

But the antialien hysteria of 1916 to 1920 had, by fueling anti-immigrant feeling in the United States, hastened the closing of the door, through passage of the immigration restriction laws of 1921 and 1924.

Ellis Island was used as an immigrant reception station until 1932, primarily for special problems because after 1924 most inspections were handled through American consulates overseas; after that it was used mostly as an internment center, doubling as a Coast Guard station during World War II. Closing finally in 1954, Ellis Island joined the Statue of Liberty as a national monument in 1965 and was reopened to the public in 1976.

Meanwhile, the millions of immigrants who passed through Ellis Island continued their journey on into the new world.

VII

INTO THE NEW WORLD

"They used to tell us on the other side that the trains in America run on rooftops! They had the Second Avenue Subway—the Second Avenue El—and the Third Avenue El. It used to run right down to South Ferry. When you got off Ellis Island at the ferry, you walked up and got the train there.

"To us it was magic! We had never seen anything like it. After the train started to go, as it traveled, you could look out the windows, and you could see people and what not. We got to this country—and then the fun began!"

❧

ARNOLD WEISS
Polish Jew, from Russia
Arrived 1921

A baggage room on the first floor held large trunks and suitcases, for people like Fannie Kligerman and Leon Solomon, who had more than hand luggage. But during the peak years, baggage often went astray, which is what happened to this Italian family.

FROM ELLIS ISLAND, they went on into America.

About one-third of the immigrants admitted went out the back of the Great Hall, down the stairs, and into the first-floor baggage room, where they made whatever arrangements were necessary for delivery of baggage. They then walked down a wire-enclosed path to the ferry from Ellis Island to the Battery. At the Ellis Island landing, they met the people who had been waiting for them. That ferry landing was for most of four decades the scene of extraordinary and joyous reunions: families long torn apart made whole again; lovers who had almost given up hope reunited; parents and children who had never seen each other before, starting a new life together.

The other two-thirds of the immigrants were going further on into America. First, most of them exchanged some or all of their money for United States currency at the money-changing counters on the second floor. Then those already ticketed went downstairs to the first-floor waiting room; the rest went to the first-floor railroad ticket offices for tickets to their destinations. Here many of them bought box lunches for the trip and then continued to the waiting room. Ultimately, all were taken by barge to railroad station, and other transportation points, for the trip further into America.

Theodore Lubik describes how it worked:

"There was a group of inspectors, young fellas only, who knew all kinds of languages. One of these young men was the leader of a bunch of immigrants. He would slip a button on you and say, 'Watch me.' You watched him, you followed him, and he took you to New York on the dock. From there, if you were going to Chicago or someplace, you went on another boat, a ferry to Hoboken.

"Then the inspector put the immigrants on the train. He knew already which cars would take them. The immigrant already had the tickets and so on paid and everything. And everyone had a place or some address where they were going. They stayed on the train until the conductor told them to get off."

One person who passed through at the time Theodore was working at Ellis Island was Irene Meladaki Zambelli. She gives a good picture of how people passed the time during the many waits on this long journey:

"Then they took us a few at a time and brought us to what I think was the Pennsylvania Station. There was a lot of us there from the ship. It was cold. I put on my coat I had with me and sat in the station for a few hours. We bought and drank beer and an Italian fellow from the ship played an accordion and sang continuously, 'Oh, Marie, Oh, Marie.' We were so exhausted that we laid on the bench and tried to sleep but he kept us awake so my cousin called, 'Hey, Italiano, stop that.' He stopped and we fell asleep. But someone came in and wakened us up and gave us a big bag full of salami, bread, cheese, and a lot of other stuff and crackers. And then put us on a train.

"We had not the slightest idea where we were going. We traveled three days and three nights, changing trains every few hours. I remember one of the stops in Cincinnati, Ohio. We stayed there awhile, went to a restaurant and ate. The food was terrible, but we laughed and joked. My cousin was a gifted comedian. He looked just like Fernandel, the French comedian. He was a street car conductor and he would imitate how a rich man sat and how he coughed, and how a poor man sat and how he coughed, how a flirt sat, how a mother with her children sat. He used to imitate my mother who was very talkative and she used her hands a lot when she talked and as the conversation went on she would raise her hands higher and higher and put them on top of her head. He could imitate her so completely and tell me some of the stories she used to tell. On the train he made fun of everyone around us, especially of his friend who never got over being seasick on the train and we ate all his bag of stuff. He followed us to New Orleans

These Italian men, waiting in the railroad room to be taken in groups
to the proper train station for the rest of their trip, have already
started on their box lunches. According to the boxes, "Fritz Brodt,
Commissary Contractor, Ellis Island," supplied these lunches in 1905.

and then we lost him. He stayed there a few days and then came to
tell us goodbye. He left for Greece.

"At the station at Canal Street and Basin Street in New Orleans,
my father met us. My cousin stayed awhile. He tried to get a job. He
couldn't. He did not speak a word of English. He took trains one after
another, going east. They put him off in every station—he had no
money to buy a ticket. He reached New York. The war had started and
they were picking up any young men that wanted to fight for their
country. So my cousin went back to Greece as a soldier. I stayed in
America until today."

THE KINDNESS OF STRANGERS

Stories—some unquestionably true—abound of immigrants being
cheated by money-changers on and off Ellis Island; of young girls

disappearing from trains bound for Chicago and other points west; of immigrants sold bad food at exorbitant prices once off Ellis Island. The newspapers of the peak immigration years are full of stories about white slavery and bodies found floating in New York Harbor.

But there was also the experience of thirteen-year-old Celia Rypinski, once a bond was posted for her, waiting for a train to Chicago, alone and unable to speak a word of English:

"Finally, they called me, and I was taken to the train by a guide. While I was at the train station waiting for the train, a little old man came and talked to me in different languages. I couldn't understand. I didn't answer. He talked all different languages. When he said something in Polish, my eyes almost popped out. And I told him my story.

"He went and he bought a ham sandwich on his own and something to drink, some kind of soda. And he brought it to me—that little old man. God give him heaven!

"And he said, 'You're gonna be hungry on the train. You're gonna ride two days and a night.' The trains weren't running from New York like they do now. He asked me if I had money. I had a twenty-dollar gold piece and some kind of change from Rotterdam. And he said, 'Give it to me and I'll change it to American money and I'll buy you a box lunch that you can have on the train, because you're not gonna understand what they say on the train. They'll come around with food, but you don't know how to handle the money.'

"He bought me a box. It was something like two dollars and he gave me the rest of the change. And he kissed me. I kissed his hands because he was Polish and he was so good to me. Oh, God give him heaven!

"And when I was on the train I had veal sausage, I had cookies, I had bread and a little container—I don't know whether it was butter or margarine they put on the bread. And I even brought home some of the food to my brother."

Celia's train and Irene's took a long time to get to their destinations because they were "immigrant trains." Immigrants were transported all together, with no other passengers, in old, poorly lit, badly ventilated cars. Immigrant trains were circuitously routed, shunted onto sidings to let other trains go through, and generally handled like only the slowest of freight trains. For all this, the immigrants were charged first-class fares, supposedly for "through" trains to their destinations.

This German family is being tagged for the railroad trip beyond Ellis Island. The tag reads "2, P.R.R., L.V.R.R.," indicating that they are taking either the Pennsylvania Railroad or the Lehigh Valley Railroad.

The Railroad Clearing House, a pool of twelve railroads, shared all traffic originating at Ellis Island and provided this "special service." And slow service it was—for many years, some immigrants were routed to Chicago via Norfolk, Virginia, to provide business to one of the railroad pool's members.

No one was able to dent the power of the railroad pool in Washington or in the state capitals. Among others, Immigration Commissioners Williams and Watchorn tried, and failed. So did the Interstate Commerce Commission, with resulting railroad promises, but no real results. It still often took twice as long for an immigrant to get to his destination as for anyone else, and under worse conditions than first-class passengers, even though they were paying first-class fares.

Undaunted, the immigrants kept coming. After the rigors of the trip across Europe, across the Atlantic and through Ellis Island, the long, slow train journeys into America seemed scarcely to have been regarded as difficult, but rather by many as a slow, interesting introduction to the new land.

After over two years Sarah Asher and her brother were delighted to be in America. They quite enjoyed their trip to Buffalo, even though all they had between them was their train tickets and the $3.20 with which they had come through Ellis Island. She remembers the immigration inspector sending them off to make their train connection:

"He was very nice. He said, 'I see you are booked to Buffalo. You have to take the train. I'll put you on the little boat. The boat will bring you to the Lackawanna Railroad.' I suppose it was Hoboken and we didn't know it.

"He called a young man to take us. So we went on the little boat that brought us to Hoboken. Everything was arranged. That was about two in the afternoon; the railroad was to start at two o'clock. So we said goodbye to the young boy.

"Our tickets for the boat covered the railroad, too, so we had them with us."

⋖§ "How much did the whole thing cost? Do you know?"

"One hundred and fifty dollars, from Germany to Buffalo.

"So we went on the train, sat down and waited. At two o'clock the train started. It was very nice. It was a slow train, a local train, not an express.

"Around four o'clock, the train stopped, and we could hear bells, just like Russian church bells. I said to my brother, 'Sounds like a Russian church.'

" 'Yes,' he said. 'There must be a church nearby.' And a few hours later, we stopped again somewhere and the bells were ringing. I said, 'They have so many churches in a free country!' We could hardly believe it.

"We were riding until about twelve or one o'clock in the morning, then stopped in a station. It was Utica, the railroad station. There we had to wait four hours for a special train we had to change to, which would bring us right to Buffalo.

"We were sitting in the waiting room, and said we would listen to the man who announced the towns. Of course, to our Russian ears the towns were strange enough, and like all train announcers, he spoke them quickly, one after another. So I said to my brother, 'You listen for Buffalo, and I'll listen for Buffalo, so maybe we will take the right train and we will land where we have to.'

"There we were at four o'clock in the morning, sitting in the waiting room. There was a beautiful buffet there, fruit and sandwiches and a lot of things. Well, they had some kinds of foods we never saw in Russia. There was grapefruit, but larger than I ever saw in Russia. There were oranges, which we had in Russia, and bananas, which we had never eaten. And sandwiches. But we didn't buy because we had only $3.20, so I asked my brother, 'Are you hungry?'

" 'Are you?'

" 'No.' But we were starved! No, not really. At four o'clock he announced the train to Buffalo. We went into the train, and it took only a few hours to come to Buffalo.

"From the train, we came into a very nice station, and we heard 'Taxi, taxi, taxi.' So my brother said to me, 'Taxi' translated into Russian.

"I said, 'Ask how much he wants and show him the address where we are going.' He wanted $3.00. I was standing there watching, and I said, 'Forget the taxi.'

"My brother said, 'But how will we . . . ?'

"I said, 'We'll see.'

"We spotted a street car. I said, 'Let's go to that street and see what is what.' We asked the conductor, and he saw that we were foreigners and didn't know where to go.

"He said, 'All right, I'll take you in my car. At a certain spot, I'll tell you where to get off and you'll take another street car that will bring you to that street.' Very nice. So how much? Twenty-five cents. Very good. We got the tickets and the transfer he gave us and when we came to a certain spot he said, 'Here you get off and wait on the corner and the other street car will come.' "

*§ "You could understand everything he said?"

"We understood very good. You see, when we studied, we studied besides Russian, German—and English was easy. I knew Latin very good, too—in our college we took Latin. And my brother knew Latin and Greek, too. The English alphabet is a, b, c, all in the same alphabet as Latin. M, n, o, p, everything. So we were reading. We read excellently. But to understand certain words, something complicated, that was a little bit hard. But we had our own dictionaries.

"Finally, he brought us to a certain street and said we should walk about two or three blocks and find that house number.

"And that's how we came to Buffalo. It was early morning. We landed about six o'clock in the morning in Buffalo. So we came to my brother's house about seven o'clock. We rang the bell, and nobody answered. They had a porch, so we knocked on the window. My sister-in-law heard the knocking. She got out of bed and came to the window and saw two people. She said, 'Oh, that must be Joseph and Sarah.' We smiled, she opened the door and we came in.

"She greeted us so nicely, then served coffee and breakfast. We were sitting and crying . . .

"My brother asked, 'How is it that you didn't let us know by telegram from the boat?'

"We told him that we were on the boat, and said, 'Who had money? Who could send you a telegram? We had $3.20, so now we've spent it on our carfare. Besides, we didn't really know when we would come, we were so long on the boat.'

"He said he was reading the newspaper a few days before we arrived, about this boat drifting in the ocean in a terrible storm and fog, and that the battleship came and couldn't find the boat and turned back. And that my sister-in-law prayed for us, and said, 'You know, Paul, your sister and brother may be on that boat.'

"He had said to her, 'Why should you say that? They would send me a telegram or letter that they were going on that boat.'

"She had said, 'You can never tell.' And she was right—we were on that boat!"

In the still neutral America of 1916, immigrants were moving into the mainstream of American life.

Samuel Goldwyn formed Goldwyn Pictures Corporation that year, later to be merged with Louis B. Mayer's company to become Metro-Goldwyn-Mayer. Born in Warsaw, Poland (then part of Russia), in 1882, he was a boy of fourteen when he came through Ellis Island in 1896, and a man of thirty-one when he produced *The Squaw Man* in 1913 with his coproducers Cecil B. De Mille and Jesse L. Lasky. One of the founders of the modern American film industry, Goldwyn produced some of the great American films, including *Wuthering Heights* and *The Best Years of Our Lives*.

Felix Frankfurter was in his second year as a Professor at the Harvard Law School in 1916. Born in Vienna in 1882, he had come through Ellis Island in 1894 with his family. He became one of the outstanding Americans of the twentieth century, a law professor, a civil liberties activist in the unsuccessful fight for the freedom of Sacco and Vanzetti, a founder of the American Civil Liberties Union, a pillar of Franklin Roosevelt's New Deal and ultimately a Justice of the United States Supreme Court.

But in 1916, with the war in Europe, immigrants in America

were cut off from the relatives and friends they had left behind. With travel restrictions in war-torn Europe, Rachel Goldman's emigration was, thus, a rare event. Her trip to Evanston, Illinois, was smooth and uneventful, thanks to the Travelers' Aid Society. But with so many people starved for news of their homeland, her arirval in 1916 turned out to be an event in its own right:

"When I got on the train, I was all by myself, and began to worry. Being that I ate so good on the ship and gained weight, I found I couldn't eat anything on the train, although I think I was more than a day, maybe two days on it. They were selling sandwiches, and I bought one but couldn't eat it. I was worried. You know, what would I do if I came all by myself and didn't know the language.

"So when we got off in Chicago, when they said I needed to change to another train, I was so surprised to hear my name called. I did have a tag with my name on it, pinned on me by the Travelers' Aid Society at Ellis Island. And I had a new blouse to change into when I got near Evanston, Illinois. But I didn't know I was near there.

"A lady said, 'Your relatives are here to meet you,' and she ushered me over to them. She also was an Evanstonian and knew my cousin and her sister, but they were not permitted to meet me by themselves. Because I was a minor, the Travelers' Aid Society had to take care of me to see that I met the right people. Which I thought was wonderful.

"Then we had a bite to eat. My cousin had an automobile and we drove out to Evanston, which was to be my home for the next six years. And it was lucky that I came then, because ours was the second to the last boat to come through for the duration of the war.

"The fellow who had sent the telegram to Evanston from Ellis Island hadn't mentioned in it what train or what railroad I was coming on, and my cousin was telling me what a time they had for two days calling every railroad and finding out if I was on it. I was on a train which took such a long time, being sidetracked all the time for regular trains, I understood it was a train that immigrants were sent on. Of course, my cousin didn't know about it. He thought I was coming on one of the regular trains . . .

"My cousin gave me a beautiful home, and since he had a fine photography studio and photographed many of the important people on the North Shore, he knew the reporter on the Tribune. And the first day I was taken to the studios, I also met the reporter. When he saw me, he said, 'Oh, Joe, please give me a picture of the little cousin.'

"I didn't know he took it, and then I appeared on the front page of the Chicago Tribune and the whole story of my coming. Being there was no regular immigration and no mail coming on account of the war, the first week I think there were at least forty or fifty people a day coming to see me at the studio to get regards from their folks, and so many were just from the entire area where we lived during the German occupation."

✑ "These people must be Jewish?"

"Most people were Jewish. One man came from St. Louis. His parents lived across the street from us and I did not know them to speak to, but I could tell him that I saw them and that they were perfectly all right, which was good.

"After all, everybody was hungry for news from the folks and to know what things were like. You know, we were just completely cut off. One man came from Detroit to see me. And I had letters, received a lot of mail, from Boston and other cities. Of course everyone was hungry to hear about how conditions were."

YOU'LL NEVER SEE YOUR BROTHER NO MORE

The trip to Chicago and other interior points was not always the way Rachel Goldman found it. Young girls were lost en route, and men did work the trains to capture and in many instances quite literally enslave the defenseless. Here is how the Immigrants' Protective League of Chicago saw the danger faced by young immigrant girls and women on their way to Chicago before World War I:

"She is carefully guarded by the federal authorities until she is placed on the train, but the government then considers that its responsibility is at an end. She may be approached by anybody en route. Through her own mistake or intention or the carelessness of railroad officials, she may never reach Chicago.

"For example, two Polish girls, seventeen and twenty-two years of age, whose experience before they started for America had been bounded by the limits of a small farm in Galicia, were coming to their cousin, who lived back of the Yards in Chicago. Her name and address had been sent to us on one of our regular lists; and, when one of the visitors of the League called at the house, she found the cousin and the entire household much alarmed because the girls had not arrived. Inquiring of others who came on the same boat we found that the girls had become acquainted with a man from Rochester on the way over, and he was 'looking out for them.' The only information the Commissioner at

Ellis Island could give was that the girls had left there and that one ticket on that date had been sold to Rochester and two Chicago tickets had been used as far as Rochester. The girls had completely disappeared, and no one was responsible for their failure to arrive in Chicago.

"Several girls had told of being approached on the trains and invited by strange men to get off at 'some big city and see the town,' but they wisely concluded to continue their journey without these gay excursions into the unknown . . ."*

Sophia Belkowski was one of those vulnerable young women who arrived in the prewar years characterized in Russian-born Irving Berlin's first big hit "Alexander's Ragtime Band." Sophia—only fifteen, and unable to speak a word of English—had been carefully held at Ellis Island for a week while her brother was checked, before she was sent on to Chicago. From the time she had walked across the Russian border at midnight, she had been helped by kind strangers. When danger appeared, however, she had to rely on her own instincts:

"After a week at Ellis Island, they put me on a train. We rode along until we came to a different place; I don't know where we were. Everybody had to get off. I saw some people get off, but nobody told me anything, so I sat in there by myself. Then a man came and hollered at me, told me to get off.

"I followed him outside. He took all of us to a basement where we waited. I sat with the people. I didn't run around because you don't know the strange place. In Europe, I never go no place, we never run around.

"I was sitting there, close to some other people, when a young man came and asked me some questions in Polish. He told me he would be better to me than my brother. Well, I never went with a boy, and I didn't know the people. He said, 'You think your brother will give you support?'

"I said, 'Sure, if my brother brings me here to the United States, he's going to support me for a while until I get a job or something.'

"Then he told me something about bringing people to the train and taking people from the train and then to someplace else. I realize now that he probably was selling girls.

---

* Extract from first and fifth *Annual Reports of the Immigrants' Protective League of Chicago*, reprinted in *Immigration: Select Documents and Case Records*, pp. 468–469, by Edith Abbott (Chicago: The University of Chicago Press, 1924), reprinted by Arno Press and *The New York Times*, New York, 1969.

"*I don't know how many hours we were waiting there. After that he brought me an apple, that Polish boy, and he said, 'I'm going to take you with me.'*

"*I said, 'No, I have to go to my brother.'*

"*Well, then the people came and took us to the train. I followed the people into the train. And then he came, and stood by me. Well, maybe God helped me somehow, I don't know. He said, 'I'm late coming for you. Now I will take you.'*

"*I said, 'Well, if you take me, I'll write to my brother and my brother will come and pick me up.'*

"*He said, 'You will never write to your brother. You'll never see your brother no more.'*

"*But then the train started moving, he jumped off, and he was gone. I was left in the train, and came right to Chicago.'*

☙ "*Did you ever find out what that Polish boy was all about?*"

"*I don't know. I didn't know how you find out. I think he sold young girls. If he had been smart enough, he should have come and asked, 'To who you going?'*

"*If I said, 'To my brother,' he should say, 'Come on. I'll pick you up and take you to your brother.'*

"*If he had taken me, maybe he would sell me—maybe I'd be in a grave a long time ago already. Who knows what he would do with me?*"

And after all that, Sophia found herself at the wrong station in Chicago, completely lost and prey for anyone who might want to take her. But there she found some people who really looked out for her:

"*After a while, a black man came. I didn't speak the English language, and he showed me his watch, and showed me five o'clock. I waited, and then he came and put me on a train. He did. He came there for me and when the train was ready to go, he put me on the train.*

"*I tried to give him a quarter. He didn't take the quarter.*

"*When I came to Chicago, a man was waiting with a horse and buggy there. I didn't see my brother—nobody was there at the station. The man spoke Polish, and I told him my brother was supposed to pick me up, and I asked him where my brother was. He said my brother wasn't there, and put me in the buggy. He rode the horse. I kept my little babushka and my wide babushka* rode with him in the front of the buggy.*

"*He brought me to Union Station, and talked in the American lan-*

---

* A bundle wrapped in large scarves, or babushkas.

guage to the man in the office there. And he said that when he brought people from the other station he usually charged three dollars. I didn't have much money. He said, 'Well, maybe you need your money.'"

The man in the station office kept her with him until her brother arrived. He, the man who wouldn't take her quarter, the hack driver who rescued her, and all the others who had helped her earlier, were as much part of the journey as the "Polish boy" who had tried to capture and sell her. They were part of the fabric of her life and time.

For some people, their strongest feeling on arrival in America was sadness. Unlike Sophia's family, who could and did go back to Poland, Martha Konwicki's family, arriving in 1914, felt that they could never return, since her father had fled the Czar's jails. So Martha thought most of the family she had left behind: "Much as I loved my father, it was only that I missed the family, my relatives. There were so many cousins that were walking distance to me, and we were so close."

The reunion was bittersweet for many, as hazy memories and impossible dreams met with reality in the new world. Catherine Bolinski's father had left for America in 1912 when she was three. After eleven years of war and waiting, Catherine was about to be reunited with the father she barely remembered, at Union Station in Chicago. She recalls her dismay:

"At Ellis Island, they put you together to be sure that you stayed in a group, which one's going where. So they divided the people who were coming to Chicago.

"We got to Chicago and they were calling out, 'Where you going? Who are you coming with?' You always had a ticket with you, so then you give the ticket to a man there, and he was calling out names. They called this one, they called that one, and we gave ours to call.

"Two men came up to pick us up at the station. So what did I do? I picked the younger one and the better-looking one for my father. I didn't know who it was."

◄§ "Was it your father?"

"No, it wasn't. It was my father's friend.

"My mother had said, 'When you see your father, go give him a hug and a kiss.' How can I go? How can I kiss a strange man at that age? So I didn't kiss anyone. I just walked over."

≈§ "What about your mother and father—did they embrace?"

"Ah yes, ah yes. After all, my mother knew my father. It wasn't that many years for her. But as a child I didn't remember him. My sister had never seen him. He had left in 1912 and this was 1923.

"We took the taxi cab. My father got some furniture and we went to the apartment. Some people from our village owned that building. My father was working in the stockyards all the while.

"So we got a cab over there, and I saw such a strange building—it was in the evening when we came to the factory sites there. I said, 'My goodness! That's Chicago? It don't look so good.' "

Other immigrants, arriving in Chicago that same year, were destined to change the look of some of America's industrial areas that "didn't look so good." Eliel Saarinen, architect, won second prize in the *Chicago Tribune* Tower competition in 1922, which gave him enough money to bring his family, including his son, Eero, over from Finland in 1923. And Eero Saarinen, thirteen years old when he came with his family to America, lived to become one of the greatest architects of our time. His extraordinary achievements include Dulles International Airport in Virginia, the Transworld Airline Terminal at Kennedy International Airport, the chapel and auditorium at the Massachusetts Institute of Technology and dozens of major structures all over the world. His innovative use of space, form and materials has helped a generation of architects, and indeed all of us, begin to understand what it will be to live with the stars, in an infinite universe.

THE TRAINS RUN ON ROOFTOPS!

For people going directly into New York City, America was often an explosion, a shock, the sudden passage from country to city coupled with a massive change of cultures. People carried handmade trunks and huge bundles wrapped in blankets into a new world of horseless carriages and trains that ran on rooftops. And their millions, largely poured into the limited space of Manhattan Island, swelled New York to the most populous city in the world in those years.

For many, the first new experience was a ride on a New York

Cleared immigrants and the people who met them waited on the dock at Ellis Island for the ferry to the mainland, with the New York City skyline in the background. In the aerial view of Ellis Island (page 146), this waiting area is under the canopy on the left side of the upper island.

elevated train, since the first subway didn't open until 1904. Frank Santoni remembers the elevated train—and the bells of a wagon that recalled his life in Sicily—on his first day in New York in 1900:

"My greatest admiration was the trains that intermingled at that time in Battery Park, the elevateds. The Ninth Avenue, Second Avenue, Third Avenue and Sixth Avenue—all met at South Ferry. I didn't know it was South Ferry, but it was Battery Park. And when I saw that, I didn't know what to think. Such an impression.

"We went to my uncle and aunt's house. While near the window I heard what I later found out was a wagon, a junk cart. You know the cow bells that they have? Now, I thought that the sheep and the goats were coming through the town, like in Campofiorito! When I looked out and didn't see goats I was kind of disappointed . . ."

253

Anna Vacek arrived on a rainy day in 1901. It wasn't quite the America she had envisioned, standing on the banks of that stream in Czechoslovakia, watching her dollies drift away to America:

"Well, then we went on a train on Second Avenue, and my sister showed me where things were—there were Indian graves, there were farms, everything.

"It was a rainy day and I said, 'Well, everything is nice; why does everyone look so sad?'

"My sister said, 'Because it's raining.'

"I said, 'When are we going to be in America?'

"She said to her friend, 'For goodness' sakes, look at that greenhorn. She don't like it here; she's asking for America!'

"I said, 'Because it rains and everything looks so wet. It should be bright, I think. This is not America. When are we going to be there?'

"Well, my sister only laughed. 'You will see America later on.'

" 'Why did they kill that McKinley?'

" 'Why are you so interested?'

" 'Because I feel sorry when there are black flags, a lot of black things hanging on the houses. What did he do?'

" 'That's a big story, child, and I'll tell you when we get home, but we all feel sorry for him.'

" 'That's too bad, why did they do it? I can't get over it that they kill such a leading man, who know kings and all that.'

"And while we were going on, I looked and saw horses looking out of a window on the fourth floor, and said, 'Oh, what is this? How did the horses get up there?'

"They all laughed, but you know, fourteen years old, I was a kid . . ."

Twenty-one years later, Marta Forman's first experience was also a ride on the elevated train. But because she was alone—an uncle met her at Ellis Island, then almost immediately left her on her own—Marta felt much less secure:

"So we went on the little boat again, and they took us to the Battery.

"That was the first time I went on the Second Avenue elevated. That was something for me. I was going up the stairs and I turned around and around and said, 'Oh my God, where are we going?'

"After we sat down on the train, the people were looking at me, and they thought, 'Oh, here's another greenhorn again.' That's what they used to call them. And I thought, 'How can people hang their wash outside from building to building?' That I couldn't get over.

"I was looking out the train window, and seeing what was going on here—it looked to me impossible—a big city like that, the people looked so neat. And it was so hot in August—people had their windows open, and the train was going by the windows. I thought the train was going to go right through their rooms. They were sleeping on the floor, it was so hot. They had no fans, nothing, so they had the windows open. They were sleeping on the floor and so many children, you know, almost naked, and the train was going by and the stations and the houses were shaking—the vibration. So I thought, 'Oh my God, how can people sleep with all that noise going on?'

"We stopped at Seventy-second Street, that was the elevated station. I got off and went down. I had my two baskets—they didn't have suitcases at that time—straw baskets, two of them. And I thought, 'What is going to happen to me now?' "

Arriving in the Czech neighborhood, she met another man from her hometown. He took her to dinner, which she ate ravenously, exhausted though she was. Then, with some difficulty, he found her a place to sleep with someone who had an apartment around the corner from the restaurant:

"She was living on the first floor and she had three little rooms, two windows facing on First Avenue. And it was so hot! In August, it is very hot here. She had the windows open and all the noise from the avenue—people yelling because they used to stay on the street God knows how many hours. They couldn't sleep inside because it was so hot.

"When she saw me, she said, 'Oh, for God's sake, come on in. Don't be afraid; I am going to take care of you.' She spoke to me in the Czech language, because she could hardly speak English.

"She said, 'You're going to sleep right here.' It was an old-fashioned iron bed painted white. The other bedroom had no windows and there she kept old suitcases and boxes from all those immigrants, all those single girls who came here to this wonderful country, who just wanted to work hard and make a living. She kept the suitcases there—a girl would take a job, and maybe the lady wouldn't like her, and why should she drag everything? She kept them there, and when you had a steady job you could always come for it. She explained it to me.

"I said, 'I'm going to wash myself.' Then I was so tired that I just flopped in that bed and slept like a rock.

"In the morning, when I got up she was making coffee in the

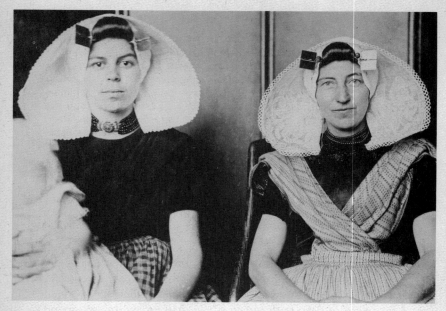

Immigrants wearing their native costumes, like these women, were often
hustled into the nearest public restrooms for a change of clothing by their
relatives, who wanted the new arrivals to dress like Americans—not to look
like greenhorns "just off the boat."

kitchen, and then when I looked around I saw the place wasn't painted
in I don't know how many years. But that old lady was very clean.

"She was very comical, a very old lady, and very honest. She even
was wearing those old skirts from the old country, you know. She said,
'Now you wash your face and I'm making the coffee. I am going to run
down across the street to the bakery and I'm going to bring something.
You sit and comb your hair.'

"So I went into the front room where she had big windows and a
long mirror and instead of paint on the wall she had post cards from
all those domestic maids that used to stay in her house. For many
years, when they got jobs they sent her post cards. She saved all the
post cards and pasted the whole front room with them. I couldn't believe it when I saw and read them.

"She said, 'You see, this is a history of all those immigrants. I don't
even know where they are, if they are still alive or not, but they all
sent me cards.'

"And it was so interesting for me."

256

So Marta found that America also had way stations run by "landsmen." Through this marvelous woman, Marta got a job as a housekeeper and children's nurse. Despite an early severe illness and hospitalization, during which her new employers helped her, she earned enough to pay back the passage money she had borrowed and to go on to build a fruitful life in America. Marta still lives in the Czechoslovakian section, only two blocks away from where she spent her first night in America.

Unexpected arrivals from the other side often posed real hardships for people who had not yet established themselves in the new country. And the new world held unexpected dangers, even when you were going to your own countrymen, as Michael Pappas found out.

In 1913 Michael and four other young Greeks from the same boat all went to one address in Manhattan, given them in Greece by the father of a young man who had emigrated to America earlier:

"Well, we went to this restaurant, they called it the Athens Restaurant. And we found the friend we were looking for. But when he saw us he was surprised. He said, 'Where are you people going?'

" 'We are going to you.'

" 'But what am I going to do with you?'

"So we begged, 'We have no other place; your father gave us your address.' That was true; his father really did give us the address.

"Poor guy, he was a laborer, and very weak and sick. He used to sell cigarettes, going from coffee house to coffee house and from store to store to make his living. So we didn't expect any financial help from him. But at least he gave us a room to sleep. He had one bed with a mattress. The rest was nothing but newspapers. So we stayed there two or three days."

◄§ "How did New York look to you when you first came?"

"Oh, I was surprised, because I was brought up in a small village. I didn't know much about big buildings. We were scared—no money, you know how it is—only sixteen years old, first time I was out of my home, and he didn't have room for all of us."

Michael's friend took three of the five young men from the boat, including Michael, and arranged for two more to sleep with another friend above a coffee house a couple of blocks away on Forty-second Street:

"Next morning, this friend in whose apartment I stayed said, 'Michael, you are the youngest; you better get out and go down to the coffee house.'

"The coffee house was a couple of blocks from the apartment where we stayed. I went down there and asked for Mr. Kyrakis.

" 'Mr. Kyrakis isn't up yet.'

" 'Mr. Kylonos sent me.'

" 'I don't know—you better go up and see.'

"There was a door, closed. You had to knock on the door and go upstairs from the coffee house to the apartment upstairs. When I opened the door I smelled something, so I went back to the coffee house. I said, 'I smell something bad.'

"Right away he noticed something was wrong. It was gas. You know, in those days there was no electricity in the houses, there was gas—they had to light by gas. So when time came to go to sleep, they were talking to these friends. When it was time to sleep in the old country, we had kerosene lamps and you put the light out. They thought they could do the same thing with the gas. So when the time came to sleep, somebody said, 'Blow the light out.' He blew it out and the light went out, but the gas was coming on all night.

"In the middle of the night they got sick—they were vomiting—but they used their heads and opened the window. They put their heads out the window. When we went up, we found them with their heads out the window.

"We dragged them out, called for help at the coffee house and started giving them black coffee. Right away we gave them black coffee and called the doctor. And they were all right."

PERIOD OF ADJUSTMENT

America was a huge, fascinating, sometimes frightening place for the new immigrants. There were the very practical problems of finding places to live, finding work, learning a new language and getting educated, all usually undertaken under conditions of extreme poverty, as the immigrants' modest resources were often almost entirely consumed by the cost of the trip to America.

And there were the often equally important problems caused by culture shock, a sudden immersion in a world of very different values, customs and perspectives; exposure to new and unknown materials and technology—all the things that make up the fabric of a culture. For these people, mainly from rural southern and eastern Europe, were suddenly set down in the heart of a modern industrial state, without the language, skills and understandings needed to make an easy adjustment to American life.

For young Arnold Weiss and his mother, the early years were especially hard:

"I went to relatives downtown. I did not stay there too long, because I had grandparents out in Lowell, Massachusetts, and they took me out there for the summer.

"My mother came to her sister, who had six children. So this aunt of mine made my mother a maid. With six small children, she always needed help cooking and cleaning. Where she lived, there was a movie across the street. On Saturday, my mother would take these small kids into the movies. And one used to run in one direction and one ran in the other direction, and the poor woman went crazy. She couldn't even converse with anybody; she was here a very short time. She didn't know the language; the majority of the people she met spoke only English.

"So one day she saw that she was in trouble. She came here—but she was worse off than in Europe. The only good thing was that I was by my grandfather. But they weren't going to keep me long, either, because a boy twelve years old you have to clothe, you have to feed.

"So she complained to her brother—she had a brother and a sister here. She told her brother, 'You know, I didn't make my life much better here than I did in Europe. At least in Europe, if I would have worked as a nursemaid, I could have stayed there.'

"He said, 'So what do you want to do? You're still a young woman.' She was thirty-eight years old.

" 'Well, I can't bring my husband back, and I have a child and I have to make a home for him. If I would meet somebody nice . . .'

"Finally her brother happened to get hold of a religious man like she wanted. He was about seventeen years older than Mama. And she went from a boiling pot of water into a boiling pot of oil. He still had his children with him, and she had me, and all in three rooms with two boarders besides. This was in New York on the Lower East Side on Cherry Street. This went on, and the poor woman finally had a child with him a year later, because she was still a young woman. And then she was really tied.

"Now the time came when I became thirteen. This man said, 'I don't want to support your son. It's time for him to go out and do something on his own.'

"She said, 'But you promised me, when I married you, you'd take care of my child. You're going back on your word!'

"He said, 'Well, how long do you think I can support him!'

"Well, to make a long story short, I came back one day—they were having a fight in the house—and I stood outside and heard what was going on. I waited until everything subsided, got quiet. I went in the house. I just let it go until finally I found an opportunity to talk with my mother. I told her, 'Look, Mama, I do not want you to fight with him. If he wants me to go out and support myself, I'll go out. I will finish school at night.'

"So I went out peddling with shoelaces, with cottons and with handkerchiefs. On weekends I traveled the trains selling the weekend newspapers and in such a way I got my support. It started with three dollars a week and went up to seven dollars a week. In the meantime, this little boy that my mother had grew up and we became very close."

Arnold Weiss survived those difficult early years, and well. He went into the garment industry and became active in the International Ladies Garment Workers Union. Later he became an independent businessman, working side by side with his wife in a silver and giftware shop. In many ways, his story is the story of so many other bright, strong, courageous young people of his generation. Thrown on their own in a totally alien land and culture, they survived and prospered. Some such "Ellis Island graduates" are:

- David Dubinsky, who was imprisoned in Siberia for union activity but escaped to come to America in 1911, later becoming President of Arnold Weiss' union, the International Ladies Garment Workers Union.
- Father Edward Flanagan, who arrived from Ireland in 1904, studied for the priesthood in Maryland, and made his way to Omaha, Nebraska, where he founded Boys' Town.
- Ben Shahn, son of a Jewish woodcarver, who arrived from Lithuania in 1906 and first achieved fame as an artist for his drawings of two other immigrants, Sacco and Vanzetti.
- Philip Murray, one of eleven children in a family that emigrated from Scotland in 1902, who became President of the United Steelworkers and of the Congress of Industrial Organizations.
- Spyros Skouras, who arrived from Greece in 1910 and, with his brothers, built the first movie theater in St. Louis, and who later headed 20th Century–Fox.

- Louis Adamic, outstanding author and chronicler of the immigrant experience, who arrived from what is now Yugoslavia in 1913.
- Elia Kazan, Greek writer and director, whose film *America, America* movingly depicted the immigrant experience, who arrived from Turkey in 1913.

And so many, many more. In a nation of immigrants, the list of those who came through Ellis Island in the early years of this century and lived to prosper and make vital contributions to their adopted country is virtually endless. The young immigrants of Arnold Weiss' generation became part of American life, their lives and futures inextricably intertwined with all those who were here before then—and all who were to follow.

They weren't all thrown on their own almost immediately, as was Arnold Weiss. But other kinds of adjustments still had to be made. Helen Barth remembers New York in the early part of the century; the many ethnic communities of the East Side, the poverty, a multitude of languages—and how the immigrants began to move into the mainstream of American life:

"New York was divided into little sections. The Chinese lived in one section, the Germans, the Hungarians, the Poles lived in other sections; and the immigrant was able to walk up and down and recognize his landsmen and speak his own language—you know—Polish, Russian, also Yiddish carried them through very much here.

"I know that my father tells a story about our family. They came through Castle Gardens and lived at Baxter Street and that was Italian at the time. My grandmother never spoke a word of English, and didn't speak Russian either, only Yiddish; she went out looking around and got lost. She was sitting on the edge of the curb, crying, she didn't know where she was, and a man came over to her and said to her in Yiddish, 'Are you lost?'

"She said, 'You speak Yiddish?' She was all mixed up.

"He said, 'What are you living here for? Why don't you live with your own people?'

" 'We have Jews here?'

" 'Sure, you have Jews here,' he said. 'Come with me.' He took her home and told her family that there were real Jews living here and that she should come there immediately to live with those people. They felt

This boarding house in Homestead, Pennsylvania, in 1909, catered primarily to Russian immigrants. As one person put it, "Coming to Pennsylvania was like coming to my village!"

very much at home among their own, you know, that they could converse with one another.

"None of our immigrants spoke English. But we had schools right away on the East Side. We had the Henry Street Settlement where we took care of our pregnant women, we had the Lillian Wald group, you know, who took up with these. Lots of doctors contributed their help. They were a real sorry lot, but I must say that within the shortest time our immigrants became self-sufficient. The mother was a hardworking woman, scrubbing and cleaning for those children, and when they were allowed to go to school, it was just the most beautiful thing you ever saw. How they appreciated this free schooling and free tutoring!

"I remember when we had the first birth control. Margaret Sanger was arrested time and time again, because she taught these poor immigrants how to keep from having more children. They were so poor and they didn't have enough to eat. I remember going into their homes on Friday, when they are supposed to make Friday night dinner—they had empty pots with just water cooking, to show their neighbors that they too have some food to give the children. That's how poor, how very poor they were.

"Of course, our styles and everything, everything was seasonal. Their work was seasonal. If they went into the shops to work it was seasonal, a little period of time. You would see them walking on the streets with great big bags over their backs, and they would bring work home for the wife and the children to help pulling threads.

"Even my own family, they were very, very poor. They would go down Friday and pluck chickens, just to make maybe a chicken for the holiday, and on Friday night anyone who happened to be in shule— that's our synagogue—would be invited home. Grandmother always had four or five very poor men my father would bring home from the synagogue to have dinner with us. First they would have to wash their hands, because we couldn't let them sit down with dirty hands and faces and unkempt beards . . ."

Not just in New York and Chicago, but also in Poznan, Wisconsin, and Cedar Rapids, Iowa—wherever the newcomers settled— they tended to stay together, supporting each other with their common language and culture from the old country. But still the new world took some getting used to. Charles Bartunek, arriving in 1914, eleven years after the Wright brothers' flight at Kitty Hawk, found farm machinery as strange and amazing as an airplane:

"Crossing the country, every piece of machinery I seen in the field, I thought I seen a lot of airplanes. The farmer had a piece of machinery in the field and it had paddles on it and I thought, 'There's an airplane.' I had never seen an airplane at that time, you know. In fact, it was quite a while before we seen airplanes in this country, until after the war.

"My brother had settled in Cedar Rapids, and that's where we all ended up and made it our home. He had friends over here that wrote and invited him over and that's how he happened to go there. That's the way it usually comes about.

"At that time, Cedar Rapids was only about 45,000 population, and they claim that 25,000 was Czechs. Of course, it still is overwhelmingly Czech population, but in years it changes a little. Czech is still spoken on the streets around here, and people coming here talk Czech to me. There are a lot of Czechs now that don't even know they are Czechs— they don't speak or understand it. I can read it and write it perfectly, from what I learned in the old country. I always had good grades there, the best that anybody could get.

"They enrolled me in a Catholic School here, and I went there about two months. But I sat there like a bump on a log and couldn't understand what went around. So I decided to work. I was fourteen years old.

"It was awful tough. If I had had a dad who could set me up in business with a couple of thousand dollars those days, I would be worth some money. But no such luck. Every penny that we got, we got the hard way.

"Over here, I had a fight about every day. They called me 'greenhorn.' That was common in those days. But I had fights with kids over there, too. Kids are kids."

After working at several different jobs, learning various skills in the early years, Charles eventually opened his own appliance business. As he put it:

"I haven't had any schooling in this country. But I am making out my own income taxes and everything else, and run a business and everything, so I am not such a big dumbbell!"

Many people had great difficulty learning English. Charles Bartunek puts the problem well:

"Well, when a person gets to be even eighteen or twenty or a little bit better than that, it is pretty hard for the tongue to twist, to pronounce some of the words. An older person never will get it. They may learn to speak and all that, but they speak it with a brogue, and you can always tell it."

At twenty-eight, fellow Czechoslovakian Vera Gauditsa might have had a hard time learning English under the best of circumstances, but arriving eight months pregnant, she was almost immediately stuck at home with a young child, with her husband often at work for twelve or fourteen hours a day. No wonder the language gave her such difficulty in those early years, but there were compensations, as Vera describes:

"If I knew the language, everything would have been perfect. This country always had an awful lot of materials. The other countries didn't have as much, and in Czechoslovakia in 1928, you hardly even saw automobiles. We had a farm, we had horses, and the horses had to work so hard. I came to this country and saw trucks. I loved them—replacing the horses!

"When I came to this country and I came to a pushcart on First Avenue, and I saw all those fruits and vegetables in February, that gave me such a lift. That I liked.

"Oh, I loved two things—the vegetables on the pushcarts and all kinds of materials, and the trucks. They gave me such pleasure.

"But the language took me a long time to learn. I had no chance until the children went to school, and then I went to work in 1934—you have to work whether you like it or not. Then I wanted to become a citizen right away and I got the papers in 1935. That was harder! The language is very, very tough. And in the city you walk between the people like you walk in the woods."

But with her characteristic ingenuity, Vera surmounted the language barrier by speaking Polish with the owner of the neighborhood meat market. That man, a Ukrainian for whom Polish was also a second language, turned out to be Mary Zuk's husband.

Once out into the working world, Vera picked up English quickly, first as part of the night cleaning crew at Rockefeller Center, and then, after her children were older, in the garment industry. Like Arnold Weiss, Vera was active in David Dubinsky's International Ladies Garment Workers Union, until her retirement a few years ago.

For Fannie Kligerman and the seven families she traveled with, America was a dream come true—but not completely. Czechoslovakian or Jewish, Cedar Rapids or New York, newcomers had to put up with being taunted as "greenhorns," until they had moved into the mainstream. Fannie's family had arrived in New York with money to spare, but they had other problems. For one thing, it was hard to find a place to live for ten people. Fannie describes her feelings on arriving in America in 1905:

"By May, we found three rooms. You can imagine the ten of us there. We couldn't fit anyplace because we had too many chldren. People wouldn't let us in. My father said, 'All right, we'll get in—no matter where. If it's only one room, we'll get in. And when we are in, we can look for other rooms.' But wherever we went, they wouldn't let us in, so we suffered. We laid on the floor, and then the furniture came, so we laid all over the furniture.

"We lived on the Lower East Side, way down. There was a saloon downstairs. My father was very much against it—he said he felt guilty. He said, 'I left Europe and I was a man. And here I am a what?'

"And you know—maybe I shouldn't say it—the bathrooms were in the yard. You heard of it? And we had such small children, two and four and six. My mother kept the place very clean and she washed the hall every day, but every time something happened, they said, 'Oh, those greenhorns did it . . .'

"Did you ever see two houses connected by one fire escape? Anyway, we looked out this window and I heard a woman cursing, 'Those greenies, they have to be shot and they have to be killed. Why did we let them into America?' and all things like that.

"Well, I didn't know why she was shouting and my mother looked out of the window and said, 'What's the matter?'

"The woman said, 'Did you have to move in with that cat?'

"Momma looked at her and asked, 'What do you mean, a cat?'

" 'It ate up my liver. I had my liver on the fire escape, and the cat ate it up.' So she was cursing. And then she felt so ashamed. She looked in and said she was sorry. We were all sitting on the luggage, because we had nowhere to pack it in. She came in and apologized. Then she said, 'Sorry, maybe your girl wants to go to work.'

"My mother said, 'She can't work. She is only thirteen.'

"The woman said, 'Nobody will ever know. I bring in the collars, from my son's factory. She'll turn them over and she'll get two dollars a week.'

"So I turned over and matched collars. When I came home on Friday with the two dollars, I thought I was the richest one!

"My father came with a big long beard and that was the trouble he had. They were chasing him, they were throwing stones. And he had a cane all his life, so he took the cane and he hit everyone. A traffic cop came and if the traffic cop hadn't come, they would have killed him. He got right on a trolley car, and went along.

"Then my father met a landsman that he went to school with, and he told us, 'He's a landlord now, and he's got an apartment. He let me in.' Oh, were we happy! Oh, we felt rich! We only had one bedroom, but we had a living room and a dining room.

"So we had struggled—it was very, very hard. But we like it, and we made it all right."

Fannie's younger brother turned to earning money, too:

"My younger brother, the little one, ten years old, but he was always doing business. Ten years old, and he said, 'Suppose I buy candy, and I'll go to the shop where they work and I'll sell.'

"And he did. He is a millionaire today. He's in Florida and he's a millionaire. But he was always business, business, business. So one day he came and said, 'I made a fourteen-cent profit.' And that fourteen cents was so good; you could get a lot of food for fourteen cents. I know my mother for one dollar bought the whole shebang for Saturday, chicken and everything."

So Fannie and her family survived—and then some. All of the seven families who had traveled out of Russia together stayed close and eventually settled in the same upstate New York town in America.

I'VE BEEN WORKING ON THE RAILROAD

Everybody worked. They worked on the railroads, ran the factories and farms, built bridges and dams, laid down roads, expanded the cities—did all the kinds of work needed to make America grow. And it was hard, very hard in those early years; work was long, difficult and dangerous, and wages were low. But it was still better than in the old country—whatever the drawbacks, in America there was a chance to change, to get ahead.

Eleven-year-old Bessie Spylios, bright, optimistic, industrious, went to work in a Massachusetts cotton mill. Full of life and pride —and without a particle of self-pity then or sixty-nine years later— Bessie tells her story:

"I came here and I went to work. I was eleven years old.

"We had to take the ferry to get off Ellis Island. It was beautiful. The lights, you know. Wondering what the heck are all these lights! And then we went to the station for the train to Fitchburg, near Boston.

"My father had some food with him. But they didn't give you anything. The tickets were in front of you and the directions where to go. From the train, you could look out at the town or the city.

"When we got to Fitchburg, they came over to tell us that we would have to get out. Then my father led the way from the station to the apartment, which wasn't too far. It was nice. A four-room apartment and a kitchen and a dining room, for $10 a month—which was a lot of money. Well, we had a good time.

"It was a Greek neighborhood. There were a lot of Greek people. And in Fitchburg, to this day yet, every nationality has their own street where they stay. We were on West Street where we stayed then, and the Jewish people were on the other side. The Italian people were on Warren Street. Everyone had his church there.

"We had a Greek church and a Greek school. Greek everything.

Everything was right there. A store—we didn't have to worry about how we would buy anything because everything was Greek there. But I was determined that I would learn the language. I didn't go to school. Both my brothers went to school and my youngest sister, she was five years old, she went to school.

"*But myself and my other sister, we didn't go to school, because we had to go to work in the cotton mills there. Six in the morning until six at night. The snow was up to my shoulders sometimes. They used to have a lot of snow. A long walk, too. A half hour walk from my house to go to work. Day and night. And we had no rubbers like they have now, no boots, nothing. Just shoes.*"

Whatever the hardship, Bessie worked to real purpose:

"*My mother and baby sister and my brother came the following year after I came. Like I said, we went to work and saved money; then we sent money and the other three came. We were three boys and two girls. And then everybody came and that's all.*"
◄§ "Did you go to meet them at Ellis Island?"
"*Oh, no, no. We couldn't afford to do that . . .*"

She kept right on working, save for some time off to have a family:

◄§ "How long did you live in Fitchburg?"
"*Well, I came in 1909 and we moved out of there in 1927.*"
◄§ "And you worked in the mill all that time?"
"*After I was grown up I got married, and my husband worked there in the same mill I worked in. We were from the same neighborhood in Greece. We both worked together, and we got married and had one child, my son . . .*

"*My husband opened a hat cleaning store. I didn't work again until 1938, when my husband died, and my son and I opened a candy store, Bessie's. We used to make all our candy, homemade ice cream and homemade candy. And we kept and we just sold the place two months ago. It would have been forty years last week in the store. My son wasn't well, and had to give up the business, or else I would be working yet. I hate to stay home doing nothing. I like to work; that is all I have ever done. I like to work. That's all, I guess . . .*"

Young people on their own—without the language, money, skills or resources—had an especially tough time making their way in the new land, in those early years. Some would gladly have returned, but for the war. Theodore Lubik describes the loneliness he felt

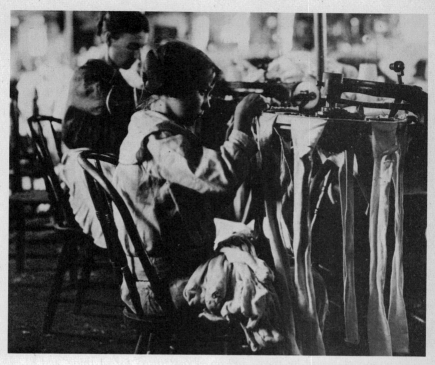

ABOVE
This eleven-year-old girl is working
in a Massachusetts clothing factory,
much as Bessie Spylios did before
child labor laws prohibited this
kind of exploitation of young
children for profit.

RIGHT
Some immigrants, like Theodore Lubik,
stayed in the coal mines only
until they were able to move on
to other work. Others, like this
Slavic coal miner near Pittsburgh,
spent their lives,
in the dark of the mines.

when he arrived in 1913 and followed his Ukrainian countrymen to the Pennsylvania coal fields:

"I came without friends. I came through Ellis Island alone. I went to Pennsylvania alone. But somehow it's all right. The first thing I learned was how to drink beer!

"But if the war didn't break out in 1914, I would have zipped right back where I came from after a year or two! Oh, sure. Positively. I was like a slave here; twelve, thirteen hours a day in the mines.

"Well, that's all right. Maybe not being in the war saved my life. I didn't have to go in the army. I guess in a way it was good. But the first year I was here working in the mines, I got blood poisoning. I had no money and no place to go, with a hand swollen like that. So my brother and cousin found me a place to live and left me there . . ."

That was the year he went back to New York, and found his job at Ellis Island. But he lost that job when the United States entered World War I, because he was a citizen of Austro-Hungary:

"When the war broke out, we had to get out—anybody who was German or Austrian. Then it was bad for me. I had nothing to do with Austria and nothing to do with Germany, but I lost the job because I came from an Austrian area. Then I looked for work in Massachusetts, Florida, and back in New York, but I got nothing. So it was again to the coal mines. I worked there, I think, a year. I couldn't get out. I had no money to pay for travel, and no money to pay for anything, and I was hooked up. Finally, my friend who was there said, 'If you want to go, take my pay advance for two weeks from now.' I signed for the money, he paid me, I beat it, and paid him back the money later. That's the way it was with me and everybody else. It was a tough life.

"One cousin of mine stayed in the mines. He had an accident in the mine—some capsules exploded in his hand and blinded him. That was a bad accident. Later he had the black lung disease. He needed this country like I need a hole in the head. His father was the biggest farmer in the whole town, with three, four, five horses, cows, and people working for him. Here he came to a coal mine!

"Carter talks about miners' injunctions and Taft-Hartley. He should go to work there a couple of weeks, or his son.

"Somehow I got hooked up with a job in New York when I got back . . ."

In those same Pennsylvania coal fields, Scottish-born Philip Murray was working as President of the United Mine Workers' local, trying to better the conditions Theodore saw there. Theodore

never went back to the mines, but worked in the restaurant industry in New York until the 1930s, when he bought a farm in upstate
New York. He and his wife, Nina, made a success of farming; after
her death he sold the farm and retired to Florida, where he remarried years later.

Like Theodore, Steve Pakan found some kinds of work unac-
ceptable, maybe even worse than what he had left behind. Steve
went to stay in Little Falls, New York, with his sister and her husband, but soon moved on:

*"He was terribly tight. He even told me not to use too much toilet
paper because it cost too much. He was an awful, awful tight guy. Of
course, my sister had good meals, but I didn't stay there too long.*

*"He helped me get a job. He had a job himself which I wouldn't
do, as much as I needed the work. It was so dusty, picking, or what
they call carding, the cotton and wool together. They tear it all to
pieces, and it is so dusty you can hardly tell a man ten feet away from
you. Finally he got sick. He had to quit the job.*

*"But after I worked a year and a half in Little Falls, I said, 'Gosh,
I'm never gonna see America here. I read so much about the Golden
West. I'm going west. I got one sister in Chicago. I'm going there.'"*

He did go west to Chicago, and later to many other places as
well. Steve taught himself to play the trombone, which his father
would not have allowed since "music was only for gypsies," and
became trombonist in a United States Army band. Later he was
for many years a master machinist, then a farmer, developing along
lines that had been closed to him in Europe.

Michael Pappas, also alone and without skills, followed his godfather to Utah and California, working at any kind of job he could
find—dishwasher, ship builder, railroad car builder, oysterman and
cook. Out around the country he worked with:

*"Hungarians, Austrians, Albanians, Turks, people from all countries,
you know. In those days the doors were open free for the States.
You could come to the States any time you wanted, as long as you had
a ticket and were in good health. Today you have to go through examinations. Then they were coming in from all over the countries."*

After four years, he returned East to join his brother, eventually
developing a successful restaurant business with a farm on the side.

Like so many "greenhorns," he helped to build America and lived to prosper with it.

People who had skills had a much easier time moving into the mainstream of a growing, developing United States.

Irene Meladaki Zambelli used her dressmaking skills in those early years, before she turned them to making needle and fabric works of art. Adele Sinko also had dressmaking skills, and they got her a very good job in her new home, so she no longer had to fear starvation:

"Oh, boy, was I lucky to get over here! I love it!"

⚞ "What did you expect the United States would be like?"

"Oh, I just figured I would get a lot to eat. That was what was on my mind. Because my brother wrote a lot about how much he liked it and even about the big beds, double beds, and all that stuff. So when I got off the boat, there was a vegetable store—and I'll never forget it. You know how nice they make them in New York, filled with oranges and this and that.

"And at that time things were very cheap. I had ten cents and I could buy something with it. Even five cents. While I was over there on the other side, you see, a lot of people lost their money because the government changed the money. I had an aunt who was quite well-to-do, but she lost everything because they changed the money. So for one or two shillings, you couldn't buy anything. But here you could with change. For a nickel. For a dime. This was something. It was beautiful here.

"I will never forget that vegetable stand, because we didn't know what oranges were, you see. I remember once when I was eighteen years old, I went to a store and saw oranges, and I bought one. I brought it home, and we divided that orange so that each one had a section . . .

"I stayed with my brother until I got a job, which wasn't hard at all. I got into a very fancy establishment. I was so surprised.

"As a dressmaker, not in a factory. In a place where they worked for private customers. Only one model, you know. You make the model and then the customer comes and looks at the model. If they like it, they want the same dress and the model gets destroyed because they were very expensive. You wouldn't want somebody else marching around with the same dress. I got in there, and I stayed there until 1932."

Education was often the key to finding decently paid, satisfying work. Sarah Asher and her brother enrolled in night school to learn

English, and were able to move smoothly into white-collar jobs in business. Irma Busch, who already knew English and had good secretarial skills as well, moved directly into well-paid, multilingual office work in New York City. Ida Mouradjian, with her teaching experience and language facility, became a French teacher.

Stanley Roszak, who had left German-held Poland to avoid the war, describes the route many people followed. Of course, for Stanley there was one hitch—during the war he was considered an enemy alien—but it turned out better than he could have hoped:

"I got my first job in Wieboldt's wrapping packages. I went to the YMCA on Division Street—they used to have a school there to teach English to Polish people. I went there so in two or three months I would know enough English to get around and get a certificate of high school graduation. I had all the education in Poland, but here it wasn't accepted . . .

"I wanted to study chemistry, but chemistry was a hard thing to do, so I settled on pharmacy. Already in Europe, in Poznan, I was an apprentice in a drug store for about two years. I used to go also to evening school to make up high school credits. After about a year and a half, I had enough knowledge so I went down to the State Board of Education, took my exam, and got my credit for high school.

"Then I went to the engineering school, to Armour Institute, that's now ITT. I started to take engineering while working and going to school evenings. I worked in the drug store still and I used to work in a bakery Friday and Saturday, putting icing on the cakes. I did everything that came along, because I had to make my money for tuition. There was no scholarship—you had to put your money down.

"Later I got a job in the preparatory school where I took classes to get my high school certificate. The professor asked me to take over the classes in German, so I was teaching German for about three years.

"But the trouble is, when I enrolled at Armour Institute, I paid the tuition, bought the books and everything—and the war broke out. So the dean called me and about twelve other fellows into the office. The government made every university campus a military camp—and because I was born in Germany, they classified me as German. I was an alien enemy so they told me to get out of school because the law was that you couldn't go within five miles of an army post.

"So that year I just happened to get work as a chemist. In the evening I was teaching myself a little Spanish. I had a job at a grocery store and a nice lady used to come there, Mrs. Garcia, and we talked a little Spanish. So she asked me what I was doing and I told her my trouble, that I couldn't go to school and I wanted to be a chemist. And she said, 'Oh, my husband is a chemist.' She gave me the address to go over.

"So I went over to this big manufacturing company and got a job there in a laboratory during the war. When the war was over I went back to the Armour Institute and studied chemical engineering, because I liked chemistry and I thought chemical engineering was the more practical aspect of it."

Once people learned the language, a little education and enterprise went a long way. Leon Solomon's father came to America with no marketable skills, and spent his early years here as a peddler in Bethlehem, Pennsylvania, as Leon describes:

"My father began as a peddler. He bought a horse and wagon and went among the farmers to buy up discarded rags, bones of cattle that had been slaughtered and consumed, discarded junk, and then sold what he had bought and accumulated to wholesalers. That was his first occupation.

"He sold to different specialists, like those who specialized in junk, the junk dealers, who in turn sold junk to factories, where the metals were melted down. Those who bought up rags, sold them to paper mills where the rags were transformed into pulp. Those who bought bones sold them to soap manufacturers, and so this was the first stage of my father's career as a bread earner in the United States.

"For a while my mother, too, went peddling. She went to a storekeeper who sold dry goods to peddlers, gave them credit, then as a peddler, she went out among the farmers and tried to dispose of the merchandise, sometimes for cash, frequently on credit. And so my father and mother worked very hard to accumulate a little bit to enable them to support the family."

But the family worked hard and grew more prosperous, and provided a good education for their children. Starting with that education, Leon Solomon became an internationally respected and beloved conservative rabbi, scholar and teacher.

Of course, in America, there were many ways to fame and fortune. In 1913, the year Stanley Roszak arrived in America, Norwegian-born Knute Rockne, then a junior at Notre Dame, was introducing the devastating forward pass to football. He went on to become head football coach at Notre Dame, the greatest football coach of his time.

In that same year, a young Italian immigrant named Rudolph Valentino arrived and started his show business career with a bit part as a dancer. Only eight years later, he was the leading screen idol of the silent era, starring in such films as *The Four Horsemen of the Apocalypse, The Sheik* and *Blood and Sand.*

And only the year before, Russian-born David Sarnoff, working for the Marconi Wireless Company, had first come to public attention for his reporting of the sinking of the *Titanic.* He later became a major figure in the broadcasting industry and president of the Radio Corporation of America.

Igor Sikorsky, developer of the helicopter; André Kostelanetz, orchestra conductor; Louise Nevelson, sculptor; Sol Hurok, impresario; Isaac Asimov, writer; William S. Knudsen, who became president of General Motors; Saint Frances Xavier Cabrini, known as Mother Cabrini, canonized for her work among poor Italian immigrants in America—these and hundreds of other major figures, whose lives and work have become interwoven with the story of modern America, were actually born elsewhere and immigrated late in the last century and in the early years of this century. Not all came through Ellis Island, not all through the port of New York, but all were part of the Great Migration that did so much to shape the America we know today.

ORPHANS OF THE STORM

Success meant far more than work and material rewards, however. It meant love, home and family as well, often with someone from the old country.

Some young men, of course, married "picture brides" they had never met, but more often they married women they met here in America. Certainly after the war a great many young women came to America looking for husbands, from a Europe shorn by war and emigration of many of its finest young men.

They found each other through their social organizations, their churches, their network of friends and relatives that stretched across the continent and often back to the old country. So Theodore Lubik married his childhood sweetheart, the girl he met once more on her way through Ellis Island; Fannie Kligerman married the "boy next door" from "the next town over" in Russia; Frank Santoni married a girl from his native Sicily; and Celia Rypinski married a boy from the old country that she met at a Polish picnic in Chicago.

Mary Zuk never knew her husband in the old country, but he came from the "big town" near her farm and they had mutual friends. She describes how people got together:

> "I met my husband in New York. Everybody goes to church, you meet people, you know. After you come out of the church outside, you talk—this one comes from here, that one comes from there, and that's the way it goes. And then one tells the other one, and this one tells another one, Mary Zuk is here, and then they all come and visit. Even if you don't know them, maybe they know your sister or brother. Well, that's it. All of us got together at somebody's house, the boys and girls, and we were happy."

Sometimes the marriages verged on the "arranged marriages" of the old country, but for young, lonely Michael Pappas, that was just fine. When asked if there were very few women in Wyoming and Utah where he had worked, Michael explained how it was: "There was women, but not Greek girls." He describes how he came to marry in America:

> "I knew my wife, Melina, from the other side. We were brought up together in the same village. Her family came to New Brunswick, New Jersey, and, through some friends of mine, I found out that they had arrived. Chester, where I was, was not far from New Brunswick, about 100 miles, I think it is. My friends and I was always talking that some day we would go and visit them. One day we went to New Brunswick and we met Melina and all that—so we knew each other—and I went back to Chester.
>
> "I moved to New York. I was an oysterman in a club there. Through another friend of mine I found out that her family had moved into New York. This friend had told them, 'I work with somebody named Michael Pappas.'
>
> "They said, 'We know the guy. Tell him to come and meet us.' So I got the address and I went up for a visit. They said, 'Michael, we have a room here. Will you come and live with us?'
>
> "So that was what I wanted, because you know, a bachelor all these

years, I liked to go with a family, with a mother, a father and a brother. I was about twenty by then—I had been four years in Utah.

"Then they decided to move to Trenton, because they had a married daughter there. I had a good job and I wanted to stay, but finally they convinced me to go with them. So I got work there and I stayed with them six or seven months.

"Sometimes my future mother-in-law told my cousin that they were thinking to fix up me and my future wife, so my cousin told me, 'You know, they are thinking to tell you to get married with Melina.'

" 'Well,' I said, 'okay.' Anyway, we got married, we lived fifty-nine years together, and had a family of six children; four girls, two boys. They are all married. They all have families. They get along nice."

Michael and Melina lived what was clearly a full and happy life together for all those years until her death in 1968.

And once in America, Ida Mouradjian's luck changed:

"When I left Ellis Island it was one happy day.

"I was put on a train to go to Rochester, New York, which I had made my destination because I had friends who had previously come and settled in Rochester. And I went there.

"After a while, my future husband—who was a childhood friend, whose sister was my classmate at boarding school and my best friend, whose family had been completely wiped out—he had heard that I was in Rochester.

"He lived in Chicago, worked and lived in Chicago. He, I guess, wanted to see the nearest thing, the person who had been nearest to his family, and he came to visit me.

"He said, 'Won't you come to Chicago, with me, where you have many other friends and countrymen?' And I consented.

"Well, should I use a cliché and say that we were two orphans of the storm . . ."

VIII

REFLECTIONS ON THE OLD WORLD AND THE NEW

❧ "How has being an immigrant affected your life?

"I don't think I felt like an immigrant. After I was here for a few years, I lived amongst American people and I was like one of them. I liked everything; I mean I was just integrated very quickly, and I never felt much like an immigrant.

"I will say that I still don't feel like one. I think in only one thing I would feel I am. I am more 100 percent American than some of the born Americans. I resent some losses of freedom more quickly. I mean I want to be proud of my country, I think more than a born American does. That way I feel that I am an immigrant. Otherwise I have never felt like one."

RACHEL GOLDMAN
Jewish, from Russia
Arrived 1916

THE PEOPLE in this book have taken a very long look back, across the whole span of their lives. Back across our whole century and beyond; back across the sea and another continent to a world that has long since ceased to exist.

They remember why they came and have a very good idea as to what their lives might have been had they stayed in or gone back to Europe. And they know what they were seeking, what they found, and what kinds of lives they have created in America.

Anyone talking to them sees clearly that the overwhelming majority are glad they came and stayed, partly because of the lives they have lived here and at least equally because of the lives they otherwise would have had to endure in the old country.

To a large extent, it's as simple as this: These are people who left places that in their lifetimes went through two world wars on their own soil, revolutions, civil wars, starvation and multiple dictatorships, to come to a place that has experienced none of those things in the last hundred years.

When you leave a land that has no peace, nor freedom, nor bread, nor hope for the future, and go to a land that has all those things for you, it is merely sane to be glad that you came and stayed. Against that, the shortcomings of the new land seem relatively insignificant. Whatever America's flaws, and they were often very clearly perceived by these people, to them America was and still is the land of the free and a land of peace and plenty.

WHAT WOULD HAVE HAPPENED?

One of the most familiar and pleasant kinds of recollections most of us carry away from our childhoods is a variation of the "what if" game. It was an after-dinner family staple, something for long winter nights, and some of our parents and grandparents never seemed to tire of it.

It usually started something like, "You know, if your grandfather and your grandmother hadn't met that day back in 1899 at the Kansas State Fair, you wouldn't be here today . . ."

The "what if" game took everyone back to a rich store of recollections, often to a thoroughly satisfying vision of other times and alternate lifelines. For those whose families had fairly recently come across the seas to America, it had and still has a very special kind of magic, embracing whole other cultures and long lost worlds.

So it is with the people in this book. Theodore Lubik knows that he would probably have been in the Austrian army during World War I. Michael Pappas was headed for the Turkish army before he escaped. Stanley Roszak might have been in the German army. Given their ages, places and times, Theodore and Stanley might easily have found themselves fighting at Tannenberg, the first great Eastern Front battle of World War I. And there, but for the migration to America, they might easily have faced Martha Konwicki's father and some of Sophia Belkowski's brothers, drafted into the Czar's army.

Martha's father escaped and most of Sophia's family came to America—but not all. Two of Sophia's brothers stayed in Poland, then Russia, as did some others of her family. Sophia remembers how it worked out for them:

"In Poland, I left my oldest brother, Casimir, and my youngest brother, Anthony.

"Anthony came here in about 1930. Somehow he came to Canada. From Canada he traveled here. But he left a wife in Europe and he didn't have any papers, so he went back to Europe in 1932."

"What happened to the brother that was in Poland?"

"He died. He died in a concentration camp, I think in 1940."

Her brother Anthony stayed in Poland, and Sophia brought his two sons to America in the 1960s. It's possible that she sometimes thinks about Anthony staying in the United States, and bringing his wife over if he had had "papers"; perhaps she wonders whether Casimir might have joined them all and escaped that concentration camp.

Rachel Goldman doesn't wonder at all. Her family had sent her to America to be sure one child was safe. Here is how it worked out for her in America and for her family, especially her sister, who stayed in Bialystock:

"My parents did not want to come over and settle someplace else. My oldest sister, after she was married, was thinking of coming here. She was the only one left at home, as my youngest sister had gone to Israel—Palestine at that time.

"My mother was sort of reluctant to see my oldest sister go, having no one around. But later times she regretted very much that she didn't let her go, because she had a visa to come to this country but couldn't get out. At that time she was a nurse and worked in a Russian military hospital. And when the Russians left during the war they didn't take her along; they left her in the ghetto for the Germans. You know what happened. It was the finish; so that's how it was.

"My sister from Israel came here after a while, so I have my one sister here in this country . . .

"It is in my nature to try and remember all the good things and to forget the unpleasant ones. But I would like to tell you the most unhappy episode of my life.

"It was when I tried to arrange for my sister, who was a trained nurse and lived in Bialystock, Poland, to immigrate here with her husband and young child. The time was about 1938. My husband and I worked on it for over a year.

"So many obstacles were put in our way. We consulted with the Hebrew Immigrant Aid Society, also with a private agency. We tried everything. We made out forms and forms. Every time we were told something new was required by the government. We were told that we did not have enough money to show to bring over three people. My husband and I both worked and had steady jobs. In conclusion, we put up a bond with Thomas Cooke and Company of Fifth Avenue, New York.

"We were permitted to bring over only one person. I wanted my sister to come first. They said only the men could come, although it would have been easier for my sister to get adjusted here and bring him over.

"*My brother-in-law arrived in 1939 and my sister and her child perished in Bialystock during the holocaust.*"

Roman Umecka had little doubt as to what his fate would have been had he stayed in Poland. During World War I, Roman and his brother were in an area occupied by Germany, so they were not drafted. However, they were active in the Polish underground, and when the war ended, they both participated in disarming the German forces then on Polish soil. He came to America in 1922, while his brother stayed in Poland.

Roman remembers the German soldiers saying in 1918, "We're going to be back here in twenty years." And back they came:

"*Then in the second war the Germans came. They killed my brother. They killed him because they had his name on a list, from when he took the arms away from the German soldiers in the first war. They had his name on the list and they had my name on the list. They were looking for me, too.*"

⋖§ "All the way back from World War I they remembered?"

"*Yes. They had a sheet with them. At that time they said they would come back in twenty years. They knew my name, my brother's, and many, many others. Those same guys came back in the second war over there, and right away they shot many, like my brother—and they were looking for me, too, but I was already in America . . .*"

THEY COULD NEVER HAVE SENT ME BACK

The old country had an enormous pull for many of those who came to America. There were families, the friends of childhood, first loves; homes, sounds, smells, tastes, belongings left behind; the unique sense and feel of the land itself.

Like Mary Zuk and Catherine Bolinski's father, many had planned to stay for a relatively short time; but the Great War changed all that. Still, many went back in the period before the war, or later between the two world wars. And shortly after World War II, people from the United States began to visit "the old country" in large and increasing numbers. Today, hundreds of thousands of Americans every year visit eastern and southern Europe, some to revisit the places of their youth, others to see the "other side," where their parents, grandparents or great-grandparents came from.

A few stay, at work or in retirement. For most, it's a visit, a reach
for youth and personal history. For Irma Busch, going back to
Germany in 1932, it started as a trip home to be married, but
became a journey to a home and culture that vanished before her
eyes:

"I went back to Germany because I was engaged to a boy whom I
had met here and we were going to get married. He went back to
Germany at the end of 1931. In 1932, I was to come over and get married. He had his mother, a widow; she lived in Berlin. And he had one
brother.

"In October 1932, I went over and burned my bridges behind me,
so to speak. Fortunately I took a re-entry permit along, just to be on the
safe side, but I gave away everything, my books, everything that I had—
and I had nice furniture—everything.

"They had taken an apartment in Berlin, in a beautiful section,
furnished and everything. We were going to get married, I met his family and all that, and then this Nazi business started.

"In fact they took me along to hear Hitler speak in a beer hall, the
second time in the sports palace, that big sports palace where he spoke.
The washerwoman had to go and reserve so many seats in the second
row for us a couple of hours in advance. And I tell you, as I sat there
and heard him speak, I started to regret coming to Berlin.

"Somebody said to me on the ship, 'What do you think of Hitler?'

"I said, 'Hitler? What do I know about Hitler? You mean that
Austrian paperhanger?' That's what I said. I was always outspoken—I
knew what I was talking about. So, okay, when you heard that man
speak, he just about hypnotized you. But, you see, with me, it was different than with the other Germans—it was different, because I had
lived here so long.

"And then, of course, it started in, you heard different things,
windows being smashed in because the owner of a store was a Jew. We
had a Jewish couple living in the building where we had this apartment.
I hadn't gotten married then, not yet. And this woman came to me one
day because she knew that I was from here and she cried so bitterly, she
was so afraid they would be arrested and all that. And for what? You
know, for what? All this bothered me terribly.

"One day I had been shopping and I came along the street. There
was a post office on the other side with an enormous swastika flag
hanging outside, and there were four or five people standing there with
their hands up, you know, 'Heil Hitler,' singing the Horst Wessel song.
When I saw that, I thought, 'What am I going to do now? If I go over
to the other side, they will see me and think I don't want to pass there.'
So I turned around and went a block down and went way, way around

to get back home. I never again walked past that post office, because if you didn't do that you would be arrested. If you weren't a Nazi, you know. You don't know how easily that could happen.

"Well, then I heard that my fiancé's brother belonged to the Nazi party. One Sunday we went to Friedrichstrasse, these beautiful cafés they have there, where you can sit in these very comfortable club chairs and have your fancy cake and coffee and your cordial and meals. They always had music—soft, nice music. And we were sitting there, talking amongst ourselves, my future mother-in-law, my fiancé, his brother and I.

"They said something about Hitler and I said, 'You know, I tell you something. If Hitler had ever traveled in other countries, especially if he would know America, then he would know he had better not start anything where America would go in and fight him.' Well, these two guys from the next table got up and came over. They were in civilian clothes, but look out! Oh my gosh! So, they wanted to know what this was. I mean, they had heard me, and who was I! So my fiancé got up, he said, 'Oh, she just came over from the other side. She's dumb. She don't know anything; that's why she talks that way.'

"I thought, 'Well, that's nice.' So his brother got up and showed that he belonged to the Nazi party. They were going to take me along, for sure, and I don't know if I ever would have gotten out—I might have ended up in one of these concentration camps. Well, anyway, knowing that he belonged to the party, and that I was just a dumb dodo, they left. Of course, we got up and went. Never again did they take me out.

"That day I made up my mind I was coming back here. I was not staying there, I just couldn't take it.

"I had made up my mind I was going back as quickly as possible. I had friends here. I didn't even have a ticket to go back, and I didn't have enough money to buy a ticket, because I had spent a lot of money while I stayed there. I stayed there from October until April 1933. The Reichstag fire was then and I was there at the time. Hitler was elected at the time I was still there, and then it came to a head. And all the Jews tried to get out.

"I had to go to the police station to get a permit to leave the country, little knowing that there was a permit for me in Hamburg, for me to get out. This friend of my uncle's had one in the American Consulate for me. Well, to be on the safe side I went to Berlin to police headquarters and here was this immense room full of people trying to get a permit. So I looked around and couldn't see that anybody was taken care of, and I wasn't going to stand around there. So I went out in the hall and marched along, looking at all the different doors, what it said on them, and I must have found the right kind of Nazi.

"*I knocked on the door—I knew he was a big shot, I could see by the sign. I knocked on the door and went in. At that time I was young and I was dressed very nicely, very just so. I explained that I was looking for a permit to leave, that I had a position here waiting for me, you know. I said friends of mine had sent me the money for the fare to come back by telegraph.*

"*This fellow said, 'Why do you want to go back?'*

"*I said, 'Well now, I lived there for a few years, I have a good position and I want to go back.'*

"*He said, 'If I give you a permit will you do something for us? Will you do something for Germany?' He put it 'for Germany.'*

"*So I said, 'Of course, for Germany, yes.' For the Nazis, no. He didn't ask me for the Nazis, I didn't say for the Nazis. For Germany, if I could put in a good word, I would. So I got my permit to leave.*

"*I got the train the next morning to go back to Hamburg, to get a ship. When I saw this friend of my uncle's in the consulate, he said, 'I have your permit for you. You can sail tomorrow.' So I said, 'I have a permit.'*

"*'How did you get it?' Because everybody was trying to get out, you know. All right, so I left.*

"*Then, on the ship, I had a good time. I said to myself, 'I will just have to forget it, that's all there is to it.'*

"*My fiancé even tried to pull me off the train, when I had to take the train from Berlin to Hamburg and oh, no. No, no, no, I was going back. I could not take this Hitler business, so I came back.*

"*I just couldn't help it. I could not stay in Germany under Hitler. If they had kept me in Ellis Island, I tell you, they could never have sent me back. They could never have sent me back! What I had seen and heard—never.*

"*This was in April 1933. The day I came back was a Good Friday, and every time Good Friday rolls around I think back, and I think what a wonderful thing it was that I came back.*"

Irma Busch was not alone in saying, "They could never have sent me back!" Theodore Lubik may have felt in 1913 that if the war hadn't come he would have "zipped right back where he came from." But the war did come, and he learned from the brothers he left behind that there was no home to return to—and he saw that for himself when he returned for a visit many years later.

"*I had four brothers that stayed over there. They stayed there and none of them got killed. That's the luck! Two wars, and all kinds of commotion—at one time, that country was under a different regime for* two or three years, then another one came in. But somehow they survived.

"But after that my sister and oldest brother said, 'We're going to leave Poland.' It was a bad place to live for the Ukrainians. Polish people would persecute them, wouldn't let them talk their language. So they said, 'We're going to go.' They went next to the city, Lvov, and there they found a nice building and everything. The other people there went on the trade—they were exchanging people. Polish people moved out north to Poland, and the Ukrainian people moved to over there. My sister and brother got a small farm—somehow they made themselves like home . . .

"When we went back to my village in 1960, they looked at us like we were wolves. They thought we were coming back to take away their property, after the wars and everything. Land that was mine or my father's or brother's, they thought maybe I came to take back. Because some people were coming back to claim property. They thought we came for the same purpose, but they made a mistake. I was disgusted. I said, 'Let's get out.'

"In this whole village, there were just two or three families that we knew. All the rest were strangers. They had switched people. They had chased people out—if you want to be Ukrainian, go ahead and be Ukrainian on the other side.

"There was all kinds of commotion there. Germans came in, Russians came in, Polish came in, and they all, the poor people, they suffered in that First World War."

Whatever the facts of the present, thoughts of the old country reflect sadness at memories of childhood in a world long gone. Theodore speaks for many when he recalls his youth in the old country:

"Oh, they had music there, they were the happiest people in the world. They were great dancers! They had music outside, pasture, houses —one or two rows, nice grass. There was geese, goats and everything. But they were happy, I know that!"

People with parents in the old country had strong reasons for returning. Adele Sinko went back to Austria in 1932 to visit her mother for what she thought would be the last time:

"In 1928 my father passed away. In 1932 I got a letter from my mother. She wasn't feeling well, and wrote, 'I can see you are not coming home to see me. I'll just tell you what I want to be done.'

"I wanted to have my citizenship papers before I went; I was here

This Czechoslovakian grandmother (left) and Italian grandmother (right), both arrived late in life, to make their home in a new land.

seven years and didn't have them yet. So I wrote to the Immigration Office and asked them if they couldn't rush them. I told them I had to go home because my mother wasn't well. But they couldn't do that, and I packed up and went home without them.

"So what do you think? In 1932 I met my husband on the boat. And in 1933 mother came over and she was with us from 1933 to 1956!

"She loved it here. You know, you have so much to eat. People here don't realize that. How you can just go and buy whatever you want. It wasn't like that there, you know. Oh, she loved it here. She never wanted to go back. She was, I think, sixty-four when she came over, and she adjusted so well.

"I went back one, two, three times. Last time, I just went back because my mother left me the family home. I didn't need it, but I had to go back to talk to the lawyer and make out the paper. So I gave it to my nephew, which was very nice, I think—to give away a house. Because America treated me very nicely. I had a happy marriage, we saved all our pennies, you know. So, that's that."

Many older people did come to America. One Italian family even tells how the grandparents held a granddaughter "hostage" until the girl's parents sent tickets for all of them to come together. The grandparents didn't want to be left behind! Some, like Adele's mother, got along beautifully in the new land. Others had a hard time with the language and felt cut off from their roots.

Vera Gauditsa's mother felt that way—she came to America to be with her daughter, but was unhappy here, so she returned after a year or two. Luckily, Vera loved to travel, and because the son she had just one month after arriving in America is a pilot, so she has often traveled back to her native Czechoslovakia. And, like others who feel strong connections with the land of their birth, she is now transferring her feeling for personal history and for roots in the old country, over to a new generation.

"My son is going there next month. He has been there five times. He loves to go there and he cannot speak that language. He can understand it, but he cannot speak it.

"This time he is taking his two boys, eleven and nine years old, and he wants me to go. I have to help him with the language, you know. He wants to show his boys where his family came from. He says many times, 'I was almost born there.'"

And Vera, like Theodore Lubik, feels a void with the passing of the world of her childhood:

"I had a different life altogether than my children had. It was a very close life, but somehow a happier life than my children had here. Because I grew up in nature and my children in the city. And I was twenty-four times a bridesmaid—twenty-four times! I was crazy about dancing. If I was born in Russia, I would have been a dancer, because in Russia they give you a chance. But not in those days.

"And you knew everybody in the town, like a whole family. There was 5,000 people in the town—you knew everybody. One way it is good, but no good because everybody knew your business. But I'm sorry for my children because there's too much studying here—they miss out on cultural things because of too much studying . . ."

Many people have passed on their language to their family, forging new links between the new country and the old. Michael Pappas describes how he has passed on his language and culture to his children:

"And we taught them Greek. We had a Greek teacher at our church, the Greek school was from two to five. I left the store where I was working at five o'clock. I used to get the Greek teacher and drive to the pig farm I had—a 105-acre farm in Monmouth, New Jersey. The teacher would teach my children Greek for two hours, every night get a

supper, and then I would bring him back again eight miles to New Brunswick. That was going all wintertime when school was open, three times a week. My wife, she couldn't speak English, so she was always speaking Greek. All my daughters and my boys—even my grandson— speak perfect Greek.

"Of course, they learned American first. Now the United States spends money and needs people to speak foreign languages. Even this is encouraged by the government, so they should speak their own language, any language, Chinese, any kind of language will help, not only yourself, it will help the country. Because nowadays we have missions all over the world, where they speak their own language. From New Brunswick, we have about ten girls and boys with good jobs in Athens, Greece, because they know the Greek language."

I AM HAPPY HERE

For Ida Mouradjian luck and life changed permanently with her coming to America. She and her husband, those two "orphans of the storm," married and settled in Chicago. As she puts it:

"I don't think we could have had a happier marriage. You see, there was need for each other. And we had two beautiful daughters. By the way, I have two daughters, two grand-daughters and two great-grand-daughters . . ."

In the United States, she became a teacher again, and threw herself into the work with characteristic dedication:

"I met a fifth grade teacher who said, 'You try so hard to have the children like you,' and I said to her, 'I am teaching them a foreign language. It's foreign goods. If they don't like the salesman, how can I expect them to like the material I am selling?'

"She just made a face and said, 'Well, you're a little pushy, too.'

"And I said, 'Well, I've got news for you. It's that pushiness that brought me from the road of exile to America. If I hadn't been a little pushy, a little daring, I would have turned into a few grains of sand, right there in the Syrian desert.'

"I could have talked to the walls, they would have understood more. She was born in America, raised in America. Her grandfather had probably come from Germany or Ireland or someplace, and that gave her a sense of superiority.

"And my being able to survive the holocaust, with the help of God and my own efforts—this gave me a sense of superiority, too.

"Let's end it by saying that miracles are done by your own efforts and also by the fact that there are men probably put on this earth to do the job of God . . ."

For Ida, as for most of the people in this book, and for the overwhelming majority of those who came in the Ellis Island years, America was indeed what they were looking for.

Sarah Asher and her brother never again faced war and revolution. Their countrywoman, Fannie Kligerman, survived, and then some. At the age of eighty-six, the woman who seventy-three years earlier had been a frightened little girl, summed up for the seven families—and for many others who fled for their lives:

"We were very happy that nobody was going to hit us. Nobody was going to kill us, and I wasn't afraid. In Europe, you were afraid they would hit you . . . But here, we knew we were through with that. And we were.

"We lived through all the troubles that people live through. All of us, thank God, came through, nicely. And my brothers are wealthy. And my parents lived long and I do the same."

People who left poverty behind them also mostly found the better life they were seeking in the new world. Casimir Cybulski returned to his homeland for a visit, and compares the old world with the land of plenty:

◆§ "Would you go back to Poland now, to stay?"

"I was in Poland in 1975. No, I wouldn't go there because it's 100 percent better here. The United States you still got everything. It's perfect. Get everything you want. That's the way the times is now in the United States.

"Over there, people are happy because they don't know any better. They think it's all right. And it's good there, too, when I was there, but not like United States. This country you can't be any better."

◆§ "The place you left, have they got running water now on the farm?"

"They get water from the well with a bucket. Put the bucket down on the rope and pull. Only improvements they got on the farm, the farmer's got an electric light—that's the only thing they got. No plumbing, you know. Everybody goes with a bucket to get that well water . . ."

Frank Santoni describes how his father felt about being in America with his family:

"When my father came to this country, he made a vow to St. Joseph that, should he get his family all in this country, he would on March 19th, which is St. Joseph's Day, make the altar. That is very commonly done in our little town of Campofiorito—you make the altar and have so many children to sit at the altar and partake of the food which is baked and cooked. The altar and all this bread that's on the altar are blessed by the priest.

"We generally had half of the living room dedicated for that purpose. We had the lumber necessary to make the altar, which consists of four or five steps and that is all decorated, naturally with the picture of St. Joseph and with different ornaments. Father used to have generally five saints—the saints were children from the neighborhood. They would be poor people, poor children, because they would get all the bread, fruit, whatever was there, besides their food for that particular day."

Bessie Spylios, too, found a better life in America and—characteristically—she never looked back:

"I never had any desire to go back to Greece. There was nobody there that I cared to see. I go to Florida every year here, for a couple of months. You see, I have my brothers there, and my sisters-in-law. If I went to Greece, I wouldn't know anybody, and I didn't care to go back . . .

"I wasn't afraid of anything coming here. Nothing bothered me. I was anxious to come here to see what it looked like, and to see different people.

"We really have everything here. Let's face it. We have more than some other nations have; and we throw away here leftovers and everything else. People can't live like that in Greece and other places."

✑ "So you have no regrets?"

"No. I am happy here."

Those who didn't find what they were looking for in those early years worked to create the America of their dreams, as Michael Pappas expresses:

"Well, the first immigrants, Greeks, Turks, Serbians, from all over Europe, we used to come here. We only had a few dollars in our pockets. We needed help, we came here, and we are the ones who built America. Because sixty years ago when I came here, America wasn't like it is today.

"I see two Americas. When I came here, America used to be a little bit like Europe. That's why many times I told my family, that was not the real America. But now the real America is today in your age."

Anna Vacek never wavered. She sent her dollies to America before the turn of the century, followed them, and blesses her luck:

"Thank God I got to America from the star. I prayed to get to this country and I love it. I stayed here and I did the best I could for this wonderful country—and I thank God daily I could stay here and do a lot, and I did. I did help. I worked hard, was honest with everybody and God always gave me luck."

Summing it up for all of them is Arnold Weiss:

"From the whole story of what I went through in all my years—and some of it wasn't very pleasant—I still love this country. There is nothing like it in the world.

"I would not want to be anywhere else. I love this country in spite of everything."

They are still coming.

Only a few immigrants come now from eastern and southern Europe; the restrictive immigration laws of the 1920s are still in force and see to that.

But they are still coming.

Some are refugees. In the 1930s, the United States welcomed some of those fleeing from fascism. On into the 1970s, it opened its doors to Vietnamese, Russians and others in flight.

But comparatively few are refugees. Today, well over a million people enter and settle in the United States every year. These are the new "new immigrants." And they are almost all "illegals," entering the United States across its southern border at night, without entry permits of any kind, and living their lives in the shadows.

Their motives in coming are precisely the same as those of the "new immigrants" of the early part of this century. They come for peace, freedom, bread and hope for the future, from lands that have little or none of those precious things to offer.

Most of them speak Spanish, have little or no English, live in Spanish-speaking communities, and hope somehow, someday, to merge into the American mainstream.

Today, somewhere between the Rio Grande and the Straits of Magellan, a little girl is putting her dolls in a brook and saying, "Goodbye, my dollies. I'll meet you in America."

Other Books of Interest

❧

Abbott, Edith. *Immigration: Select Documents and Case Records.* New York: Arno, 1969; reprint of 1924 edition.

Commager, Henry Steele, ed. *Immigration and American History.* Minneapolis: University of Minnesota Press, 1961.

Corsi, Edward. *In the Shadow of Liberty.* New York: Arno, 1969; reprint of 1935 edition.

Cowen, Philip. *Memories of an American Jew.* New York: Arno, 1976; reprint of 1932 edition.

Garis, Roy L. *Immigration Restriction.* New York: Ozer, 1971; reprint of 1927 edition.

Handlin, Oscar. *A Pictorial History of Immigration.* New York: Crown, 1972.

Heaps, Willard. *Story of Ellis Island.* New York: Seabury, 1967.

Howe, Frederic C. *The Confessions of a Reformer.* New York: Scribner's, 1925.

Howe, Irving. *World of Our Fathers.* New York: Simon and Schuster, 1976.

La Guardia, Fiorello. *The Making of an Insurgent.* Philadelphia: Lippincott, 1948.

McCabe, Cynthia. *The Golden Door: Artist-Immigrants of America 1876–1976.* Washington, D.C.: Smithsonian, 1976.

Namias, June. *First Generation.* Boston: Beacon, 1978.

Neidle, Cecyle S. *The New Americans.* New York: Twayne, 1967.

Novotny, Ann. *Strangers at the Door.* Riverside, Conn.: Chatham, 1971.

Palmer, Carleton H. *Report of the Ellis Island Committee.* New York: Ozer, 1971; reprint of 1934 edition.

Pitkin, Thomas M. *Keepers of the Gate: A History of Ellis Island.* New York: New York University Press, 1975.

Safford, Victor. *Immigration Problems.* New York: Dodd, Mead, 1925.

Shiloh, Ailon, ed. *By Myself, I'm a Book!* Waltham, Mass.: American Jewish Historical Society, 1972.

Tifft, Wilson and Dunne, Thomas. *Ellis Island: A Picture Text History.* New York: Norton, 1971.

Wakin, Edward. *The Immigrant Experience.* Huntington, Indiana: Our Sunday Visitor, 1977.

Index

◆◊◆